AMERICAN
ARMY
LIFE

AMERICAN ARMY LIFE

Col. John Elting,
U.S. Army, Ret.

CHARLES SCRIBNER'S SONS • NEW YORK

Copyright © 1982 John Robert Elting

Library of Congress Cataloging in Publication Data

Elting, John Robert.
  American army life.

  1. United States. Army—Military life—History.
I. Title
U766.E45   355.1'0973   82-5472
ISBN 0-684-17500-2   AACR2

1 3 5 7 9 11 13 15 7 19   Q/C   20 18 16 14 12 10 8 6 4 2

Printed in the United States of America.

Contents

Acknowledgments

My first thanks go to my wife and help-meet, Ann, who typed and edited my text. As for the illustrations, they would have been impossible to assemble except for the unselfish help of good friends and kindly strangers. The first include Mrs. John Nicholas Brown; Josephine Burke; Philip M. Cavanaugh; Gordon Chappell; Rene Chartrand; Dan J. Cragg, William Guthman; Richard Harrington; Col. Bruce Jacobs, ARNGUS Ret.; Col. Dale M. King, USA Ret.; Richard E. Kuehne; John P. Langellier; Michael J. McAfee; Thomas McGuirl; Col. John L. Marsh, Jr., USAR; Lt. Col. Edward S. Milligan, USAR; Michael Moss; Mrs. Harold Peterson; Carter Rila; Brig. Gen. Edwin H. Simmons, USMC Ret.; Michael J. Winey; Lt. Gen. William P. Yarborough, USA Ret.

The second group (some of whose military members undoubtedly have been promoted and transferred while this book was in gestation) includes: David A. Armour, Mackinac Island; Maj. Peter Blake; John O. Curtis, Old Sturbridge; Sp. Joel P. Day; Anthony Dean, Yellowstone Park; Joseph M. DeCotis, Fort Adams; James P. Finley, Fort Huachuca; Lt. Col. Robert W. Frost; Sp. Steven L. Geary; Col. J. E. Greenwood, USMC; Gillett Griswold, Field Artillery Museum; Dr. Jean Humbert, Musée de l'Armée; Lt. Paul J. Jacobsmeyer; Leon Kelly; Alfred V. Konecny, PAO, USMA; Sp. Raleigh Kraft; Col. Jean Martel, Musée de l'Armée; Montana Historical Society; Maj. Jack E. Mooney; Bernice Z. Parkes, US MP School; Public Archives of Canada; F. G. Renner; Barbara A. Shattuck, *National Geographic;* SM Sgt. O. E. Williams, EUSA PAO.

Preface

This is not a book for professional military historians—though it certainly will do them no harm to read it. It concerns itself with battles, campaigns, and great captains only incidentally, as they have touched the daily life of the American soldier.

I saw my first soldier as a very small boy in Yellowstone Park. My father and uncle had gone off fishing, leaving my mother and aunt to set up camp. A tall cavalryman came by on patrol, saw they had started their cooking fire on top of a bed of pine needles, and quickly and politely showed them the way it should be done. He still rides his powerful bay horse through my memories.

It was a good time for growing up in Billings, Montana. There was a former army scout, a fleshy old man with a water-fall mustache and the aroma of Old Rye, and a local character who had been General Custer's civilian hostler. At political rallies, Crow chief Plenty Coups, a daring young warrior with General Crook in the 1876 Rosebud campaign, would warn all politicans, "Keep whiskey away from my people!" A favorite uncle sometimes could be brought to tell of Cuba and the Philippines. His praise of Spanish soldiers and blunt devaluation of Rough Riders and Cuban insurgents alike were my first lesson that newspapers and popular history might not always be repositories of truth. And so, in my turn, I came to be a soldier. It began with "Cannoneers' Hop" around a French 75mm gun, and ended with nuclear weapons war games.

Except for major wars which became

national crusades, the American soldier has been something of a man apart. For most of our history he was poorly paid, fed, and equipped, and thrust out to the fag ends of this nation and the globe to stand guard and fend for himself. Today he is much better cared for, but he has greater needs. He and his army have changed during the last fifty years, just as the United States has changed. The uncomplicated, rather threadbare army I came into had more in common with "Mad Anthony" Wayne's 1792 Legion of the United States than with today's complex, high-technology organization. The soldier is better edu-cated, more ambitious, more frequently married, and usually just out of an adolescence ignorant of the hard physical work and familiarity with wind, cold, and rain so many young Americans knew a half-century ago.

American Army Life is an attempt to tell any interested American citizen something about the American soldier: his origins, the conditions under which he served, and his many peacetime contributions to the United States—some of them almost unknown. No one book can do all this. I have had to leave out many things. But this at least is a beginning.

1

The Colonial Soldier

The Americans are in general the dirtiest, most contemptible cowardly dogs that you can conceive. There is no depending upon 'em in action. They fall down dead in their own dirt and desert by battalions, officers and all.
BRIG. GEN. JAMES WOLFE, 1758[1]

There have been soldiers in North America since the coming of the first explorers and settlers. For the English colonies, soldiering began with the settlement of Jamestown in 1607. Despite hunger and sickness, that colony maintained its military organization. Its martial laws of 1611 provided that all soldiers must be drilled daily in complete equipment and armor, "... least in the field, the souldier do find them the more uncouth strange and troublesome"; and that sentries should "... stand with careful and waking eye."

When the Declaration of Independence was signed in 1776, America had already experienced nearly two centuries of military activity. The first North American settlers were rough men in a rough new land; their tiny colonies grew stubbornly between the forest and the sea amid constant wars between the British, Spanish, French, and Dutch: the wars between England and Spain (1585–1604); the first Dutch War (1652–54); the second Dutch War (1665–67); the War of Devolution (1667–68); the third Dutch War (1672–78); the War of the Grand Alliance, also known as the War of the League of Augsburg and, in North America, as King William's War (1689–97); the War of the Spanish Succession, known in America as Queen Anne's War (1701–13); the War of Jenkin's Ear (1739–41); the War of the Austrian Succession (1740–48), and the Seven Years' War, or French and Indian War (1754–63). These great struggles raged in Europe and often across half the world. Although North America at this time was of less importance to the European powers than the sugar islands of the West Indies, soldiers died just as hard here as did those on the battlefields of Europe.

Treaties brought little peace to North American frontiers, where rival fur traders and fishermen bickered and undeclared wars flared up: in 1686–87, for example, the Spaniards ravaged South Carolina, and the French seized English posts along Hudson Bay. Piracy periodically spread northward from the West Indies; ships were taken and seacoast farms and villages were plundered.

At the same time, the colonists faced the long run of Indian troubles—from minor thefts to grim conflicts, such as King Philip's War, which ravaged New England from 1675 to 1676, and the Yamassee devastation of Carolina from 1715 to 1716. These were probably the deadliest wars of American history in terms of the casualties inflicted upon the population.

Many of the Indian tribes in eastern North America were strong nations, living in fortified towns and flourishing corn fields. They often waged savage wars among themselves for control of hunting grounds and trade routes, frequently seeking white men as allies against their tribal enemies—just as the colonists sought Indian allies in their international wars.

Through all these dangers the colonists had to provide for their own security. They had brought with them from England the militia system that originated in King Henry II's Assize of Arms (1181), which required that every free man provide himself with proper arms and armor and undergo periodic military training "for to keep the peace." Most settlers came to America so armed and equipped, and the average group took care to have at least one veteran captain—men such as John Smith, Miles Standish, and John Underhill—to train and lead them. Wealthy men were expected to provide weapons

for their servants, and in some communities, no man could set himself up as an independent householder until he had the requisite arms and armor. The amount of training varied, but was as often as once a week. Failure to attend these musters or to come properly armed and equipped was punished with heavy fines.

In Virginia and the more southern colonies, with their plantation economy and thinly spread population, the militia was organized by counties, its officers appointed by the provincial governors. In New England and New York the town was the basic geographical unit, each having one or more "trainbands," or companies, which elected their own officers. Eventually, beginning with Massachusetts in 1636, these separate companies were grouped into regiments. Pennsylvania was the only undefended colony, since a Quaker minority maintained control through clever political juggling and resolutely prevented any military preparations. In 1747, however, after French privateers had raided up the Delaware River, Benjamin Franklin was able to establish the Associators, a force of volunteers.

The colonial militia's original system of drill and weapons was that of sixteenth- and seventeenth-century Europe. The companies were divided into pikemen and musketeers (also known as "shot"), and most men wore light armor. This might not seem effective for Indian warfare, but the militia also had to be prepared to meet the Spanish, French, or Dutch. Moreover, in their first clashes with the Indians, the flash, roar, and smoke of the militia's matchlock muskets usually sufficed to frighten them away whether or not many were hit.

Gradually, weapons and then tactics changed. Pikes were discarded, and all men were ordered to carry firearms. The cumbersome matchlocks—8- or 10-gauge weapons weighing up to 20 pounds that had to be fired from a rest—proved too heavy, slow to load, and inaccurate for woods fighting. (One officer observed that they were designed for soldiers with three hands!) They would remain adequate for European armies into the early eighteenth century, but by the 1670s, most colonials somehow had found the means to purchase the newer "snaphaunce," or flintlock, muskets, which were far lighter and handier. By contrast, armor, since it would stop arrows, remained in use in America until the 1650s (by which time many Indians had acquired firearms), although "buff coats" of heavy leather or canvas coats "quilted with cotton wool" increasingly replaced the steel corselets. During King Philip's War between New Englanders and five Indian tribes, Capt. Benjamin Church and others worked out more flexible tactics, borrowed in part from the Indians, employing special "independent companies" of both colonial and Indian volunteers.

Militiamen were immediately available in time of danger, and could put up a stout fight with their backs—sometimes literally—to their own front doors, while the women tended the wounded and loaded spare muskets. When the French and Spanish came against Charleston in 1706, the militia not only routed the invaders but rowed out and captured a large French warship by boarding.

For longer operations, which would keep men away from their farms and trades for weeks, it became customary to form temporary units by levying a quota on each militia company. If there were not enough volunteers, the requisite number were drafted, though a drafted man might be allowed to hire a substitute, or avoid service by paying a fine. A militia captain who went out in Sir Edmund Andros' expert 1688–89 winter campaign remembered the experience:

> Officers and soldiers carried their own provision in a leather knapsack; a few pease, a few bisketts and a pice of salt pork were our provision and stores: marched out 250 miles upon the snow four or five foot deep under us, our drink was snow melted in our mouths, never saw one house, at night cut down some spruce boughs to lye upon, and if it chanced to snow we lay the warmer under it, while the [Indian] fort was burning down I was warm.

During the unusually long peace from 1713 to 1739—between the War of the Spanish Succession and the War of Jenkin's Ear—the English colonies increased greatly in size and population. The militia system remained, but training was relaxed. Except along the farthest frontiers, knowledge of Indian warfare was forgotten. Still, as the War of Jenkin's Ear blended into the greater War of the Austrian Succession (or King George's War) in 1744, the New England militia accomplished the major feat in June 1745 of capturing the great French seacoast fortress of Louisbourg, in present-day Nova Scotia. Hurriedly organized, their expedition obviously was based on excellent intelligence concerning the Louisbourg area, the state of its fortifications, and the weak and mutinous condition of its garrison. New England merchants knew how to move men and supplies. Almost four thousand volunteers were raised from the militia of Massachusetts, New Hampshire, and Connecticut; Rhode Island sent a sloop-of-war; and a small squadron from the Royal Navy arrived to blockade Louisbourg. Reaching shore against light opposition, the Americans dragged their siege guns by sheer grit and muscle through bogs impassable even for ox teams. They were half-trained and less disciplined, fond of straggling and pillaging, and most reluctant to risk their necks except on their own terms. There was a "great want of good gunners that have a disposition to be sober in the daytime."[2] But they stuck to their work through miserable weather until Louisbourg capitulated.

IN THE KING'S PAY

The Seven Years' War, or the French and Indian War, as it was known in America, saw the first large-scale employment of British troops in North America. These were Regulars, who enlisted for twenty years of service—in effect, for life. As a whole, they represented England's and Ireland's offscourings and "odds and sods," ranging from convicted felons, impressed into the army, to gullible farm boys whom knowing recruiting sergeants had tricked into it. Officers were a mixture of tried professionals and careless dilettantes, mostly gentlemen (at least by birth) and very brave. Between officer and private was an iron cadre of veteran sergeants and corporals, expert in making soldiers out of the most unlikely human material.

The British Army was a collection of regiments, differing considerably in uniforms, efficiency, and actual systems of drill. But even the newest-raised of them had a corporate integrity and its own rigorously observed customs. The older regiments had over a half-century of proud tradition from the great wars of Europe, where they had proven themselves almost invincible. Thousands of Americans enlisted in the first regiments that arrived in North America, and a number even secured commissions in British units. They passed into a disciplined military world, and appear to have served efficiently; by 1756, in fact, over half the enlisted men of a half-dozen regiments were American born. There *was* some awkwardness that year when Americans captured at Oswego were later exchanged and drafted into the 1st Regiment of Foot. The 1st, or Royal Regiment, was a senior and rigid outfit; it found its new acquisitions a "most irregular sett of people,"[3] but proceeded to make proper privates of the Royals out of them by liberal application of the cat-o'-nine-tails (using up most of the local supply of whipcord in the process).

British discipline was strict and enforced by flogging—as many as a thousand lashes was the sentence for serious military offenses such as open insubordination, theft, or desertion. (Only habitual deserters were likely to be executed, as it was difficult and expensive to find replacements for them.) Punishment for officers varied from reprimands to "cashiering"—being dismissed from the service in disgrace. One especially mutinous captain had his sword broken over his head in front of his assembled regiment as a prelude to cashiering. Officers and men guilty of crimes against civilians normally were turned over to civil courts for trial.

The British Army subscribed to a complex system of pay apparently designed to make the soldier support himself. The cost of his uniform and camp equipment, plus fees to assorted paymasters, surgeons, and officials, was deducted from the soldier's pay, leaving him with little cash on hand. If his shoes wore out halfway through the year they were supposed to last, he was docked again for their replacements. In England he also had to pay for his food; but in North America foodstuffs were so expensive that he received free rations. (Brig. Gen. James Wolfe opposed this benefit, asserting that it left the soldier too much to spend on rum. The sum involved was fourpence a day, but rum was one of the few reasonably priced items available.)

With each of these trim-gaitered, pipe-clayed, impressive regiments came a draggle of women, each of whom, somewhere along the line of march, had "packed up her placket and followed the drum."[4] Some were legal wives; others, married only by the ancient camp rite of "jumping the sword." Officially, six women of good character were allowed for each company. There were usually more than six, and all were accustomed to the rigors and hardships of the soldiers' life. Most of them were expert foragers, or even thieves; they often bootlegged bad liquor; and their conversation made sergeant-majors blush.

The regimental women cooked, sewed, washed, and mended for their husbands and their comrades. They also helped the regimental surgeon as the wounded staggered back from the firing line, and sometimes dodged screeching forward through the smoke with their aprons full of cartridges, when the supply in their men's pouches ran low. With women about, there also were children, who had to be cached somewhere when a campaign opened. It did no good to order the women to stay behind; they would turn up anyhow, despite orders or guards.

Some Provincial troops followed British custom and were accompanied by their women; others, especially New England regiments, were more virtuous—and were rewarded with dirty shirts and indigestion from too much fried salt pork. They had chaplains aplenty, but these reverend gentlemen neither cooked meals nor took in washing.

Because the Regulars' first campaign under Gen. Edward Braddock ended in disaster at the Monongahela in 1755, an American legend soon developed that these haughty Redcoats were helpless without American guidance and protection. Like most legends, this was mostly exaggeration. Had the miserly, squabbling colonial governments given Braddock the proper support in transportation and supplies, his campaign probably would have been successful. (Some two months after Braddock's defeat, a strong column of Provincial troops—though accompanied by Mohawk scouts—walked carelessly into an ambush near Lake George, New York. If their casualties were not as heavy as Braddock's, it was because few of them paused to make a fight of it!)

In fact, the British Army adapted itself to the American wilderness with amazing rapidity, modifying its organization, tactics, dress, and weapons. The average Englishman was never as handy in the woods as the best of the Americans, but it was the British who won the decisive battles, did the planning, and took care of the army's supplies.

Newly added to the British service and much admired by commanders as different as Henry Bouquet and James Wolfe were the kilted Highlanders. Their discipline had much of the patriarchal relationship of chieftain and clansman; and their pipers, customs, and dress made them a marvel to all beholders. In addition to the Highlanders, there were the badly misnamed Royal Americans, who were mostly culls from the British regiments in Ireland, plus miscellaneous Germans, Bohemians, Poles, and some assorted Americans. Their officers included Bouquet and a number of other excellent Swiss and German officers, one of whom, Capt. Simon Ecuyer, remarked that he never had "seen such a tribe of rebels, bandits, and hamstringers."[5] Also, there was the brown-uniformed 80th Regiment of Light-Armed Foot, the first light infantry regiment in the British Army, formed in America in 1757; most of its men were Americans and of a better type than the average recruit.

If sick or wounded, the Regular could expect what was, for the eighteenth century, decent care. Each regiment had its own surgeon, assisted by one or two "mates"; nurses were obtained from the regimental women. These regimental hospitals were supported by "flying" (mobile) hospitals, which followed the armies in the field, and by well-equipped "general hospitals" in such cities as Halifax, New York, and Albany. Special isolation hospitals were set up for men with smallpox, a major medical problem of the time. Army surgeons and physicians were gravely ignorant by modern standards, but they knew from experience the importance of cleanliness and order.

Provincial medical personnel might be

no less educated, but they lacked experience in taking care of men in the field. Moreover, it seemingly was difficult to persuade American doctors with established practices to abandon them for almost a year; consequently, medical care varied greatly from one Provincial regiment to the next. On occasion, sick or wounded Provincials might be admitted to the general hospitals.

The weekly ration for a British soldier during the Seven Years' War was 4 pounds of pork or 7 pounds of beef, 7 pounds of bread or flour, 3 pints of dried peas, 6 ounces of butter, and ½ pound of rice. (Provincial troops usually had somewhat more ample allowances, which included rum, molasses or sugar, and ginger.) The meat might be fresh or salted—any knowledge eighteenth-century military leaders had of nutrition was entirely empirical, but it was generally understood that fresh meat prevented scurvy, and that it was wise to feed troops salt meat at least occasionally during hot weather. Combat rations were salt meat and flour; fresh meat would be available only if herds of cattle could be brought up behind the army and some steers slaughtered daily. These rations were generally of passable quality, but naturally there were complaints, especially concerning the butter, which was usually Irish-made and heavily salted to preserve it. The men compared it to whale oil. Occasionally there was fresh game or greens gathered in the forest. When the situation permitted, wise commanders planted gardens to provide fresh vegetables and procured seines to catch fish from nearby lakes or streams.

The ideal preventative for scurvy (which always appeared when the troops went too long on salt rations) was spruce beer. This was made by boiling end twigs of the black spruce, adding molasses to the liquid, and allowing it to ferment. Regulars would receive a half-gallon a day, but their pay was docked for the cost of the ingredients, the brewing, and transportation. Spiking spruce beer with rum produced "Calibogus," a potent brew that could enliven even a Nova Scotia winter.

To cook their rations in the field or in garrison, soldiers clubbed together in small messes of five to eight men, each with its own camp kettle. Here, as in other aspects of military housekeeping, the Regulars usually fared far better than the Provincials. Their camp women were old hands at converting government rations into something reasonably tasty, as well as at snapping up any available trifles that would make their mess kettle "boil fat." Another difference prevailed—Provincial troops insisted on having hot breakfasts.

When they had money, soldiers could buy rum, tobacco, and extra food and clothing from the sutlers who followed the army, filling the need met by today's post exchanges. These men were traveling merchants, who were engaged in a risky business and charged accordingly. Some were licensed and subject to some degree of inspection, but there was also a plague of unlicensed peddlers who offered "vile liquors," dealt in stolen government property, and were otherwise troublesome.

Finding quarters for troops en route to the front or brought back from the frontier for the winter was a constant problem. In England, they would have been quartered either in permanent camps or in the larger inns and public houses. America lacked both, and there was no clear legal guidance in the matter, resulting in much bickering between military officers and civilian officials. Some of the colonies built barracks, others allowed the quartering of troops in civilian homes in emergencies. Even the traditional British allowance of candles, firewood, cooking utensils, vinegar, salt, and 5 pints of "small" beer daily usually was provided for troops so quartered, though the beer often was replaced by cider.

Citizens might board their enforced

guests for the value of their rations. On occasion the hospitality could be excessive: Fraser's Highlanders found "good quarters" in Connecticut during the winter of 1757–58 and were introduced to New England rum. Accustomed to nothing stronger than their native *usquebaugh*, the regiment reportedly was drunk for three days. (One householder complained that the stalwart bearing and unusual dress of the three Scots officers quartered in his house were arousing undue curiosity among the womenfolk of his family.) By contrast, South Carolina—after demanding that more troops be sent because of trouble with the Cherokees—refused Montgomery's Highlanders proper shelter, firewood, or bedding in winter weather until half the regiment was sick and many were dying.

With the Regulars were other units, raised in America but also in the king's pay. These included companies of carpenters and artificers, skilled workmen who did the expert's work in opening roads and building forts and shipping. Probably most important were the forty companies of New England sailors and whalers, called batteauxmen, who handled the tricky, double-ended, flat-bottomed boats that were the army's principal supply vehicles along the northern rivers. Their commander was wrathful, cantankerous Col. John Bradstreet, Regular officer, logistical genius, and driving leader in irregular operations; they worked armed and under military discipline, ready, willing, and able to whip any French and Indian raiders who might get in their way.

THE RANGERS

And there were the rangers, special troops for raiding and scouting missions, already a well-known type of American fighting man. Most of the colonies had formed such units from time to time to patrol their frontiers, watch Indian activities, escort surveyors, and intercept fugitive criminals, runaway slaves, and straying cattle. Georgia had a strong force in the 1740s, including one mounted company in "full Highland dress." John Gorham's company was enlisted for service in Nova Scotia in 1744, and was taken into the Regular establishment in 1751. The most famous—probably because their service was in the war's main American theater, between the Hudson River and Lake Champlain—were a varying number of companies grouped under Maj. Robert Rogers.

Rangers were organized as independent companies; enlistment was for one year. While their service was hard and unusually risky, their pay was correspondingly high and could be increased by bounties for scalps. The original companies were largely composed of skilled woodsmen, but as casualties mounted and the number of companies increased, they had to flesh out their cadres of experienced rangers with volunteers from Regular and Provincial regiments and whatever recruits were available. In 1756 Rogers had to make do with "Irish Roman Catholicks and others mostly Sailors and Spaniards."[6] Such men naturally could not match the woodscraft of Indians or French Canadian partisans.

Good ranger officers were rare and had short life expectancies; enlisted rangers often were undisciplined and hard to handle. General after general complained of their behavior and periodic irresponsibility—still, they were indispensable. Indian scouts were far less reliable, Regulars were helpless in the trackless forests, and the

Provincials were incapable and often unwilling. Even James Wolfe sufficiently overcame his disdain for Americans to take six companies with him on his expedition against Quebec. He dismissed them as "little better than *la canaille*" and "the worst soldiers in the universe," but used them with ruthless effectiveness.[7] In addition to these quasi-Regular rangers in the king's pay, there were a number of Provincial ranger companies, of varying efficiency. Probably the best known was Israel Putnam's "spy company" of men selected from the Connecticut regiments.

One section of the army that remained completely civilian was the drivers of supply wagons and packhorses, who were hired locally, if possible through contractors who could provide them in reasonably large numbers. It was a difficult task, as civilians disliked risking their farm equipment and livestock, and the process of getting reimbursed if either were lost could be slow and involved. On the other hand,

farmers and contractors demanded impossible prices, furnished rickety old wagons and ancient crowbaits in place of the sound vehicles and strong horses specified in their contracts, and sometimes disappeared in the middle of a campaign.

Finding sufficient feed for the horses was always a problem. As they weakened from hunger, their loads had to be reduced. Pack horses could carry 200 pounds in rough country, one-fourth of this being corn for their feed; four-horse wagons were expected to haul approximately a ton, but bad weather and ruined roads might reduce that by half or even more. The army also hired horses and civilian drivers for its artillery, but furnished the necessary harnesses and equipment.

(Artillery had a limited part in these wars. It could make short work of the average timber-built frontier fort, but it was damnably troublesome to move, unless easy water transportation was available.)

THE PROVINCIALS

Provincial troops formed the majority of Americans under arms. They always had been an uncertain commodity, but capable—as in Louisbourg—of considerable independent effort. Unfortunately, the quality of Provincial regiments was in decline by 1756. The average militiaman was a property owner, taxpayer, and voter—and was not inclined to go off to the wars, year after year. As a natural result, men drafted out of the militia for active service were those their fellow citizens felt most able to spare.

The Provincial soldier enlisted for a year's campaign, which meant only five to eight months of actual service. This short period was too brief to afford much effective training, even for the more conscientious officers and men. In particular, it

seems to have inhibited the development of effective noncommissioned officers who, as in the British Army, could show both new recruits and new officers what was to be done and how to do it. Even so, there were some Americans who came to like soldiering, turned out for each campaign to "go up to the lakes," and served to the best of their abilities. Some of these mastered the soldier's trade; given commanders who understood them, they were capable of feats such as Bradstreet's daring raid across Lake Ontario to destroy Fort Frontenac in 1758. That same year, Gen. John Forbes got good service out of some of his Virginians (his subordinate, Col. Henry Bouquet, concluded that the Provincials' "good men" were better at woods fighting than his Regulars). Unfortunately, he found most Provincials "a gathering from the scum of the worst of people."[8]

There was reason enough behind comments such as Forbes'. William Pitt, a politician of vast ambition but limited comprehension, became England's secretary of state in 1757 and thereafter attempted to run the French and Indian War by detailed orders from his London office. The results in North America were too often compounded confusion, but—as often happens in such cases—he thereby acquired a reputation for energy. Pitt somehow convinced himself that victory in North America required more Provincial regiments and that the best way to obtain them was to meet whatever expenses the colonies claimed for raising them. The colonial governments were delighted: they offered higher enlistment bounties for one-year service than the Regular got for his twenty-year hitch, as well as higher pay and allowances. The Provincial soldier's pay, moreover, was not subject to the deductions for clothing and equipment that ate up most of the Regular's; and he usually took home the equipment issued him. The civilian officials responsible for raising these troops voted themselves excellent salaries, and colonial merchants made a good profit out of supplying clothing and equipment issued them. The British taxpayers footed the entire cost, which probably contributed to their subsequent insistence that the American colonies be taxed.

Most of the men who enlisted in these new Provincial regiments were "loose, idle" fellows—vagabonds, petty criminals, free blacks, "domesticated" Indians, and others not considered suitable for membership in the militia.[9] These had been the Americans most likely to "take the King's schilling" and enlist in the Regulars, who had made soldiers of them; but now they found it far more profitable to join a Provincial unit. This dried up the Regulars' American recruiting, without noticeably aiding the war effort.

The Provincial regiments were slow to muster and slow to reach the front. Generally, there were too many of them, and supplying them strained the army's logistical system. They deserted in large numbers. Worst of all, they were not the "backwoodsmen . . . every man a woodsman and a hunter" that early American historians such as Francis Parkman proclaimed them and that British commanders were anxious to secure.[10] The average Provincial was as inexperienced at Indian fighting and as helpless in the woods as any Redcoat. In emergencies he too often lacked the discipline and esprit de corps that held the Redcoat firm. He did not know how to take care of himself in camp.

Undoubtedly, the Provincials' ineffectiveness resulted primarily from the unmilitary character of their officers, the majority of whom were "utter Strangers to Military life" and differed but little from their enlisted men in education and social background.[11] Captains and lieutenants who had been elected by the men of their companies seldom attempted to enforce any sort of discipline, relying on coaxing and wheedling instead of commanding. John Forbes, one of the best English generals and a man of endless patience, damned his Virginia and Pennsylvania officers as "an extreme bad collection of broken inn-keepers, horse jockeys and Indian traders."[12] Contemporary orderly books are filled with directives that Provincial officers wear proper uniforms and swords when outside their regimental areas, so that they would not be mistaken for stray civilians; that they see to it that their men had "their hats Coked [cocked] & with shoes and stocking on" when they paraded; and that their men stop firing muskets at random in camp or on the march.[13]

Men often were killed before they even saw the enemy, because of their officers' ignorance and incompetence. An inspector wrote that Fort William Henry in 1756 "stinks enough to cause an infection, they have all their sick in it. The camp is nastier than anything I could conceive, their necessary houses [latrines], kitchens, graves and places for slaughtering cattle all mixed through their encampment."[14] As there was no hospital, the sick had been jammed into dank, unaired rooms, where six or seven men died every day, demoralizing the increasingly sick survivors. The troops did not even police their areas, but left filth of all sorts to fester in and around their tents.

The colonial governments frequently neglected the men they had raised. New England troops who relieved the Quebec-bound Regulars in Nova Scotia in 1759 were "a poor mean ragged set of men." Their "sober modest" officers wore blue uniforms with scarlet facings and gilt buttons, laced hats and waistcoats, but the enlisted men had "no uniforms nor do they affect any regularity."[15] The miserable Pennsylvania levies of 1758 were "in the most frightful disorder. Their guns are entirely unfit for use, more than three-fourths unfit to fire, the wood in pieces, and the screw plates attached to the guns with string. They have no tents, neither the officers nor the soldiers. Not a single kettle, axe, or tomahawk. No ammunition or provisions, and no one to furnish them." The nonchalant Pennsylvania authorities finally were prodded into providing new weapons, whereupon "the new guns . . . burst; and not a soldier dares to fire them. The rest are old rusty muskets as heavy as two of our guns." The New Jersey Regiment was considered something of a rarity, being sent into the field at its full authorized strength, "completely cloathed in a handsome uniform & furnished with all necessaries."[16]

In one respect Provincial troops admittedly were far superior to Regulars: most of them knew how to handle an ax or a shovel. Clearing timber, building roads, moving supplies, herding cattle, and providing the muscle for constructing fortifi-

cations were tasks they could do well when properly supervised, and these were the tasks they customarily received—inglorious, but necessary. One British officer put it most unkindly: "the Works that in inhabited Countrys are performed by Peasants."[17]

The king's armies in North America served in a strange and hostile place. From the Atlantic coastal settlements west to the Mississippi River, most of the land was ancient forest—a somber world of few trails, where death might wait behind any tree, and even competent woodsmen could lose their way. Soldiers from Europe or the American seacoast farms and towns found it daunting, sometimes terrifying. A hundred feet or less in any direction, the trees shut out the rest of God's creation; the enemy struck suddenly out of them and then vanished. Capture often meant death by torture, or being forced to drink from a pot in which a comrade had been cooked. Daily existence itself was hard enough. It is not surprising that Bouquet, that Swiss expert at wilderness campaigning, wanted "a little rest" for his battalion of Royal Americans in the autumn of 1763; they had been in the forests for six years and "their spirits [were] much cast down."[18]

Those endless forests made road building extremely difficult. There were few open "intervals" to provide forage for domestic stock, limiting the use of draft or pack animals. Bulk transport of men and supplies thus was much restricted to navigable lakes and rivers, where cargo had to be shifted into progressively smaller boats as it was moved farther upstream. The portages—places where boats and cargo had to be taken from the water and carried or hauled around impassable rapids or from one body of water to another—vastly increased this labor. Asked what would be necessary to move 5,760 barrels, containing a month's rations for 20,000 men, approximately 80 miles from Albany to Lake

George, Colonel Bradstreet reported that it would require three weeks of good weather and the services of 1,000 bateaux, 1,000 ox carts, and 800 wagons. Each barrel would have to be loaded or unloaded five times.

Away from water transportation, men carried their own rations for several days. Bouquet had the actual weight of a grenadier's load determined: including his uniform, weapons, equipment, spare socks and shirts, toilet articles, blanket, full canteen, twenty-four cartridges, tomahawk, and six days' rations, it came to 63 pounds, 3 ounces. Since grenadiers had short cutting swords in addition to a musket, bayonet, and tomahawk, this was 2 pounds, 3 ounces more than the average infantryman of a battalion company could carry. (At this time, the standard British infantry regiment consisted of a single battalion with two elite companies—one of grenadiers and one of light infantry—and eight battalion companies. The Royal Americans had four such battalions, which usually served separately; the Royal Highland Regiment, or Black Watch, had two.)

For all this hard marching and labor, rum was the universal comforter, an incentive and a reward. It was issued to men who worked on roads and fortifications or had returned from dangerous duty. Usually it was dark authoritative stuff from the West Indies that made a soldier feel someone had pulled a tomcat down his gullet by its tail. Rum was considered essential to protect the soldier's health against chills and damps, and officers swore that a ration of rum—or even the less-respected American whiskey—reduced the sicknesses caused by drinking "Quantities of bad Water."[19] Very likely it did. At the least, it worked wonders for the soldier's morale.

Through all the colonial wars, no American officer above the grade of colonel really distinguished himself, except for William Peppenell, who led the 1745 conquest of Louisbourg. But some American officers, like Col. George Washington of the 1st Virginia Regiment, did gain invaluable experience and self-confidence. They painfully learned the art of command, the intricacies of logistics, and the essentials of military hygiene. Not all of them would devote these skills to the service of the new United States in 1775; a number—for example, Joseph Gorham and Robert Rogers, the senior ranger officers—would remain the king's men. (But some Regulars would marry and settle in America, and thereafter give it their allegiance.)

These wars taught the soldiers the need for careful preparation before action and for adapting military organization and tactics to fit the country in which the war was fought. They learned the value of individual initiative and individual marksmanship, and of small, lightly equipped units that could endure great hardships and yet move swiftly and fight skillfully across difficult terrain. (Unknown to Americans, Hungarian hussars and Croat irregulars were spelling out the latter lessons across Germany and Bohemia on a larger scale at that same time.) These were, in fact, universal lessons, applicable to almost any campaign, but they were the first given the American soldier.

Judging American military capabilities by the hapless Provincial regiments, British soldiers tended to agree with Wolfe, Forbes, and Bouquet that Americans made "very bad" soldiers and that it should be no great trouble to keep the American colonies in a proper state of subjugation, no matter how rebellious they might become. The Americans, on the other hand, made much of Braddock's defeat and other British reverses, telling themselves that British armies would be helpless against Americans employing ranger-style tactics in rough, wooded country. Both groups would experience many unpleasant surprises when their theories were put to the test of battle in 1775.

Sometime between 1758 and 1763 a column moves into the wilderness, through the hot afternoon stillness.

Ghost silent, half-naked, grotesquely painted, a half-dozen Indian scouts weave through the trees and disappear. Then open files of rangers appear, one in the trail, others flanking it on either side. They move with a wary ease, their green or black uniforms merging into the forest's shades.

The minutes pass quietly, punctuated only by the occasional crash of a felled tree. Almost as quietly as the rangers, a company of light infantry passes—small, agile men in jaunty caps and snug jackets, moving in open order, their short muskets half-poised. Behind them rides an engineer officer with a small party of guides and couriers; as he goes he marks trees for felling or notes that a stream crossing must be improved. At his heels are a company or two of carpenters, felling axes in hand, muskets slung across their backs, extra tools in small carts or on pack horses. They swiftly widen the trail into a rough 12-foot road, so that wagons and cannon can use it. With them as a rallying point is a company of tall grenadiers; off in the woods to either flank are files of light infantry. A drum taps quietly, and several battalion companies of infantry slog by; there is a light field gun or two, tended by blue-uniformed Royal Artillerymen, who keep an eye on their uneasy civilian drivers.

This advance guard moves on, and the road is empty. Then more drums tap and a snatch of pipe music skirls through rising dust across the shrill snarl of a fife. These are the regiments, Regular and Provincial, and the guns of the main body, marching in close order. Somewhere near the head of their column rides the commanding officer with a small staff. (In 1758 John Forbes rode in a litter slung between two horses, dying by inches, but never faltering.) Beyond the regiments are supply wagons with reserves of ammunition, salt meat, flour, and rum. Other wagons carry the mobile hospital and forage for the column's horses. There are forge carts, where artificers can shoe horses and repair weapons, tools, and vehicles. In among these wagons, bent under heavy bundles, trudge the regimental women. A baby's wail sounds plaintively from amid their chatter. After the wagons, whip-cracking drovers push along a complaining herd of cattle. A company or two of infantry close the column. Half-glimpsed through the trees on either hand go the last of the patrols that have covered the column's flanks.

Again there is empty road and quiet for a short space. Then more drums lead on the rear guard, which sweeps the woods to both sides of the road to flush out stragglers. Only a fool would drop out of the column when enemy Indians and French irregulars haunt the forest, but there are always fools, and sometimes good soldiers taken too sick to keep up.

Finally, if the commander is wise, a detachment of light infantry or rangers follows the rear guard, chins on their shoulders as they watch to the flanks and rear. And then the new-cut road is vacant once again, except for a frightened unlicensed sutler, driving a bony nag loaded with bad rum and tobacco, and, perhaps, an enemy war party, looking for such easy prey.

These are field soldiers; their clothing is worn, their shoes battered, their hair cropped short. They have trimmed the brims of their hats short, and wear them slouched instead of fashionably cocked. Officers have discarded their distinctive sashes, gorgets, and aiguillettes, and many wear enlisted men's dull red coats, cut short, in place of their usual scarlet. Some regiments have packed away their heavy uniform coats and march with waistcoats open over checkered shirts. Most have replaced their tight, many-buttoned gaiters with "Indian stockings," made of several layers of rough woolen cloth, reaching from the instep to well up the thigh. One battalion of Royal Americans has these made of bright green baize, tied with red garters. Highlanders have given up their belted plaids for the "little kilt" or even canvas trousers made of old tents. Heavy packs have been left behind; soldiers carry their spare clothing and rations ranger-style, inside a rolled blanket slung across their left shoulder and fastened under their right arm.

Their weapons have also changed. Musket barrels are shorter and browned. Only sergeants and grenadiers still wear the short infantry sword, and the sergeants have replaced their traditional halberds with muskets and bayonets. Finding their broadswords an encumbrance in the underbrush, the Black Watch has stored them away. By contrast, the rangers now have bayonets, which give a man who missed his shot as the ambush broke a second chance against the whooping painted foe that rushes him. Officers have light, handy muskets called "fuzees." Here and there along the column, selected marksmen cradle rifles—probably the stubby, heavy-barreled German type that was the ancestor of the American rifle. Both officers and men carry tomahawks, useful both as a weapon and a tool.

This column does not fit the common image of a British army in the field, but there is no mistaking the disciplined surge of it. Over half the men who pass by are Americans, whatever regiment they belong to or uniform they wear. They and their fathers before them have served the king for almost two centuries; this is the last war in which they will.

1. Gorham's Rangers, 1761. Recruited in New England, Gorham's Rangers served in Nova Scotia and Canada from 1744 to 1764. This ranger wears a leather "jockey cap" with an oak leaf painted on its left side as a recognition symbol. His coat has an unusual design: As worn here, it is brown with red cuffs and lapels; turned inside out, it becomes a dressy red coat with brown trimmings. On his legs he wears "Indian stockings," modified to button snugly around his shoe tops. His weapons are a light flintlock musket, bayonet, tomahawk, and knife.

2. "All Gentlemen Volunteers, and Others." Recruiting announcement for Gorham's Rangers.

All Gentlemen Volunteers, and Others.

THAT have a Mind to serve his Majesty King GEORGE the Second, for a limited Time, in the Independant Companies of Rangers now in *Nova-Scotia*, may apply to Lieutenant *Alexander Callender*, at Mr. *Jonas Leonard's*, at the Sign of the *Lamb* at the South End of *Boston*, where they shall be kindly entertained, enter into present Pay, and have good Quarters, and when they join their respective Companies at *Hallifax*, shall be compleatly cloathed in blue Broad-Cloth, receive Arms, Accoutrements, Provisions, and all other Things necessary for a Gentleman Ranger : And for their further Encouragement, his Excellency Governor CORNWALLIS has by Proclamation lately published, promised a Reward of *Five Hundred Pounds*, old Tenor, for every *Indian* Scalp or Prisoner brought in, which Sum will be immediately paid by the Treasurer of the Province, upon the Scalp or Prisoner being produc'd.

N. B. Lieutenant *Callender* has obtained Leave from His Honour the Lieutenant Governor, to beat up for Rangers in any Part of this Province.
Boston, September 8. 1750.

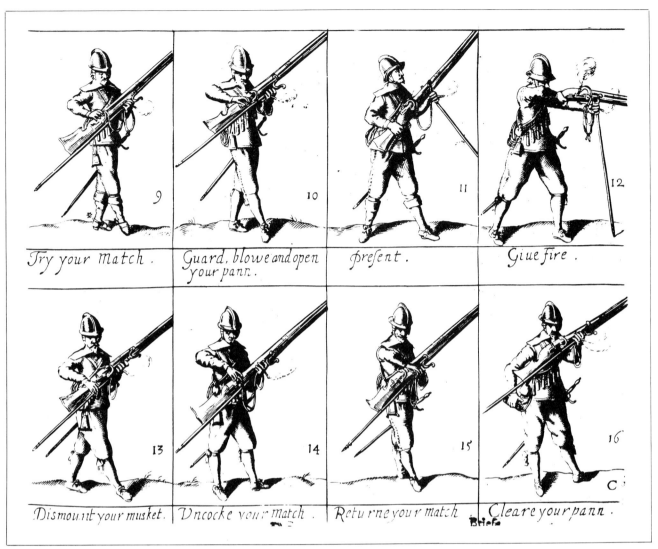

Try your match. | Guard, blowe and open your pann. | present. | Giue fire.

Dismount your musket. | Vncocke your match. | Returne your match. | Cleare your pann.

3. Infantryman, early seventeenth century. These illustrations show part of the complicated drill necessary to load and fire a matchlock musket. The musketeer wears a steel helmet, and his coat is probably of stout leather. The containers hanging from his shoulder belt or "bandolier" hold individual loads of black powder; his bullets are in the small pouch at the bottom of the belt. (In action, he would hold several bullets in his mouth for faster loading.) The small flask hanging from the belt below the bullet pouch contains fine "touchpowder" for priming the musket. In addition to the yard of "match" (a loosely twisted cord, impregnated with saltpeter) he carries looped around the middle fingers of his left hand, with both ends lighted, he has a reserve supply coiled around the back of his bandolier.

4. The pikeman. The pikeman in these illustrations wears a corselet with tasses to protect his thighs. His pike, only part of which is visible, is 14 to 18 feet long. Only a strong man could wield it effectively; consequently, pikemen were selected from the biggest and most robust recruits.

Order yor Pike.	*Aduance yor Pike in three motions. The first Motion.*	*the seacond Motion*	*the third Motion being Aduanced*
Order yor Pike in 3 motions. the first Motion	*the 2^d Motion*	*The 3^d motion being ordered*	*Shoulder yor Pike in 3 motions The first Motion*
The seacond Motion.	*The 3^d motion being Sholdred*	*Port yor Pike in 3 motions. the first motion.*	*The 2^d Motion.*
The 3^d motion being Ported.	*Charge yor Pike*	*Advance yor Pike.*	*Sholder yor Pike in 3 motions. The first Motion.*

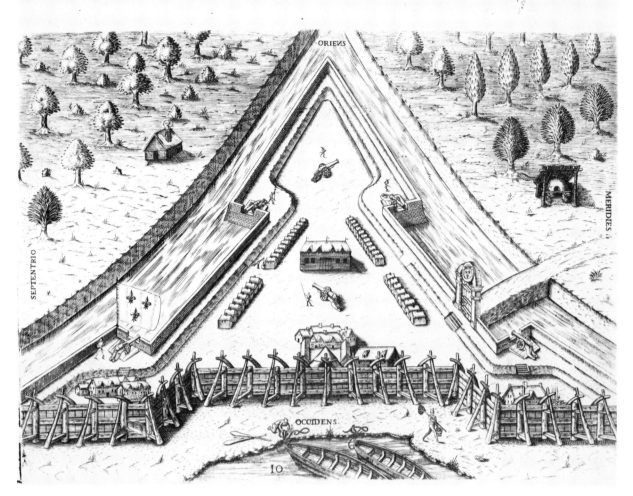

5. Fort Caroline. On landing, the early colonists' first action was usually the construction of a fort as a defense against both Indian and European enemies. One of the first ones was Fort Caroline, built by French Huguenots in 1564 near present-day Jacksonville, Florida. (Note that the bakery is outside the fort to lesson the chance of fire.) Spaniards surprised Fort Caroline in 1565, butchered all the men they could catch, and converted it into a Spanish stronghold. Three years later vengeful Frenchmen burned the fort and hanged their Spanish captives for committing robbery and murder.

6. The danger of Indian attack. Frontier settlements lived with the constant danger of attack by Indians. War parties might strike suddenly from out of the western wilderness and then vanish with the scalps and plunder they had taken before any effective pursuit could be organized.

7. French infantryman, circa 1740. This crude print shows details of camp life that would be typical of most armies into the middle of the nineteenth century. The sentry in the foreground is in full dress, with his hair neatly plaited and powdered. The collar, cuffs, and turnbacks of his white coat are bright blue, as are his waistcoat and breeches; his buttons and braid are yellow. He has a flintlock musket and carries paper-wrapped cartridges in the leather pouch on his right hip. A bayonet and sword hang from his waist belt. Behind him one of the regimental women is cooking the usual *soupe* or stew over an open fire. A soldier, probably a sentry just off duty, has removed his hot gaiters and is being served a bowlful. Each tent in the background accommodates approximately ten men. Two soldiers seem to be playing a French version of horseshoes. At the left a fatigue detail in waistcoats and forage caps collects firewood. In the left foreground is a stubby mortar, used for siege warfare, and two of its shells. To the right is a clumsily drawn field gun with five solid shot. The implement leaning against the gun's tube is probably the "ladle" used in loading the gunpowder.

8. Moses Marcy, circa 1750. Marcy's service apparently consisted of helping to raise, equip, and pay Massachusetts Provincial regiments. Yet this painted overmantle from his house in Southbridge shows him in a smart brown uniform, trimmed with silver lace. He has a black military cockade on his laced hat and an officer's distinctive crimson scarf over his left shoulder.

9. Portrait of Maj. George Scott. An English officer with a knack for irregular warfare, Major Scott commanded units of light infantry and rangers at Louisbourg and Quebec. This portrait, attributed to John Singleton Copley, shows him in a uniform modified for North American service: His coat is cut short and is without lace, and the cocked hat has been replaced with the leather cap in his right hand. Part of his equipment—a cartridge box and a powder horn—can be seen under his right elbow.

10. American powder horn, circa 1758. Soldiers filled idle hours by decorating their powder horns with intricate carvings. This one has the two common themes—the British coat of arms (right center) and a map of the rivers and forts between New York City (bottom) and Canada. The double-headed eagle (lower left) may well be the arms of Frederick the Great's Prussia, then a British ally.

2

Soldiers for Independence

The genius of this nation is not in the least to be compared with that of the Prussians, Austrians, or French. You say to your soldier "Do this!" and he does it; but I am obliged to say "This is the reason why you ought to do that"; and then he does it.

BARON VON STEUBEN [1]

So wrote Baron von Steuben from Valley Forge in 1777. Four years later, however, while trying to get Gov. Thomas Jefferson and the state of Virginia to take effective action against the ravages of Lord Cornwallis' invading army, he wrote that America was a country "where every farmer is a general, but where nobody wishes to be a soldier."[2]

The U.S. Army began on June 14, 1775, with the Continental Congress' decision to raise six companies of expert riflemen, its subsequent adoption of the New England volunteers then besieging Boston as the "Continental Army," and its appointment of George Washington to command all American forces. These "Continentals"

formed the country's first regular army, and from beginning to end they carried the major burden of the Revolutionary War. Congress placed the responsibility for raising, maintaining, and clothing Continental regiments on the various states in proportion to their size and population. Massachusetts and Virginia were each assigned fifteen infantry regiments; Pennsylvania, twelve; Delaware and Georgia, one apiece. Each state named the officers for the Continental regiments of the contingent (or "Continental Line") it provided, which was an unfortunate but probably inescapable factor in overloading the army with officers whose only merit was the favor of some local politician.

Congress initially attempted to form too

many infantry regiments (often called battalions); in September 1776 it authorized a total of eighty-eight, but few, if any, of these could be brought up to full strength. Consequently, in 1780 their number was reduced to fifty. The other Continental units consisted of four regiments each of artillery and light dragoons, one of artificers (skilled workmen, probably never fully organized), the "partisan corps" or "legions" (small units for scouting and raiding) of Lt. Col. Charles Armand Tuffin and Maj. Henry Lee, a Provost Troop (military police), and Washington's guard.

The first Continentals were excellent raw material—"Young, stout, healthy, zealous, and good humor'd and sober," wrote Maj. Gen. Charles Lee, the eccentric former British officer who helped greatly in organizing the army but finally fell victim to his own mental instability.[3] In recommending their soldiers to Washington in 1775, the Massachusetts Provincial Congress described them honestly:

> The greatest part of them have not before seen service; and though naturally brave and of good understanding, yet, for want of experience in military life have but little knowledge of divers things most essential to the preservation of health and even of life. The youth of America are not possessed of the absolute necessity of cleanliness in their dress and lodging, continual exercise and strict temperance to preserve them from diseases.[4]

These men were enlisted for only one year. The hardships they suffered in Canada and in the winter fighting in New Jersey disabled many and left many more disinclined to reenlist. In fact, their appearance and the stories they told on their return home discouraged recruiting in general.

As the war against England lengthened and enthusiasm dwindled, the quality of the recruits declined. In 1777, Maj. Gen. Philip Schuyler complained that the New England regiments serving under him in New York were "one third negroes, boys, and men too aged for the field."[5] A French observer noticed many soldiers who were "small and thin, and even some children twelve or thirteen years old."[6] A sprinkling of free blacks served in the Continental regiments from the first days of the war, and their numbers increased as the war went on. Rhode Island purchased the freedom of slaves willing to volunteer, and other states promised freedom to those who served faithfully for three years. Some blacks came into the militia as substitutes for gun-shy masters who had been drafted for service. In August 1778 there were some 755 blacks in an American army of approximately twelve thousand. After 1776 the 1st Rhode Island Regiment was composed in large part of black soldiers, who were noted for their smartness, discipline, and bravery. Only North Carolina, South Carolina, and Georgia did not accept black recruits, although some blacks were with Francis Marion and other partisan leaders in the Carolinas. Black soldiers served well, and their service undoubtedly had much to do with the abolition of slavery in New England and Pennsylvania and the outlawing of the slave trade in all states but South Carolina and Georgia.

In 1776, Congress raised the term of service to three years "or the duration of the war." To fill empty ranks, some states began enlisting deserters from the British Army, and even British and German prisoners of war. Such men frequently deserted again, often carrying off horses and equipment, as well as information. At the same time, some veterans came back into the service; other recruits might have had some active service with the militia. Although there never were enough men, the Continental regiments of the last years of the war were composed of hardened professionals, generally the equals of any European troops.

Sectional differences made army life uncomfortable during the first years. During the siege of Boston, New Englanders brawled with riflemen from Pennsylvania, Maryland, and Virginia. At Ticonderoga in 1776, New Englanders looked on the morals of the "Southern troops" (mostly Pennsylvanians) with great misgivings; the Pennsylvanians, officers and men alike, were disgusted with the "leveling" tendencies among the "dirty, lousey Saints" and their town-meeting style of discipline.[7]

THE INFANTRY

The internal organization of a Continental infantry regiment varied considerably from state to state, and sometimes from colonel to colonel. Some regiments followed British custom in forming elite companies of grenadiers and light infantry. Light infantry was especially adapted to the rugged American terrain, especially after the American riflemen (from whom so much had been expected) proved comparatively ineffective. In 1777, Washington formed his first large light infantry units by drawing selected men from all his infantry regiments and grouping them in temporary battalions. In early 1778 the Continental infantry regiments were standardized at 585 officers and men, in nine companies. The ninth company was light infantry, made up of men who were young, strong, active, 67 to 70 inches in height (taller than the average soldier), good shots, and preferably veterans. They were specially trained to use their bayonets and became the elite of the Continental Army. In the spring these companies were detached from their parent regiments and combined into a "corps" of several provisional regiments for outpost operations or special missions, such as the storming of Stony Point in 1779. When the army went into winter quarters, the companies were released to their respective regiments.

RIFLEMEN

The companies of riflemen raised in 1775, with their half-Indian dress and deadly long rifles, were the most characteristically American troops of the Revolutionary period. Freeborn frontiersmen, much given to strong drink, riotous behavior, and desertion, they could hit a single Englishman at up to 300 yards—a distance at which an infantryman armed with the usual smoothbore musket would be lucky to hit a massed regiment. The Americans had expected that their riflemen would shoot the British Army to pieces, but had overlooked the facts that loading a rifle took twice as long as loading a musket and that the rifle did not have a bayonet. The British quickly developed the tactic of giving American riflemen a volley and then charging through the smoke with the bayonet, catching them in the act of reloading. So rushed, riflemen would break for the rear, throwing the regular infantry behind them into disorder. As a result, no new rifle units were enlisted, and some seem to have been rearmed with muskets.

In 1777, Washington formed a provisional Corps of Riflemen, under Col. Daniel Morgan, with picked marksmen detached from Pennsylvania, Virginia, and Maryland Continental regiments. They were sent to deal with the Indians who had been raiding in the Hudson Valley as part of an invading British army under Gen. John Burgoyne. Working in close cooperation with the American light infantry, Morgan employed his riflemen with great effectiveness as sharpshooters in the battles around Saratoga. This "corps" was broken up during the winter of 1777–78 and never reactivated. Other rifle units, mostly militia or state troops, served usefully in the south, especially in fights such as King's Mountain, against Tory forces of

THE CONTINENTAL NAVY

The Continental Army was amphibious. During the siege of Boston, while Congress still was debating the creation of a navy, Washington organized a fleet of six schooners manned by officers and soldiers from New England regiments. This new navy raised considerable havoc with the British ships bound for Boston harbor, capturing much-needed supplies for the Continental Army and helping to keep the besieged British short of food and fuel through the bitter winter of 1775–76. On Lake Champlain, Maj. Gen. Philip Schuyler and Brig. Gen. Benedict Arnold built up a naval squadron of small warships that supported the unsuccessful American invasion of Canada in 1775–76, and delayed the British counterinvasion of New York in 1776 by forcing the British to build a stronger fleet at the north end of the lake before risking an advance. New England regiments, especially Col. John Glover's Massachusetts regiment of former seamen from Marblehead, evacuated the defeated American army from Long Island in 1776, and manned the boats that ferried it across the ice-filled Delaware River for the attack on the Hessians at Trenton during Christmas that same year. One of the war's most daring exploits was Col. Return Jonathan Meigs's whaleboat raid across almost 50 miles of Long Island Sound from Guilford, Connecticut, to Sag Harbor to capture a Tory foraging party and a twelve-gun schooner. The army also supported David Bushnell's nearly successful hand-powered submarine, the *Turtle*, in 1776 and his floating torpedoes in 1777.

STATE REGULARS AND MILITIA

In addition to the Continental Army, the various states had their own land forces, which consisted of state regulars and militia. (Most of the states also had their own navies.) The regulars, often confusingly termed the "State Line," were enlisted for from one to three years of service. Usually in uniform, they were employed for garrisons, seacoast defense, frontier operations, and the preservation of law and order; in emergencies, they might be attached to Continental forces. The militia, consisting of able-bodied citizens of military age, was often called up for varying periods of service, but seldom for more than three months.

Regarding themselves as sovereign and independent, the states usually gave their own regulars and militia higher pay than they did their Continental regiments. This naturally made it more difficult to secure recruits for the Continentals—why endure three years of hardship and danger when you could earn far more for a shorter period, under much easier discipline, near your home?

On active service, the militia (or "Long Faces," as the Continentals called them) often were more of a hindrance than a help. Washington described them as "badly officered and under no government. They come in you cannot tell how, go, you cannot tell when, and act you cannot tell where, consume your Provisions, exhaust your Stores, and leave you at last in a critical moment."[8] Maj. Gen. Nathanael Greene compared them to the "locusts of Egypt" because they wasted the country-side without performing any useful duty. In battle they usually broke and ran as soon as things got dangerous.

The militia had to be used in large numbers, however, because of the weakness of the Continental Army. In states like New Jersey that were fought over repeatedly, militiamen acquired appreciable military skills and were very effective in harrying British foraging parties and detachments. They also were useful in suppressing Tory activities, and militiamen formed the guerrilla bands of Francis Marion and other partisan leaders in the Carolinas. In the end, the militia was very certain that only its own skill and courage had won the war.

OFFICERS

Except for a scattering of veterans of the French wars, the officers of the Continental Army had to learn their new trade from scratch. Few of them were dismayed by the prospect. Though they generally admitted that engineer, and possibly artillery, officers did require specialized training, freeborn American citizens naturally assumed themselves equal to any military assignment. They might study such standard books as Humphrey Bland's *Treatise on Military Discipline,* but these could give them little help with their primary problem, which was to organize, clothe, feed, and discipline several hundred individualistic young Americans with no sense of subordination and somewhat less of sanitation. In this task they lacked the three major advantages enjoyed by British officers: the mutually accepted class system that set the British officer apart from and above his enlisted men, the established administrative services that supplied and paid the British Army, and the assistance of veteran noncommissioned officers. The colonies did have their own social systems, but they were flexible and counted for little in New England and along the frontier. The British administrative services might have been corrupt but they worked in their archaic way; Americans had to improvise theirs or live hand to mouth without them.

In the New England regiments that Washington took over around Boston, many officers originally had been elected by their men; most of them were, in Washington's words, "nearly of the same kidney with the privates."[9] Sardonic Charles Lee thought them "defective"; a Connecticut captain agreed that the Massachusetts officers were a "most despicable set." They were, in fact, old friends and neighbors to their enlisted men, business associates, relatives, and in-laws. As such, only the strongest characters among them had much control over their men, coaxing instead of ordering, and dodging the enforcement of unpopular regulations which might affect their popularity. Others indulged in various swindles; they might claim pay and rations for more men than they actually had, and pocket the difference. A good many of these officers had behaved disgracefully at Bunker's Hill, and some subsequently were broken from the service as an example for the rest. It was noted that Col. John Glover's regiment, made up of seamen commanded by former ships' officers, was the most exact in its discipline.

To George Washington, both as a soldier and a Virginia aristocrat, such conduct as the often-cited example of a captain shaving one of the privates in his company was unendurable. He wanted "gentlemen" for officers, meaning men who would accept responsibility, lead, command, and set an example, but to the end of the war the Continental Army's major weakness was the quality of its company and regimental officers. Crusty Schuyler thought many of them "a disgrace to the most contemptible troops that were ever collected,"[10] and Nathanael Greene agreed. Baron von Steuben noted that they considered their duty, after the English fashion, to be only to mount guard and to put themselves at the head of their men when going into action. Few colonels or captains knew how many men they commanded; fewer still had an accurate idea of what weapons, camp equipage, and accoutrements their men possessed. The internal administration of a regiment and a company was completely unknown.

The army's paperwork normally was in something of a muddle. When Washington took command of the army it took him eight days of hard work to get an approximate count of its numbers. For the first year he had a competent adjutant general, a former British officer named Horatio Gates, to handle administrative matters, but Gates' ambition soon took him off to field commands and then into almost open opposition and insubordination. Thereafter a group of intelligent, hard-working young officers drafted letters, rode errands, and generally helped out around the headquarters, but Washington never had a functioning staff in the modern

sense. Most of the burden of simply keeping the army in existence, planning its operations, commanding it in action, championing it against those congressmen who suspected every general of being a would-be Caesar, and handling any other difficulty that arose became Washington's personal responsibility.

Congress chose the general officers, often without consulting Washington. Each state had an unofficial quota, based on the troops it provided. Competence and experience might be considered, but usually only along with political expedience. Proven fighting men like Benedict Arnold and John Stark of New Hampshire would have less qualified officers promoted over them. Fast-talking foreign officers such as Thomas Conway might bedazzle congressman into giving them undeserved rank. Too many of Washington's overcrowded hours had to be diverted to dealing with the resulting hurt feelings, quarrels, and resignations.

Promotion at lower levels was handled strictly within the state contingents. Capt. Robert Kirkwood of the Delaware Continentals, much praised as an outstanding officer, was one example. He could never be promoted: Delaware provided only one regiment and that—after Gates wasted it at Camden—never had more than two companies. Kirkwood led them for over a year, foremost in every battle and in constant raids and patrols between battles, and went home still a captain. But it was officers of his same stamp, taught by years of defeat and suffering, who held the thin Continental regiments together and made them unconquerable. Whatever the fortunes of war, they marched with their battered Continentals, enduring with them, looking after them, and getting the last gasp of effort out of them on the march and across the battlefield. A work or two on the art of war—Steuben's "Blue Book" or a translation of Frederick the Great's *Military Instructions*—was usually tucked in among the worn shirts and darned stockings in their haversacks, to be studied by the evening campfire.

Foreign officers appeared in large numbers. Many were worthless adventurers who scented prestige and profit. Later came those who were purposely recruited by American agents in France to fill specific needs. Some, such as Steuben and Louis du Portail with his fellow French engineers, had essential skills no American officer possessed. Others were excellent officers who served loyally, whether adventurers such as Jean de Kalb (born Hans Kalb) or idealists like Thaddeus Kosciuszko, jackleg engineer and military handyman extraordinary. The charming young Marquis de Lafayette was in a class by himself, a useful friend and sometimes an overambitious nuisance. The Polish cavalryman, Count Casimir Pulaski, was brave, but never comprehended either the English language or the art of handling Americans. Thomas Conway, from an Irish regiment in the French Army, was competent, but also a greedy troublemaker. Most of them wanted promotions and choice commands which American officers also desired, creating more teapot tempests that Washington had to adjudicate. There is little evidence as to what the enlisted Continentals thought of these foreigners. Those who were useful and plainly concerned with the soldiers' welfare were accepted and even popular, especially if they were entertaining. Lafayette seems to have been liked; although men might weary of Steuben's constant drilling and inspections, but not of Steuben himself. De Kalb's Continentals followed him to the death.

There can be no denying that the war bore heavily upon the officers. They provided their own uniforms and equipment out of a pay that never was particularly generous and rapidly became next to worthless as the value of Continental paper money declined. Families of enlisted men were entitled to some assistance from the local authorities if in want (which does not mean they always received it, as such charity was likely to raise the local tax rate a few pence). Officers' families were not eligible, and letters "filled with the most heartaching tender complaints a woman is capable of writing" drove many a good officer to resign his commission.[11] Others hung on, drawing on their personal fortunes, selling property, borrowing, often using their own money to get their men some desperately needed food or clothing. Toward the end of the war a captain's whole pay for a year hardly would buy a new pair of boots, and a common day laborer could earn more.

WOMEN OF THE REGIMENT

As in the French wars, women followed the Continental drums, sewing, mending, washing, cooking, nursing—and also pilfering. Some stripped the dead in the night after a battle, and might not be too tender with a dying or badly wounded man in the process. Some passed from the Continental Army to the British and back again with the fortunes of war. Washington complained that pregnant women and those with small children were clogs on the army's movements, but he usually allowed them rations because many had come from areas since occupied by the British and so had no homes to which they might return. They included respectable wives and mothers, as well as professional whores in such desperate circumstances that they would follow an American army for their livelihood. Two of these women achieved considerable fame: Margaret Corbin took her husband's place when he was killed serving a gun at Fort Washington in 1776. Congress later gave her a small pension, and she was a local character and sometimes a problem at West Point for years afterward. "Molly Pitcher"—actually Mary Hays, wife of a gunner in the 4th Continental Artillery Regiment—was praised for her courage in carrying water to gun crews under fire even though a British cannon ball tore off the lower part of her petticoat. More famous camp followers were Martha Washington and the wives of some of the senior officers, who joined their husbands when the army went into winter quarters and exerted a civilizing influence on the American war effort. Tradition, apparently better founded than usual, credits Martha Washington with quiet deeds of gentleness among the sick and suffering at Valley Forge.

BARON VON STEUBEN

Until the winter camp at Valley Forge, the Continentals had been handicapped by the lack of any standard system of regimental organization and drill. The more conscientious colonels had developed their own systems, but the inevitable results were delay and confusion when the army had to occupy a position or maneuver in the face of the enemy. Camps were poorly organized and carelessly policed, to the great detriment of the soldiers' health. Overburdened as he was, Washington could not have time for everything; his repeated orders on camp cleanliness were ignored by many of his brigade and regimental commanders.

The soldier who would correct these faults arrived at Valley Forge on February 23, 1778. Friedrich Wilhelm Ludolf Gerhard Augustin, Baron von Steuben, some years previously a captain in the Prussian army, came as a volunteer, asking neither rank nor pay until he had proven himself worthy. He had an honest claim to the title of Baron, though no estates went with it. His military credentials (much inflated by Benjamin Franklin and the French officials who had assisted him in his wish to serve America) represented him as having been a lieutenant general and an aide-de-camp to Frederick the Great. Brief, expert service at Valley Forge made him a major general and Inspector General of the Continental Army.

In hard fact, Steuben was completely qualified for his new duties. He had been one of Frederick's *quartiermeisterleutnants,* a small, highly select group of young staff officers who were responsible for collecting intelligence, organizing and supervising the army's marches, selecting and laying out its camps, and maintaining order and discipline. Before that he had been an officer in one of Frederick's "Free Battalions," which were mercenary light infantry units recruited from Europe's dregs, notorious for their wildness and brutality. The most raunchy American recruits would be promising material to an officer who had served successfully with such irregulars.

Steuben gave the Continental Army "invariable rules for the order and discipline of the troops, especially . . . a uniformity in their formation and maneuvers and in the service of the camp."[12] By untiring personal example he taught American officers to train their own troops instead of leaving that work, after the English fashion, to their sergeants. Occasionally he was resented; the better officers disliked giving up their own systems of drill, the lazy ones hated being forced to bestir themselves and keep exact records on the state of their units. But the army as a whole approved highly of its new teacher, who cursed thunderously in three languages and worked tirelessly, "like a lieutenant anxious for promotion." His "Blue Book" (official title, *Regulations for the Order and Discipline of the Troops of the United States*) became the army's secular bible.

Steuben was Prussian-born, but his drill and discipline contained nothing of the Potsdam parade ground. Everything was simple and practical, designed for field service and not ceremony. Colonels were told in the "Blue Book" that their soldiers' health should be their "first and greatest care," captains that their first object should be "to gain the love of [their] men, by treating them with every possible kindness and humanity," privates that they must conduct themselves as befit good soldiers and shoot straight. At the same time, discipline was strict and the too-prevalent American practices of straggling and going absent without leave were sternly punished. Possibly somewhat to its own surprise, the Continental Army discovered that it could be smartly military even though ragged, maneuver swiftly and efficiently, and use the bayonet as bloodily as any Redcoat. Out of this came a surge of self-confidence and high morale.

LIFE IN THE REVOLUTIONARY ARMY

Rations

Mostly young men from farms and small towns, the first Continentals were accustomed to regular and hearty meals, and Congress intended that they should be fed accordingly. The ration that it established on November 4, 1775, provided each soldier with a daily issue of 1 pound of beef or salt fish (or ¾ pound of pork), 1 pound of bread or flour, 1 quart of cider or spruce beer, and ½ pint of milk. This was to be supplemented by a weekly issue of 3 pints of peas or beans, and either ½ pint of rice or 1 pint of Indian (corn) meal. The beef and pork might be either fresh or salted. Every hundred men also were to receive 6 pounds of hard soap and 3 pounds of candles each week. If beer could not be procured, every hundred men would be issued 9 gallons of molasses a week in place of it. Small quantities of salt and vinegar "if it can be had" also were issued from time to time, as were fresh vegetables. In the more permanent camps, markets were set up so that nearby farmers could offer produce for sale.

As the war went on, there were various minor changes. As there never was enough milk, even for the sick, it soon was dropped from the ration (not to reappear for over a century), and a gill (4 ounces) of rum or whiskey was added, much to the satisfaction of the troops. But too often the real problem was not what to feed the troops but how to find them any food at all. Winters were hungry times: at Valley Forge the chant "No bread, no meat, no soldier" went echoing down the straggling lines of makeshift cabins; at Morristown in the dire winter of 1779–80, with snow 4 feet deep, the half-naked soldiers endured "five days on half a pound of salt Beef and half a pint of Rice without any other kind of support whatever."[13] In 1780 the army was even on short rations most of the summer: "five or six days together without Meat; then as many without bread, and once or twice, two or three days together without either."[14]

Service in the southern states was even harsher. Continentals marching across North Carolina in early 1780 moved out "with only a half-ration for today and not even a half-ration for tomorrow," subsisting mostly on green apples, peaches, and corn gathered along the road and "often fasting for several days together."[15] An occasional bony wild cow was a feast. Through late 1780 and 1781 American light infantry campaigned for weeks on frogs, which "abounded" in the swampy Carolina lowlands, and a little rice; some tried alligator meat. Beef, when it could be found, was "simply carrion," sometimes too stringy and tough even for famished soldiers. Still worse was the constant problem expressed in a young officer's letter, "We have not had a drop of Spirits in Camp."[16]

Of course there were times when food was plentiful, though these often were of the army's own making. The spring shad runs, such as that up the Schuylkill past Valley Forge, gave soldiers fresh fish in brief plenty. Sometimes game was available; in 1781 Greene's little army rejoiced in a camp at Round O, South Carolina, where rice was plentiful and the hunting and fishing were excellent. Maj. Gen. John Sullivan's troops lived well during their devastation of the Iroquois territories in western New York in 1779. Inspecting his regiments, Sullivan found his men carrying pompions (pumpkins) or melons on their fixed bayonets, while their shirts were stuffed with corn, nuts, and beans. (They came back with their worn-out clothing streaming in tatters behind them, but their hair elegantly powdered with surplus flour.) When possible, camp gardens were planted; Chaplain Enos Hitchcock noted "Radishes with breakfast" at Ticonderoga in early 1777, as well as meals of venison, beef, veal, and fish. (He also had a private stock of 20 gallons of the best rum and brandy, with a dozen nutmegs for spicing, all of which he had to abandon

when the Americans evacuated the fort to avoid being trapped by "Gentleman Johnny" Burgoyne's invading army.) Sometimes there were spirits enough to give soldiers an extra allowance, especially after unusual exertions or when promised food failed to arrive. It made going to sleep in wet clothing on a cold hillside at least possible if not entirely pleasant. Even at Valley Forge and Morristown some regiments fared far better than others, because their officers were more efficient in the use of available supplies or able to discover unofficial sources for extra food.

Whatever the ration, it was issued directly to the individual soldier each day. He either could cook it himself or club together with a "mess" or "squad" of his comrades. As in the French wars, the regimental women helped. Each company supposedly had a mess kettle for every six or eight men, though twice that number might have to share one, especially after a lost battle or a hard march. In established camps the best cooks in a company often were detailed to prepare all of its meals, and detachments of bakers were organized to convert the flour ration into decent bread for the whole army.

Camp cooking was apt to be slovenly. Connecticut surgeon Albigence Waldo jotted in his diary, "There comes a bowl of beef soup—full of burnt leaves and dirt, enough such to make a Hector spew— away with it, boys—I'll live like the chameleon upon air."[17] Eating utensils were simple: a wooden bowl or plate, a wooden or pewter spoon, a cup, probably made from a cow's horn, and some sort of knife. Maryland bought bowls and spoons for its troops at one time; other states may have done as much, but the soldiers probably provided most of this equipment themselves.

In the field, soldiers might spit their individual bits of meat on their bayonets or ramrods and broil them over the campfires. (This was a habit officers had to check, since such use ruined the bayonet.) Flour or corn meal was puddled with water to make little "fire cakes" that were baked in hot ashes. Sometimes the soldiers had to thresh and grind wheat themselves to provide the flour, or grate corn into corn meal. When available, baked squash or pumpkin might be mixed into the fire cakes to give them a better taste. Such cooking was a rough-and-ready business. As one soldier noted in December 1777,

> We had no tents, nor anything to Cook our Provisions in, and that was Prity Poor, for beef was very lean and no salt, nor any way to Cook it but to throw it on the Coles and brile it; and the warter we had to Drink and to mix our flower with was out of a brook that run along by the Camps, and so many a dippin and washin [in] it which maid it very Dirty and muddy.[18]

The ability of the Continental to march and fight on such a sparse diet is not the least testimony to his innate toughness. Some American commanders had enough practical experience to know what their men needed to stay healthy, and did their best to procure it. A steady diet of fresh meat with little or no bread, salt, and vegetables was unhealthy, especially in summer. Schuyler reported in July 1777 that he needed salt meat; what little he had on hand he was issuing only to his scouting parties. Washington constantly was pleading for vegetables, "proper drink," and vinegar. (Vinegar was valued for "mellowing" water or seasoning food. Naturally Continental officers did not comprehend that it was a powerful antiseptic—they knew only that its use had beneficial results.) Greene considered salt the one item troops would not do without for a long period. It was so rare and valuable in the south that Francis Marion used it to pay his irregulars.

Clothing

Clothing the Continental Army was almost as difficult a problem as feeding it. In 1775 most of the New England army that formed around Boston turned out in civilian dress, with only two small units having any sort of uniform. In order to tell the officers and noncommissioned officers from the privates, Washington set up a simple system of identification: sergeants were to sew strips of red cloth to the right shoulder of their coats, corporals green strips; lieutenants were to wear green cockades in their hats, captains yellow or buff, field officers (majors, lieutenant colonels, or colonels) pink or red. General officers would be distinguished by ribbons worn across their chests—pink for brigadier generals, purple for major generals, and light blue for Washington. Aides-de-camp had green ribbons.

In late 1775, Congress decided that the army's coats were to be brown, a color that had already been adopted by Massachusetts and Connecticut. But the army had to wear what it could get, as much of the cloth for its uniforms had to be imported. Dark blue was a favorite color in the more southern states, but the supply was very limited since little, if any, cloth of this color was produced in North America. New York wanted blue coats for all four regiments it raised in 1775, but ended with one each in blue, light brown, gray, and dark brown; a fifth regiment (raised in what is now Vermont) got green coats. A Maryland regiment appeared in scarlet, which they replaced with brown hunting shirts when in action. The artillery's traditional uniform was blue faced with red, but black cloth frequently had to be substituted instead.

From 1776 on, clothing became more and more a matter of improvisation. America was a rough place for campaigning. Uniforms wore out faster than they could be replaced. While some Continentals at Valley Forge were almost naked except for "an old, dirty blanket around them attached by a leather belt around the waist,"[19] Boston merchants would not sell any of their stocks of clothing except at a profit of 1,000 percent or better, with payment in cash. Incompetent quartermasters, bad roads, and a shortage of transportation hampered replacements. Stocks of purchased clothing might rot in storage or be sold by embezzling commissaries.

The 2nd Rhode Island Regiment had been neatly uniformed when formed in early 1777, but by late summer it was "scandalous . . . in ye view of everyone, and has because of this incurred . . . ye disagreeable and provoking epithets of the Ragged, Lousy, Naked regiment. Such treatment . . . does effectively unman ye [men] and render them almost useless to ye army."[20] Sometime later it was given fringed white hunting shirts and overalls, which a French observer noted they kept extremely clean and neat. The single Delaware Regiment had a smart blue-and-red uniform in 1776, and was again fully outfitted when reraised in 1777. It got yet another uniform in the general distribution of 1779. In 1780 North Carolina somehow found it hunting shirts, overalls of blue-and-white striped ticking, and rough shoes. The 2nd Rhode Island did not get another complete uniform until the war's end in 1783. Col. Samuel Webb secured captured British uniforms for his regiment, which thereafter went proud in scarlet coats faced with yellow, earning a reputation as a first-rate fighting outfit. Washington usually tried to prevent the use of captured British uniform coats, but the 4th Regiment of Continental Light Dragoons also was allowed to wear red from 1777 to 1779.

To keep the troops clothed after a fashion, Washington and his officers utilized a variety of measures. They asked civilians to contribute spare garments or cloth from which army tailors could make uniforms; the hides of cattle slaughtered by army butchers were bartered with cobblers in nearby towns for finished shoes; forced requisitions were levied from the country-

side; and captured clothing was utilized. The cheaper, more easily made hunting shirt, a loose garment gathered in at the waist by a belt, was substituted for the uniform coat. Overalls, which were long trousers often cut to strap under the instep and fit snugly around the top of the shoe, replaced knee britches, stockings, and gaiters. Overcoats were rare—infantrymen wrapped themselves in their blankets instead, though each regiment tried to have a number of heavy "watchcoats" for their sentries in bad weather. Mounted men had, or were supposed to have, long cloaks.

The Revolutionary uniform had several very characteristic features. The cockade, a rosette of ribbon worn on the left side of the hat or helmet, was the recognized badge of a soldier. For some reason, Americans retained the black cockade worn by the British; in 1780 it became black and white in honor of the alliance with France. (The French cockade was white.) Another item was the "stock," a band of black leather or cloth worn around the neck for warmth and smartness. It could be thoroughly uncomfortable in warm weather, but endured, especially for full-dress occasions, into the Civil War.

Shelter

In the field the Continental Army lived in tents whenever possible. Its tentage came from different sources—captured from the English, domestic manufacture, imported from France—and varied in size and style. A wall tent approximately 6 feet square was supposed to suffice for six enlisted men, but on occasion eight to twelve men might be jammed into one. Tents of this size had to be hauled by wagon, and if possible, the men's packs were also. Usually this worked well enough unless the tactical situation made it necessary to send the wagon train to the rear, in which case the soldiers slept in the open, or made themselves crude shelters out of brush. (Without tents during his delaying action southward along the Hudson River from Ticonderoga in 1777, Schuyler secured a large number of planks to build huts. When he fell back to a new position, the huts were dismantled and the planks formed into rafts, which were floated downriver to the new site and there reassembled.) Senior officers had larger tents, often called "marquises" or "marquees." These not only gave them more living space but also provided room for their maps, papers, and staff work. Steuben stressed that every effort must be made to keep the tents clean. Soldiers were not to eat in them except during bad weather, and company officers were to inspect them every day. When worn out, tents were converted into trousers and other garments.

Blankets were a highly valued article but frequently difficult to provide. If carried in the regimental wagons with the tents and packs, they might be stolen by "the Rogues and whores that went with the baggage."[21] If the soldiers carried them, large numbers would be discarded whenever there was a fight.

On several occasions the American supply system broke down completely, despite the size of the departments of the quartermaster general and commissary general. (In 1780 approximately nine thousand men, mostly civilians, were supposedly engaged in "supplying" the army, which at that time did not have that many Continentals fit for duty.) After his most urgent appeals to Congress, the state governments, and influential citizens failed to bring relief, Washington was forced to require contributions of food and clothing from the surrounding districts. Whenever possible this was done through local officials. However, if continued for any length of time, this could be as devastating as an enemy invasion, as it stirred popular resentment against the army and strained the discipline of the soldiers engaged in collecting contributions.

Medical Care

The army's medical service or "Hospital Department" was organized on the British model, and consisted of regimental surgeons, a "flying hospital" to move with the main army, and several more or less permanent general hospitals. However, it operated under unusually severe handicaps. To begin with, the Americans did not have enough competent surgeons and physicians, and practically all medical supplies and equipment had to be imported from Europe. Worst of all, Congress turned inexplicably miserly toward the Hospital Department, denying its personnel decent pay and sufficient supplies, and meddling constantly in its organizaton and functioning. Some devoted doctors did their best, but too many were mere quacks. The general hospitals especially had a bad reputation for killing off their patients. Seriously wounded soldiers might be crowded into a room with others suffering from infectious diseases; dead men might be left among the dying and still living for twenty-four hours or more. Even in properly managed hospitals there might be no medicines, nothing but sour bread for the patients to eat, and a shortage of firewood. The continual shortage of transportation made movement of the sick and wounded slow and painful. Consequently, any sick or wounded man who still could walk usually tried to stay with his regiment, where friends might be able to help him.

Sickness ravaged the American armies. On an average, almost one man out of five was ill. In early 1777 there were seven men in the hospitals to every ten still well enough to do duty. Smallpox was a particular scourge. It could be prevented by "inoculation," which involved implanting material from a skin lesion of a smallpox patient into the skin of a well person, who then developed a mild case of true small-pox that left him thereafter immune. Unfortunately, this artificially induced smallpox was just as contagious as the actual disease, and could be transmitted to others in its original severe form. To be effective, inoculation had to be carefully controlled, which was difficult in an American army.

The treatment of wounds was still primitive. Some doctors appreciated the value of cleanliness; many understood that opium would deaden pain. But medical supplies were few. A soldier facing the amputation of an arm or leg—and there were many of those because of the way in which heavy, soft-lead musket balls splintered bones—was lucky if he got a slug of "stinking whiskey" before the surgeon's mates pinned him down, and the surgeon went to work with knife and saw. Sometimes he was given a musket ball to bite down on for relief from pain. (Hence the old expression "to bite the bullet.") General medical treatment included much bleeding and purging, which was considered essential to cleanse the patient's system, but usually succeeded in weakening an already weak patient.

Pay

By 1780 Congress' ability to support the war effort through the issuance of Continental currency and foreign loans had collapsed. It therefore resigned the responsibility for paying and feeding almost all of the army to the separate states, but the states failed to take care of their regiments. Through that year there were minor mutinies over shortages of food, rum, and clothing. Feeling abandoned and despised by the prosperous civilians around them, troops were increasingly ready to take what they needed from them at bayonet point. The mutiny of the whole Pennsylvania Line on New Year's Day 1781 shook the states into momentary awareness. New Hampshire, for example, suddenly realized that its troops "have had no pay for near twelve months" and so decided to "send forward some hard money by way of a present."[22] This improvement lasted through the Yorktown campaign, aided by a new loan from France and a reorganization of the U.S. financial system. After Yorktown, with victory and peace obviously at hand, Washington believed the army to be better "organized, disciplined, and clothed" than ever before, but rations were always a question and pay, even in worthless paper money, was long in arrears.

In 1782 Brigadier General Glover had received no pay for almost two years; Daniel Morgan was in debt and his remaining clothing sadly threadbare; and Maj. Gen. Arthur St. Clair, who had been a great landowner in western Pennsylvania, reported himself penniless and dependent on his rations to keep his family from starvation. Younger officers grumbled that pretty girls had no interest in "a picture of poverty" like themselves, being too busy catching stay-at-home civilians who had gotten rich from speculation and profiteering. Lt. Col. Ebenezer Huntington was moved to an inclusive damnation:

> I despise my countrymen. I wish I could say I was not born in America . . . the insults and neglects which the Army have met with from the country beggers all description. . . . I am in rags, have lain in the rain on the ground for 40 hours past, and only a junk of fresh beef and that without salt to dine on this day, received no pay since last December . . . and all this for my cowardly countrymen who . . . hold their purse strings as though they would damn the world, rather than part with a dollar to their Army.[23]

Given these conditions, the final disbanding of the army became a serious problem. Enlisted men had neither been paid nor compensated for clothing promised them but never issued. Congress had promised the officers half-pay (retired pay) for life after their discharge, but had taken no measures to implement this offer. Various ambitious politicians, such as Alexander Hamilton, sought to make capital out of the army's discontent. Some hot-headed young officers who had spent most of their adult lives in the army talked of turning their weapons against Congress; Horatio Gates, the second-ranking general with the army in the northern states, quietly encouraged them.

Washington agreed that the army had been cheated, but set the example of loyal military subordination to civilian government. He put an end to these maneuverings with his famous "Newburgh Address"—a simple appeal urging the officers not to "lessen the dignity and sully the glory you have hitherto maintained." Some recruits mutinied in Philadelphia, frightening Congress into moving to Princeton, but were quickly put down. The soldiers were gradualy furloughed, with the understanding that the signing of a peace treaty with England would end their service. By financial sleight of hand enough cash was found to give some of them three months' pay, but many did not get even that. Congress did, after some debate, let them keep their muskets.

The American soldier, Continental or militiaman, had had much to learn. From the start he generally could outmarch, out-dig, and outshoot the enemy, being far more familiar with tools and weapons in his daily life than was the average British or German soldier. He also could outsuffer them—a virtue his fellow citizens practically forced him to develop. Order and discipline came hard to him; officers were as green and individualistic as the men they led. But they endured and learned until they could match British infantry—proud regiments that had been almost invincible through a century of European wars—in open battle.

A leaven of patriotism, conscience, and professional pride worked within the thin American ranks. Nothing else could have held soldiers to their colors through "Seven Years of painful life in the Field." European officers marveled at their patience and devotion, half-naked in the snows and frost, unpaid, hungry amid plenty, defeated yet rallying to fight again. They fulfilled the old proverb "Nothing ever has been made until the soldier has made safe the field where the building shall be built, and the soldier is the scaffolding until it has been built, and the soldier gets no reward but honor." But for them the noble words of Jefferson, Adams, and Madison would have been futile. No other American army has suffered so grimly and so long, or achieved so much.

Autumn of 1781 in the Carolinas, somewhere west of Charleston—a warm day ending and long glints of sunlight reaching through the pine woods into a half-overgrown clearing. Two years earlier this had been a fat plantation, but its owner was a patriot. Lt. Col. Banastre Tarleton passed by with the green-uniformed Tories of his British Legion, and left nothing but the smoke-grimed rubble of its chimneys.

A dragoon comes suddenly out of the trees where a narrow road breaks the clearing's western rim, riding tensely, his stubby carbine raised and ready. Others appear to right and left of him. They are gaunt men on gaunt, powerful horses; sweat-marked white jackets and black leather helmets mark them as Col. William Washington's Continental dragoons. A white-plumed officer shouts an order. Putting their horses into a canter, they scout the clearing with swift efficiency and probe on into the woods on its far side. Cavalry of "Light Horse Harry" Lee's legion in faded green follow. Behind them come Lee's and Kirkwood's Continental light infantry, worn down to bone and sinew, tattered and battered, yet striding easily. A company of volunteer back-country riflemen pad silently past on moccasined feet, fringed homespun shirts open for coolness, long rifles carried every which way.

They follow the dragoons into the far tree line. A mile or so farther on they will halt on favorable ground and set up an outpost line for the night. Now into the clearing trots a knot of horsemen—the quartermaster general of Greene's little army, the quartermasters of its different brigades, and the colonel commanding the infantry advance guard. Quickly checking the clearing, the quartermaster general lays out a campsite, assigning areas to each of the brigade quartermasters in the order in which their brigades will arrive. The advance guard commander selects positions for the camp's guards and sentinels, which will form a "chain" around the camp to keep out curious strangers and to prevent soldiers from straggling off into the woods to forage on their own or possibly desert. With the advance guard march the regimental quartermasters and pioneers. The brigade quartermasters show them their respective areas, where they begin marking the sites for their tents, kitchens, and sinks (latrines). (Steuben's "Blue Book" gave detailed instructions, complete with diagram. Such a uniform system made it easy for soldiers to find their way around the camp, or turn out and form up ready for action, in complete darkness.)

The road fills with the main body of Continental infantry, dusty, weary, marching at ease. The regiments are tiny, some down to less than a hundred men. Many soldiers are half-naked and have tied pads of Spanish moss to their right shoulder and hip to relieve the chafing of their musket and cartridge box. But they move like veterans, having learned that the man and not the uniform makes the soldier. As each regiment enters the clearing the command "Carry Arms" rings out, drums crash into a marching beat, fifes shrill, and the ranks close up and march in cadence. Its regimental quartermaster meets it and guides it to its area. Sentries are posted. The soldiers stack arms, clear their tent sites, and begin digging kitchen pits and sinks at the spots marked by the pioneers.

Behind the main body is the wagon train with each regiment's lame and sick and—unofficially—its women, all under the charge of its quartermaster sergeant. (In some regiments he may be assisted by a fife-major whose particular duties are to train fifers and keep the women in some sort of order.) As soon as the quartermaster sergeant brings the regimental wagons in, the tents are pitched, including one or more isolated ones for the sick. Wood smoke lifts through the dwindling daylight. Horses are unsaddled and un-hitched and fed; in an efficient regiment they also are groomed and their hoofs are carefully checked. A few light field guns trundle in and are parked near the center of the camp. Last comes the rear guard, tired and out of sorts and hoping it will have time for supper before dark. Chattering shrilly, the women have clustered at the company kitchens and started food cooking while regimental adjutants have sent details, each under two responsible noncommissioned officers, to collect firewood, water, forage, and other "necessaries." They also will keep an eye out for any vegetables or stray chickens that may have survived two years of war, and any edible berries or greens. Meanwhile, the regimental commander has examined his area, paying particular attention to whether he has easy communications with the regiments on either side of him. If necessary, the pioneers will rough out roadways and improve stream crossings. The soldiers take their muskets into their tents; if the weather is threatening, or they will occupy the campsite more than one night, they dig small ditches around their tents, taking "great care that they do not throw the dirt up against their tents."

With sunset, after a scanty meal, the drum beat for "The Retreat" echoes across the camp, beginning on the army's right flank. The regiments fall in for roll call; the orders of the day and the names of officers and men assigned to tomorrow's details are read to them. With darkness, drums beat "The Tattoo," the signal for men to go to their tents where they must remain (except for necessary visits to the sinks) until "Reveille" the next morning. A quarter of an hour after "Tattoo" the sergeants "visit their respective squads . . . see that they are all present and retired to rest; and make their report to the commanding officer of the company." Then all is darkness and quiet, except for occasional challenges as officers go the rounds to check the sentries.

11a. General Washington and his men. From a hilltop west of Boston, Gen. George Washington, newly appointed commander of the new Continental Army, surveys the British fortifications around the seaport. To his left is Maj. Gen. Artemas Ward, who had commanded the army before Washington's arrival; to his right is a young aide-de-camp. All of them wear the black military cockade in their hats and the broad ribbons indicating their respective ranks. Behind them are some of Ward's New England regiments—a "mixed multitude of people" in a motley assortment of civilian clothing, uniforms, and semiuniforms. The men carrying halberds (a combination of spear and ax head) are sergeants.

11b. The American soldier, 1781. Under a chill drizzle in the fall of 1781, a column of Continental infantry from North or South Carolina (identifiable by their plain blue coats) moves against the last British footholds in the southern states. In the foreground stand a captain (distinguished by the silver epaulette on his right shoulder) and a lieutenant, who has pushed his hat back and sideways for comfort. The more ornately uniformed Continental artilleryman on the right has a blue coat faced with red and trimmed with yellow lace; he also wears "overalls"—long trousers cut to fit around his shoe tops, with straps under the insteps.

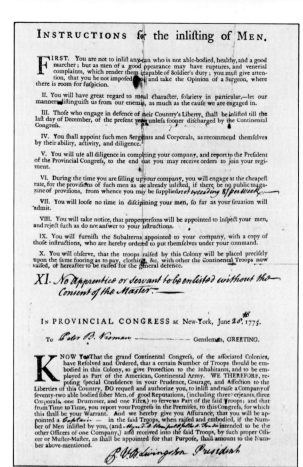

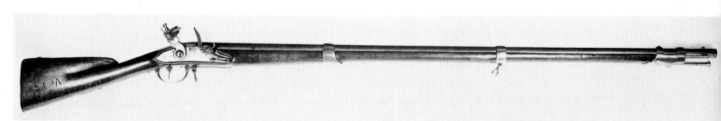

12. Raising troops. A common method of raising troops in 1775 was to authorize would-be captains to recruit their own companies. These are the authorization and instructions given one such officer by the Provincial Congress (state legislature) of New York.

13. The Charleville musket. The Revolutionary War infantryman's favorite weapon was the Charleville musket, thousands of which were furnished by the French government. There were several different models, but all were caliber .69, and lighter and better designed than the British "Brown Bess." The Charleville musket had a maximum range of approximately 1,000 yards; when well cared for, it was effective against formed bodies of troops up to 200 yards, and against individuals to 80 or 100 yards. A well-trained soldier could load and fire it four times a minute for short periods and two or three times a minute during a longer conflict.

14. Continental Army uniforms. The best contemporary pictures of the Continental Army's enlisted men were the work of foreigners. (American artists seldom depicted them, except as obscure background figures.) The four shown here were painted by a French officer, Jean Baptiste Antoine de Verger, late in the war. The figure on the left, wearing a white uniform and oddly shaped cap front with anchor insignia, belongs to a Rhode Island regiment—probably the 1st, which had many black soldiers. The soldier beside him in a black coat with red facings and red waistcoat and overalls is probably from a New Jersey regiment. Next is a rifleman in a dark green hat, fringed brown "rifle" shirt, and overalls. The figure on the right, an artilleryman in a blue coat with red facings, holds a linstock for firing a cannon.

15. Trooper and officer. These two figures are from a German source. (**1**) is a trooper of the 3rd Regiment of Continental Light Dragoons. His white uniform has light blue facings and a vest of the same color; his black leather helmet is bound with red cloth and has a foxtail for a plume. (**2**) is an officer of George Washington's picked headquarters guard company; his coat is blue, faced with buff.

16. Cavalryman. Also painted by de Verger, this smartly uniformed cavalryman in buff and blue is from the 2nd Regiment of Continental Light Dragoons, raised in Connecticut.

17 and 18. Indian allies. Most Indian tribes supported the British, but several, especially the Oneida of central New York and the Stockbridge group in Massachusetts, were loyal and useful allies of the Americans. Of these two contemporary paintings by de Verger of friendly Indians, the rendering of the figure on the left may have subconsciously been influenced by classical art, while that on the right looks more realistic.

19. "Rifle dress." This crude print, based on sketches by German officers serving with the British Army, shows two American soldiers in "rifle dress" of light blue linen, fringed with white. (The fringing shown is probably more elaborate than usual.) Because of the constant shortage of uniforms, this style of clothing—initially the frontier dress of army riflemen—frequently was worn, as here, by regular infantrymen of the Continental Line. It was comparatively cheap and easy to make; in winter, it might be made of woolen cloth. Usually it was white or brown, sometimes with fringes of a contrasting color, but it might be gray, blue, green, purple, black, or even orange. This print also illustrates the army's frequent lack of shoes.

20. Artillerymen on the march. This realistic engraving on a Revolutionary War powder horn shows American artillerymen on the march with a light fieldpiece, drawn by two horses hitched in tandem. The driver is a hired civilian who is unlikely to risk himself or his horses in action; consequently, the cannoneers will have to tug, push, and grunt their gun from position to position.

21. French field gun. This French 6-pounder bronze field gun was one of the Continental artillery's better weapons. A muzzle-loading smoothbore, it could throw a 6-pound solid shot accurately for approximately 800 yards; with grapeshot (a packet of small iron balls which spread like buckshot when fired) it was effective up to 500 yards.

22. Trenton, 1776. American artillery goes into action on the morning of December 26, 1776, to sweep the streets of Trenton. The men in the foreground are taking a round of grapeshot from an ammunition chest.

23. Yorktown, 1781. French siege artillery in action at Yorktown, 1781. Serving such heavy cannon was hard work: Since they lacked the recoil system of modern guns, they rolled backward when fired, and the artillerymen had to manhandle them back into position again. The cannoneer in the center is using a handspike to shift the gun's trail to the left, thus moving its muzzle to the right.

24. Baron von Steuben. The system of drill established by Baron von Steuben was used by the army for almost thirty years. Cheerful, generous, and extravagant, Steuben became an American citizen, dying in 1794 on the farm New York had given him near Utica.

25. French military engineers. At the beginning of the Revolution, the United States had no trained military engineers. It therefore secured the services of several officers from the French Corps of Engineers, then considered the world's most expert. Here two of them, assisted by three rodmen, are preparing to survey the trace of a seacoast fortification. One of the French engineers, Maj. Pierre L'Enfant, later laid out the new capital city of Washington, D.C.—and, ironically, died in poverty there.

26. West Point. Built to command a narrow bend in the Hudson River, the fortress of West Point was considered the key to North America since it barred any British advance from New York City to link up with their forces in Canada. This print shows the view looking downstream (south) from the fortifications (**A**) on Constitution Island. (**B**) is a heavy iron chain, stretched across the river on log floats; (**C**) is Fort Clinton (originally named Fort Arnold before that general's treason); (**D**) is Fort Putnam. There were other forts and batteries farther south. At the far left, two redoubts crown hills on the Hudson's east bank. Once heavily forested, this area has been completely logged for building materials and firewood. All of these fortifications were built by soldier labor, under the direction of Col. Thaddeus Kosciuszko and various French officers. It was grinding work, and the builders were often on short rations without even a dram of "stinking whiskey" at day's end. Some soldiers called the place "Point Purgatory."

27. The *Turtle*. Also known as "the famous Water Machine from Connecticut," the *Turtle* was the invention of David Bushnell. An egg-shaped wooden craft, it had separate hand-powered screw propellers for horizontal and vertical movement, and held a half-hour air supply for its one-man crew. It submerged by letting in water ballast through a foot-operated valve in its keel; to surface, the crewman used two hand pumps to eject the water. When submerged, he navigated by a compass illuminated fitfully by "fox-fire" (luminescence in decaying wood). The *Turtle* was armed with a waterproof "torpedo," containing 130 pounds of gunpowder and a twenty-minute clockwork delay fuse, which was to be attached to the hull of an enemy vessel by a sharp screw, operated from inside the *Turtle*. The Continental Navy had no interest in this craft, but the army attempted to use it against British warships in New York Harbor. One autumn night in 1776 a heroic sergeant, Ezra Lee, actually got under the British warship *Eagle*, but the screw was not sharp enough to pierce its copper sheathing. Short of time and air and pursued by a British barge, Lee had to cut loose his torpedo and crank furiously to make his escape.

28. Washington crossing the Delaware. This picture of Washington crossing the Delaware River early on December 26, 1776, has been ridiculed, often unjustly. Though the boats shown are too small, and it is far from certain that the "Stars and Stripes" actually were carried that early in the war, Emmanuel Leutz, the artist, did considerable research for the painting. He certainly caught the spirit of that desperate venture, in which the Marblehead sailors of Col. John Glover's Massachusetts Infantry Regiment got Washington's small army across through cold, hail, sleet, wind, and floating ice.

29. The myth of the militia. The Revolutionary War created its own military traditions, perpetuated in myth, art, and even serious history. The most pervasive of these was that all free-born Americans would spontaneously rise in arms to meet and crush any foreign invasion—a belief well expressed in this painting of militia rushing to meet the British. (Fortunately, the actual militia had better weapons than the collection of farm implements shown here!) In cold fact, there was no large-scale rallying during the Revolution, but the myth endured.

30. Hardship at Valley Forge. By contrast, the tradition of hardship bravely endured at Valley Forge through the winter of 1777–78 is based on actual fact, though undoubtedly the army's hardest winter was that of 1779–80 at Morristown, New Jersey. But it was at Valley Forge, despite its sufferings, that the Continental Army was trained and inspired into what one French observer praised as a "well-disciplined army, presenting in every detail the very image of order, reason, training, and experience."[24] This primitive print somehow captures the army's growing pride and self-confidence.

3

The Frontier Soldier, 1784-1845

*I am deceived; I enlisted for a soldier.... I never wa.
given to understand that the implements of agricultur
and the mechanic's tools were to be placed in my hand
before I had received a musket or drawn a uniform
coat. I never was told that I would be called on t
make roads, build bridges, quarry stone, burn brick an
lime, carry the hod, cut wood, hew timber, construct i.
into rafts and float it to the garrisons, make shingles
saw plank, build mills, maul rails, drive teams, mak.
hay, herd cattle, build stables, construct barracks
hospitals etc. etc. etc.... I enlisted to avoid work, an.
here I am, compelled to perform three or four times th.
amount of labor I did before my enlistmen.*

AN UNHAPPY RECRUIT, 1838

THE FIRST AMERICAN REGIMENT

On June 2, 1784, as the Continentals straggled homeward, still largely unpaid, Congress decreed that

standing armies in time of peace are inconsistant with the principles of republican governments, dangerous to the liberties of a free people, and generally converted into destructive engines for establishing despotism.... Resolved, that the commanding officer be ... directed to discharge the troops now in the service of the United States, except twenty-five privates to guard the stores at Fort Pitt and fifty-five to guard the stores at West Point ... with a proportionable number of officers, no officers to remain in service above the rank of captain.

The next day Congress called on Pennsylvania, New York, New Jersey, and Connecticut for seven hundred men to form a regiment of eight companies of infantry and two of artillery to serve for one year. Its purpose was to secure the Northwest Territory (roughly, today's "Middle West"), protecting surveyors, evicting squatters, and occupying frontier posts that the British still held at the end of the Revolution. Because of the nation's shabby treatment of the Continental Army, few men would enlist. Those who did were mostly "the offscourings of large towns and cities; enervated by idleness, debaucheries and every species of vice."[2] Lt. Col. Commandant Josiah Harmar gave his new unit the ringing title of "the First American Regiment." He worked devotedly to make good soldiers out of such unpromising material, but got little help from the national government. Poorly fed and clothed and irregularly paid, the regiment was scattered in the forts it built along the Ohio River from Pittsburg west to Louisville and Vincennes. It is not surprising that few men reenlisted when their year was up.

Almost immediately, the First American Regiment was involved in Indian troubles. The tribes of the Northwest Territory had sided with the British during the American Revolution. Their warriors were veteran fighting men, and their war chiefs were intelligent and daring. They had no intention of yielding any land to American settlers, and in their defiance they had British support. Judging the United States too weak to take effective action, England refused to evacuate Detroit and the other western forts as stipulated in the peace treaty. The immediate objective of the British was continued control of the Northwest's rich fur trade; their long-range hope was to convert the territory north of the Ohio River into an Indian state under British protection. Encouraged, and sometimes assisted by British advisers, Indian war parties raided American settlements north of the Ohio and frequently crossed that river into Kentucky. Kentuckians in turn raided back across the Ohio, ignoring Harmar's efforts to keep the peace. At best their hit-and-run raids inflicted little real harm on the hostile tribes; too often they struck friendly tribes and made new enemies of them.

In a spasm of economy Congress reduced the army's pay. (A private's was cut from $4 to $3 a month, and he was docked an additional dollar a month for his uniform and "hospital stores.") This made recruiting even more difficult. Yet a second infantry regiment was added in 1791. That same year a hastily assembled, ill-supplied army of some 1,400 Regulars (most of them raw recruits), levies (temporary Regulars enlisted for six months), and militia under Maj. Gen. Arthur St. Clair was cut to pieces by a smaller force of Indians near the present site of Fort Wayne, Indiana.

THE LEGION OF THE UNITED STATES

The need for an effective army having been bloodily demonstrated, Congress authorized the Legion of the United States, a flexible, balanced force of all arms, commanded by Maj. Gen. Anthony Wayne. A harsh perfectionist, Wayne put his dispirited veterans and apprehensive recruits through months of incessant training, teaching them to maneuver easily in the woods, shoot straight, and carry themselves proudly. His legion never could be brought up to full strength, and he was constantly sabotaged by his second-in-command, Brig. Gen. James Wilkinson. But he was able to defeat the Northwestern tribes at Fallen Timbers in 1794, and the British then gave up their frontier forts.

THE ARMY IMPROVES GRADUALLY

In the following years the army's strength and organization constantly fluctuated, as new regiments were raised for every crisis and then quickly disbanded. There were gradual improvements—better pay, a more effective staff system, and the creation of a Corps of Artillerists and Engineers. The "Quasi-War" with France (1798–1800) inspired the construction of coastal fortifications, a program that would continue hit-or-miss through World War II.

In 1802, President Thomas Jefferson cut the army to two regiments of infantry and one of artillery, plus a corps of engineers consisting of seven officers and ten cadets. (Out of the last a straggling school for officers developed at West Point.) Jefferson also began using the army to explore the western reaches of the United States. In 1808, with another war looming with England, he tried to rebuild the army, adding eight new regiments, including one of light artillery and one of dragoons. He did not bother, however, to provide either of them with horses and equipment. Secretary of War Henry Dearborn did manage to have Capt. George Peter equip and train one company of the artillery properly; and the company amazed everyone by its ability to march from Washington to Pittsburg in sixteen days. Shortly thereafter James Madison succeeded Jefferson as President, and appointed as his secretary of war, the mouse-skinning William Eustis, who promptly sold the army's horses to save the cost of their hay.

STATE MILITIAS

Because of the extreme reduction of the Regular Army after the Revolution, the state militias became the strongest part of the armed forces of the United States. Most Americans considered this proper and a true guarantee of their just-won liberty. The Constitution gave Congress the authority to call these militia into federal service to "execute the laws of the union, suppress insurrections, and repel invasions"; the second amendment stated that "A well regulated Militia, being necessary to the security of a free State, the right of the people to keep and bear Arms, shall not be infringed."

To ensure that the militia was indeed "well-regulated," the Militia Act of May 8, 1792, required the enrollment of every free, white, able-bodied male citizen between eighteen and forty-five in the militia of his state. (Federal officials and such persons as the states might specify were exempt.) He was to provide himself with a weapon, basic equipment, and ammunition, and to appear with them when called out for drill or service. Each state would organize its militia into companies, battalions, regiments, brigades, and, "if convenient," divisions and appoint the necessary officers; units of cavalry and artillery were to be organized from volunteers; the infantry was to include elite companies of grenadiers, light infantry, and riflemen. Each state also was to appoint an adjutant general who would report the condition of its militia annually to its governor, with a copy for the President.

It was a weak piece of legislation—there were no penalties for failure to comply with the act, and no federal standards were set for training, except that Steuben's 1779 "Blue Book" was to be used.

Another act passed shortly thereafter gave the President the authority to call out the militia in case of an invasion, without going through the governors. It included penalties for noncompliance, but softened these by providing that offending militiamen would be tried only by courts-martial composed of militia officers, and that the militia could not be called into federal service for more than three months in any one year.

In practice, no two states were alike in their military organization. Officer selection methods varied; usually the company officers were elected by their men. Generals and staff officers customarily were appointed by the governor or the state legislature. Militia commissions became convenient political small change and militia generals as common as dog catchers. All states allowed a militiaman to be excused from service if he provided an acceptable substitute. Records were poorly kept, and frequently there was no urgency to see that men actually reported for drill. Training seldom was exacting; one participant noted: "The militia were in a double crooked straight line in a great big field and were armed with shot guns, and rifles, and muskets, and sticks, and cornstalks, and thrashpoles, and umbrellas, and they were standing up and setting down, or on the squat, or playing mumble-peg, and they hollered for water half the time, and whiskey the other."[3]

It was 1802 before the federal government was able to obtain a partial idea of the militia's strength and organization. It took eighteen months to gather this limited information, and even then Maryland, Delaware, and Tennessee did not reply. There were approximately 525,000 enrolled militiamen but only 249,000 weapons; the best-armed states were Connecticut and Massachusetts, the worst Virginia and Georgia. South Carolina had the only effective militia system in the South; North Carolina did not even have an adjutant general. There was a serious shortage of artillery. Accordingly, in 1808 the federal government began to supply the states with weapons and equipment.

To its credit, the militia was good enough to put down Shays's Rebellion in 1786 and the Whiskey Rebellion in 1794, these being uprisings that responsible citizens opposed. Since militiamen often were the only armed force available, they were much engaged in the early Indian wars, especially along the southwestern frontier. There the indomitable frontiersmen fought off raids on their settlements from 1776 through 1789. Usually they were mounted riflemen, using their horses for swift movement, fighting dismounted, Indian-fashion, from tree to tree. They were almost as undisciplined and individualistic as the Indians they fought, apt to plunge into a probable ambush to prove their courage or to quit in mid-campaign and go home. Men such as John Sevier, James Robertson, and George Rogers Clark, however, could lead them on amazing raids, which never have received proper historical attention. But such frontiersmen were very few. The Kentucky militiamen who marched with St. Clair in 1791 were mostly newcomers to the West, unfamiliar with woods fighting and poorly armed. Even Clark's last campaign in 1786 broke down in squabbling, mutiny, and desertion.

Militia participation in the War of 1812 was often farcical, although units fought courageously at Bladensburg and Baltimore in 1814 and at New Orleans in 1815. Usually the militia ran away as soon as possible, or refused to turn out in the face of an enemy invasion. Several promising operations collapsed during 1812 and 1813 because militia refused to cross the Canadian frontier or to serve outside their native states. Even Andrew Jackson could accomplish little against the Creek tribes with only Tennessee militia. Moreover, many militiamen in upper New England and New York were involved in the illegal supply of foodstuffs to the British forces in Canada. (A British officer recorded that he bargained with an American militia officer "in full uniform" for the purchase of beef cattle. The American closed the deal by remarking that he wasn't supposed to trade with the enemy—but that he couldn't believe that anyone who offered such high prices for his cattle *was* an enemy!)

During the subsequent long period of peace the ordinary militia withered away. Its place was taken by the "volunteer militia"—groups of citizens interested in military matters who formed their own organizations, ranging from single companies to strong regiments. Normally these groups had a strong social background and were organized as military clubs; they chose their own members, selected their own officers, and established and enforced their own regulations. Some had existed before the American Revolution, the oldest undoubtedly being the Ancient and Honorable Military Company of Massachusetts, chartered in 1638. Even before 1812 they formed most of the militia's artillery and cavalry units as well as its companies of grenadiers, light infantry, and riflemen.

Many volunteer militia organizations, such as the Philadelphia City Troop, Albany Burgesses Corps, Richmond Blues, and Georgia Hussars, were formed from the socially elite and wealthy. Others were organized by immigrant groups, especially the Germans and Irish. Hundreds of such units—Fusiliers, Cadets, Light Guards, Grays, Greens, Gunmen, Rifles, Fencibles, Lancers, Dragoons—appeared, dwindled away, consolidated, or flourished. A few remain today as National Guard units. They favored impressive uniforms and often frankly gorgeous ones. A good many were efficient military units and took their training seriously. Some traveled widely, visiting similar organizations in other sections of the country for drill competitions. They also assumed an important civic duty. In an era of small and ineffective police forces, they maintained law and order when domestic disturbances got out of hand. In times of epidemics and natural disasters they enforced quarantine regulations, carried out rescue operations, and prevented looting. They were a flare of pomp and color in the hard-working life of the average citizen, and in national emergencies they were available for service—whatever their actual military skills.

THE ESTABLISHMENT OF A PROFESSIONAL ARMY

The War of 1812 saw a frantic build-up of the army to the equivalent of fifty-five regiments, but it is doubtful that more than 35,000 Regulars ever were on duty at one time out of the 62,274 authorized. An equal number of militia volunteered for four months to a year of active duty. Some were good troops (in particular the regiment of Kentucky Mounted Volunteers raised by Col. Richard M. Johnson in 1813). In general, though, both Regulars and Volunteers lacked competent officers and proper training until 1814, the last year of the war.

Following the war, the army again went through a series of reductions that left it without cavalry or ordnance troops. But the Black Hawk War and the need to concentrate troops to overawe South Carolina's threat of nullification (both in 1832) showed that the army was too small to meet its many responsibilities. Also, as the United States expanded westward across the Mississippi, infantry could not deal with the mounted warriors of the Plains Indian tribes. A battalion of mounted rangers who were to provide their own horses, weapons, and equipment was enlisted in 1832, but proved unsatisfactory. It was replaced the next year by the U.S. Regiment of Dragoons, which soon became an elite unit; a second dragoon regiment was added in 1836. It was at this time that the Topographical Engineers (explorers, surveyors, and map makers) were established as a definite branch of the service, the Ordnance Corps was revived, and an Artillery School was opened at Fortress Monroe and an Infantry School at Jefferson Barracks.

Warfare with the Seminole Indians in Florida from 1835 through 1842 again led to an increase in the army's strength. This was essential, for the unhealthy Florida climate was deadlier than the Indians. The fighting flared up so suddenly that the artillery commander found himself short of powder bags. He met the problem by borrowing flannel underwear and nightshirts from officers and men alike. Maj. Gen. Winfield Scott, commanding the Regular troops, donated his flannel underwear— and promptly caught a bad summer cold. Once the Seminole campaigns ended, the inevitable reduction in army strength reoccurred, but this time largely in the sensible form of reducing the number of men in each company rather than disbanding whole regiments.

Soldier-Frontiersmen

The average American soldier of this period was something of a roughneck. As one Indian agent complained, "all [his] feelings and habits run on extravagance & carnal intercourse with loud profanity."[4] Public opinion regarded him as a ne'er-do-well, too lazy for honest work, and in fact a large proportion of American-born recruits did come from the "idle and improvident." Also among them were better-educated men who had sought refuge in the army after business failure or woman trouble, or were seeking adventure, but these were comparatively few. The lack of suitable native-born recruits was partially made up by immigrants who by 1845 formed close to half of the enlisted men.

Most of these were Irish, with Germans next in number, followed by smaller groups of English and Scots. On the whole they were good soldiers, but their presence gave the army an increasingly foreign aspect, setting it still further apart from the American public. Attempts to prohibit or limit their enlistment had to be abandoned because they were often the only acceptable recruits available.

The enlisted Regulars' major sins were drunkenness and desertion. Discipline in isolated frontier posts had to be strict; a private caught smuggling whiskey into a fort might be sentenced "to carry ten six-pound [cannon] balls packed in his knapsack and strapped on his back, for fifteen days and nights every alternate two hours."[5] The older punishment of "running the gauntlet" passed away, but flogging was freely used as a punishment for insubordination and desertion. (It was prohibited in 1812 but reintroduced in 1833.) A good deal of the punishment was informal; noncommissioned officers, and even officers, might use their fists to convince a troublemaker of the error of his ways. The soldiers themselves normally dealt out justice to barracks thieves without bothering higher authority.

To make frontier duty more bearable, every established army post maintained a library, usually financed by a tax on the post sutler. Amateur theatricals were popular. Post schools sometimes offered instruction for illiterate soldiers as well as for children. The special holidays were observed with as much festivity as possible. By tradition dating from Valley Forge, all "Sons of Saint Tammany" were excused from duty on St. Patrick's Day. (The rest of the garrison was supposed to stay sober.) At Fort Mackinac at least, the non-Irish soldiers were given a holiday on April 30, and the Irish in turn "had the duty." In 1838 Congress authorized a chaplain for each post; their work was difficult, but many of them managed to develop sizable congregations.

Officers

In its first years the new army was officered by Revolutionary veterans, and not always the best of those. Few had any experience in Indian fighting but there were some good men among them. In St. Clair's defeat, Capt. Robert Kirkwood "... died as he had lived ... brave, meritorious, unrewarded. ..." It was his thirty-third battle. Capt. William Eaton had been discharged from the Continental Army in 1783 as a nineteen-year-old sergeant, and had worked his way through Dartmouth College before securing a commission in Wayne's Legion. He would be U.S. Consul to Tunis and would climax his career in 1805 during the war with Tripoli by leading a rag-tag column of Levantine mercenaries and Arabs—stiffened by seven U.S. Marines—from Egypt across 500 miles of Libyan desert to storm the city of Derna.

Political backing was essential in securing a commission or desirable assignments, and most officers sensibly sought it. But it also could be helpful to a scoundrel, such as James Wilkinson, who succeeded Wayne as the commanding general of the army. Gifted with an ingratiating personality, quick cunning, and an endless ego, Wilkinson was a natural confidence man. During the Revolution he served as an aide-de-camp first to Benedict Arnold and then to Horatio Gates. In 1779 he accepted the position of Clothier General, but neglected his duties and resigned before the end of the war. Seeking fortune, he went out to Kentucky and established himself in business, politics, and militia affairs, soon becoming a leading citizen. He also involved himself in Spanish intrigues to detach the western territories from the United States, swore allegiance to Spain, and became a paid agent of the Spanish government. Failing in business, he magnified his services in a minor militia raid across the Ohio sufficiently to get a Regular commission. Thereafter he did his best

to undercut Wayne's authority and blacken his reputation. He retained his Spanish ties, probably carried on treasonous correspondence with the British, possibly was involved in French intrigues, and definitely was a party to Aaron Burr's murky schemes to set up an independent state in the Southwest. Always suspected, repeatedly court-martialed, constantly seeking an easy dollar, he infected the army until he was swept out with other incompetent generals in 1815. But before that he had the support of dozens of influential citizens, including John Adams and Thomas Jefferson.

Politics also ruled in 1798 as the army was increased (because of the "Quasi-War" with France). Alexander Hamilton, who lusted after a military career and so got himself appointed Inspector General, was careful that all new officers were trusty members of his Federalist party. This brought screams from members of Jefferson's Democratic-Republican party, who accused him of planning a military dictatorship. But the officers appointed out of civil life when Jefferson increased the army in 1808 were practically all deserving Democratic-Republicans!

The constant fluctuations in the army's strength simply ensured that—a few devoted individuals aside—those officers who could make a living elsewhere left the army. (In the 1802 reduction, for example, 76 officers out of a total of 248 were released from the service with one month's pay and allowances for each year they had served.) Those who remained were generally overage, without interests beyond their daily routine, poorly educated, and sullenly resentful of any change. Their discipline was harsh but erratic, and drunkenness was common. The influx of new officers in 1808 did not improve matters. Winfield Scott, then a captain, who was one of them and usually of generous temper, described his fellows as "swaggerers, dependents, decayed gentlemen ... totally unfit for any military purpose whatever."[6] Scott himself began as a clumsy hand with his company payrolls and was suspended from the service for a year for publicly declaring that serving under Wilkinson was like marrying a prostitute, and similar insubordinate remarks.

The incompetence of too many Regular officers showed in the succession of American defeats during 1812 and 1813. However, combat gradually developed first-rate leaders; some, like Jacob Brown and Andrew Jackson, emerged from the militia, knowing little about the art of war but always ready to fight. In early 1814 Scott, by then a new brigadier general, was able to establish a camp of instruction at Buffalo, New York, for the "Left Division" of the U.S. Army. Reverting to Steuben's techniques, he formed all of his officers into an oversize, awkward squad and personally drilled them until they were capable of drilling their men. In addition, he hammered a knowledge of tactics, deportment, and military hygiene into them, unhesitatingly disciplining those who were not ". . . decent and emulous of improvement." A few months later Scott's own brigade routed an equal force of British Regulars in a stand-up fight at Chippewa, and the war's aspect changed abruptly.

The post-1815 army embodied a sense of newly proven national independence. Its officers were individualistic, competitive, and highly contentious. They had survived three years of war and also the brutal reduction at the war's end. (Congress casually cast off over three-fourths of the officers—many of whom had served honorably but were no longer physically "competent"—with three months' pay.) The tenacity and ferocity with which they wrangled over questions of rank and assignment are almost beyond modern comprehension, but was thoroughly typical of their generation of Americans with its hair-trigger readiness to settle personal differences by the *code duello.* Their patriotism was instinctive and uncompromising. In 1816 Scott and other Americans visiting Paris held a well-advertised banquet, under the nose of the Duke of Wellington and a British army of occupation, to celebrate the anniversary of the Battle of New Orleans, sitting armed at table in case any Englishman wanted to make something of it.

West Point

Almost imperceptibly, however, a major change was taking place among the army's officers. For years Washington, Steuben, and others had urged the establishment of a military academy based on the French model to train young officers. In 1794 President Washington had secured the creation of the grade of "cadets"—young officer candidates assigned to the Corps of Artillerists and Engineers at West Point, where they were to receive a combination of classroom instruction and on-the-job training. Unfortunately, the corps' officers were lazy and ignorant, and cadets were given every opportunity to do their routine work for them, but nothing more. When Lt. Col. Stephen Rochefontaine took command in 1796 and attempted to give officers and cadets instruction in fortification, a mysterious fire destroyed the school building and all its equipment.

President Adams could find no Americans competent to teach the necessary subjects, but President Jefferson finally opened the school in September 1801 with a civilian mathematics instructor and twelve cadets of all ages and backgrounds. The instructor soon had to be dismissed. But in March 1802 Jefferson, hoping the school would provide America with civil as well as military engineers, secured passage of a law authorizing a separate Corps of Engineers to be stationed at West Point and constitute a military academy.

The first year, instruction was given in artillery, fortification, mathematics, and "natural philosophy" (physics); French and drawing were added the next year. There were no entrance requirements and no regular curriculum. Few books and little scientific equipment were provided. The cadets themselves were a mixed lot, from eleven to thirty-four years old, strong believers in their personal rights. One appeared with a wife; another was one-armed. Some mastered the course of instruction in one year; others ("Uncle Sam's bad bargains") might attend for six or more years and never do satisfactory work.

The Academy barely survived the War of 1812, as most of the instructors were transferred elsewhere. Capt. William Partridge, one of its earliest graduates, was left in charge and held it together with a fierce devotion. Unfortunately, he was totally lacking in method and ready to quarrel with his own shadow. In 1816 Partridge refused to hold the required final examinations, then put all the professors under arrest and attempted to teach their classes himself. With some difficulty he was replaced as superintendent in July 1817 by Maj. Sylvanus Thayer—much to the displeasure of most of the cadets.

Thayer established discipline, organized the cadets into military units under cadet officers, developed a standard four-year curriculum, improved the quality and variety of its courses, and provided both theoretical and practical military training. His innovations included exact systems of grading cadets' performance and small classes to permit daily recitations and individual instruction. Beyond that, he set an example of professional competence, personal integrity, and self-discipline.

Under Thayer's guidance, the Academy flourished until the election of President Andrew Jackson in 1828. Flash-tempered, autocratic, and impatient of all rules, Jackson also had nephews and protégés who wished to be army officers, preferably without overworking themselves. Jackson made no bones about demanding special privileges for them; if they were dismissed for academic failure or misconduct, he ordered them reinstated. Eventually he became the champion of the cadets against Thayer and the Academy staff. Realizing that he had become the focus of Jackson's anger, Thayer resigned the superintendency in 1833.

For years thereafter, West Point was under attack as unnecessary and aristocratic. When new regiments were raised, Congress would officer them with civilian applicants, such action being both politically profitable and also an expression of the popular belief that any American citizen had the innate ability to command armies. Meanwhile, Academy graduates left the army by the hundreds, and had little trouble finding employment. West Point was the nation's only technical school; its cadets learned such useful mechanical arts as stone cutting and machine construction as well as engineering. In the arm or out, West Point graduates built roads, canals, and railroads; carried out river and harbor improvements; and mapped the wilderness. In the army they provided a cadre of self-confident young soldiers, uniformly taught and indoctrinated and accustomed to working together.

FRONTIER SERVICE

Rations

The First American Regiment's rations were similar to those of the Continental Army: 1 pound of bread or flour, 1 pound of beef or ¾ pound of pork, 1 gill of "common rum." Every one hundred men were to receive 1 quart of salt, 2 quarts of vinegar, 2 pounds of soap, and 1 pound of candles. The regiment also went hungry almost as frequently as the Continentals had done. Its food and clothing were supplied through contracts let by the Treasury to the lowest bidder, who was responsible for their delivery to the various forts along the Ohio Valley. As might have been expected, many of these contractors were dishonest or incompetent, or both. Even reasonably competent ones could have trouble getting their shipments down the Ohio through floods, early freezes, and Indian war parties. During the winter of 1786–87 the regiment might have starved if Harmar had not spent his own money to buy flour from local traders and to hire hunters who brought in "Venison, Bear, Turkey, Raccoon, Panther, etc, etc." in great plenty. The garrison at Fort McIntosh was thankful for "an abundance of fish" to replace the beef they did not receive.[7] One low point in the regiment's supply problems came on Christmas Day of 1788, when there was no rum in store, and the commissary had to borrow enough whiskey to give each soldier a half pint. But worse was to follow. In addition to cutting the soldier's pay, the Congress in its economy drive of 1790 also halved his liquor ration.

The quality of this contract food seldom was more than passable. Pork usually came in the form of bacon and in short measure—10 ounces per man instead of the 12 that were authorized. The beef ration often was delivered "on the hoof"—as live cattle, which required feeding and guarding until they could be slaughtered. This, in turn, depended on the availability of salt to preserve the meat in hot weather. Some of the officers experimented with "jerking" venison or drying it, Indian fashion, in the sun. Whenever possible the troops planted vegetable gardens.

At best, supply by contractor was an uncertain matter. At worst, it could fatally cripple the army. In 1791, while St. Clair was attempting to mount his offensive against the hostile tribes, the responsible contractor was William Duer, an avid and dishonest speculator in western lands, government bonds, and bank stocks. He was too engrossed in those concerns to supply the army. St. Clair had hoped to begin his advance in July, but could not move out until September as "there was so small a stock of provisions on hand, that, had the army moved on, they must have eaten their fingers."[8] This delay meant that frosts killed the grass, making it useless as forage for the army's horses and oxen, which grew steadily weaker. The men were incompletely clothed, often on reduced rations. Part of the Regulars had to be sent back to guard some expected pack trains of provisions against hungry deserters and stragglers. The Indian attack on St. Clair's camp struck men weakened and disheartened by hunger and hardship.

Somewhat enlightened by these years of Indian warfare, Congress decided in 1794 that all soldiers on frontier duty were to get an extra ration of 4 ounces of beef, 2 ounces of flour, and ½ gill of rum or whiskey. Further fiddling followed; in 1799 the liquor ration was entirely abolished, though the commanding officer of any detachment was authorized to issue "from time to time, rum, whiskey, or other ardent spirits, not to exceed ½ gill per man per day, except on extraordinary occasions." This permission seems to have been fully exploited. In 1802 a new ration gave each man 1¼ pounds of beef or ¾ pound of pork, 18 ounces of bread or flour, and 1 gill of whiskey, rum, or brandy; each one hundred men now received 2 quarts of salt, 4 quarts of vinegar, 4 pounds of soap, and 1½ pounds of candles. There were no further modifications until 1818, when soldiers stationed in the South were to get "In lieu of whiskey . . . ½ pint of peas, beans, or rice per day." Fourteen years later coffee and sugar replaced the liquor ration for good, and "ardent spirits" became part of the "hospital stores." The results were mixed; Americans of that period drank freely, and soldiers probably more than the average. The abolition of the liquor ration removed hard liquor, except for officers' use, from army posts, but it left the enlisted man who wanted strong drink no choice but to patronize the dives (somewhat later given the highly descriptive name of "hog ranches") that always sprang up on the edges of military reservations. There he was sold foul whiskey, treated with tobacco or lye to give it "bite" and soap to give it "bead." If he had no money, the proprietors would happily barter their liquor for stolen clothing, blankets, or tools. At West Point one captain's anger over such proceedings led him to roll out a field piece and almost demolish the tavern of one "Esquire North."

Uniforms

The dress of the American soldier changed greatly during this period. The First American Regiment was initially clothed in an assortment of hand-me-down Revolutionary uniforms. Harmar was angry over the shirts ("of a sleezy linen, very scanty"); shoes ("too small, fit only for boys . . . and of a bad quality"); hats ("too small and badly worked"); and coats ("of the worst quality") furnished his men in 1786.[9] He wanted long coats, but the secretary of war decided that short ones were more "proper for the service of the frontiers." Ordinarily soldiers had "hunting frocks" to wear on fatigue details. Wayne gave each of the four "sublegions" of his Legion of the United States a distinctively colored binding for its hats and otherwise made its uniform as smart and practical as possible.

During the period 1800 to 1815 the shako replaced the cocked hat; coats lost their customary red collars, cuffs, and lapels; and ordinary trousers were issued in place of the snug-fitting overalls. The expansion of the army in 1812 caught the administration unprepared to clothe so many additional men. The summer uniform of white linen jacket and overalls could be rapidly produced and so was issued extensively to the new regiments. For winter, since the United States produced very little blue woolen cloth, the infantry regiments got black, drab, brown, blue, or gray coats, with woolen overalls "of a dozen different colors." Because of supply difficulties some regiments on the western frontier (Indiana and Ohio) received no winter uniforms and so campaigned in the snow wearing their worn-out linen summer dress.

In the summer of 1814 American troops on the Canadian frontier were issued coarse gray woolen jackets and trousers of unbleached linen. Tradition has it that their exploits in this plain uniform led to the adoption of a gray uniform for the Corps of Cadets at West Point. After the war, the tendency was to develop very smart and elaborate uniforms for ceremonial occasions and simple and practical ones for work details and field service.

In early 1801 there had been another major change in the appearance of the American soldier. Until then, he had worn his hair long and clubbed into a queue; for parades, reviews, and inspections it had been rubbed with tallow or soap and then "powdered" with flour. This custom had been abandoned in the French Army during their Revolution (though Napoleon's Old Guard revived it) and was considered old-fashioned and reactionary by American liberals, probably including President Jefferson. Consequently, Wilkinson decided that the queue was "filthy and insalubrious . . . inconvenient, expensive, and unnecessary," and ordered all hair cut short.[10] Logical or not, his order was unpopular with a good many officers, who considered their queue the badge of a soldier and a gentleman. Veteran Lt. Col. Thomas Butler was twice court-martialed for refusing to cut his off; dying of yellow fever just before the end of the second trial, he told his friends to bore a hole in his coffin under his head "and let my queue hang through it" as a final gesture of defiance to Wilkinson.

Medical Care

Medical attention remained a haphazard affair and improvement was slow. The First American Regiment had one surgeon and four surgeon's mates to look after the garrisons of nine or ten widely separated posts. Wayne secured a higher proportion of medical personnel for his Legion, and established a model general hospital with two "industrious humane and honest matrons to assist in nursing and cooking for the sick," but subsequent army reorganizations cut this establishment back to one surgeon and two mates per regiment. The Office of the Surgeon General was formed in 1818 to provide centralized direction of the army's medical activities and to supply drugs and equipment, but it was 1832 before candidates for appointment as army surgeons had to pass an examination as to their physical condition, morals, and professional competence.

In practice, this meant that the average isolated post had no permanent medical personnel. Usually one of its officers functioned as acting physician and surgeon, and would be thankful if he had a few of the most basic medical supplies. Most posts had a small "hospital" room or building where the sick could be isolated under whatever care was locally available. Soldiers might doctor one another or try Indian remedies. Not surprisingly, disease killed four or five soldiers for every one killed in combat, and left many more unfit for duty for days or months.

The Ohio and Mississippi valleys were often unhealthy country, especially in autumn when the streams ran low. "Ague" (a type of malaria) and various other "fevers"

(frequently typhoid caught from contaminated water) were common afflictions, as were "fluxes," "diarrhoeas," and scurvy during the winter months. An epidemic of Asiatic cholera swept the northern United States in 1832, gutting a force of Regulars Scott was bringing from Buffalo, New York, by steamboat to take part in the Black Hawk War. Hitherto unknown in North America, cholera was terrifying—in a few hours a healthy soldier might be a dehydrated, discolored corpse. Scott's chief surgeon soon died, and another got dead drunk; Scott found himself head nurse as well as general. The epidemic burned itself out during 1833, becoming less virulent. Its weakened form may have been the "bilious fever" that disabled half of the U.S. Regiment of Dragoons in 1834 during its first long patrol into the western plains.

These sicknesses baffled contemporary doctors who, knowing nothing of their causes or methods of transmission, were uncertain as to whether ague and the other "fevers" were different diseases or simply different manifestations of the same one. They felt that the "miasmas" from swamps and stagnant waters, sudden changes of temperature, or some dangerous quality in the night air must be a major cause of such illness, never suspecting the swarms of night-flying mosquitoes that bred in the stinking swamps. Giving good advice for the wrong reasons, they might urge that camps and forts be situated well away from marshy areas and that soldiers be kept indoors until after sunrise. Smallpox could be controlled through innoculation and, after about 1806, by the safer method of vaccination; but, as a contemporary English soldier despairingly noted, "The ague, the yellow fever, and the plague will appear; and all that human ingenuity has hitherto suggested in prevention or mitigation, of these dreadful maladies, amounts to very little."[11]

Possibly the ancient army tradition of

"spit and polish" did more to keep soldiers healthy than all their surgeons. Steuben had stressed cleanliness; Wayne was a grim believer in the importance of military hygiene; and Scott carried on their work. Medical officers were amazed that Scott's insistence on rigid cleanliness in his 1814 camp of instruction had eliminated "even the demon diarrhoea." Throughout his long service Scott continued to insist on "Sobriety, cleanliness of person, cleanliness of camp and quarters, together with care in the preparation of the men's messes."[12] Unfortunately, the most conscientious surgeons and generals never dreamed that the clearest stream or lake might well be loaded with typhoid or cholera germs.

In dealing with wounds or accidental injuries the army surgeons were more self-confident. They knew little concerning the interior of the human body except for the major bones, muscles, nerves, and organs, and believed that suppuration in wounds was necessary and should be encouraged—the "laudable pus" thus produced was supposed to free the body of harmful substances. However, they made more use of antiseptics and anesthetics than is generally realized, using hot wine, vinegar, or even cauterization with hot irons for the former and opium for the lat-ter. Most of them appreciated the importance of cleanliness, but had no comprehension of the degree needed for properly sterile conditions. To avoid shock to the patient and danger of hemorrhage they stressed speed and dexterity; a good surgeon could amputate a leg and have the stump properly bandaged in about three minutes.

Indian wars were merciless affairs. Wounded soldiers had no hope for survival if they were not carried along with their comrades to the safety of a fort. Surgeons and their mates went armed, ready to defend the sick and wounded in their care. Death by prolonged torture—a fire kindled on his belly, or his intestines plucked slowly out of his body—was usually all a wounded soldier could expect after a lost fight. (The great Shawnee war chief Tecumseh was merciful, but there were few like him.) Some of the wounded St. Clair had to abandon to save the rest of his army loaded their muskets "with a coolness and a deliberation" as their comrades left them and "where they could pull a trigger they avenged themselves," as Indians stormed into the abandoned camp.[13] St. Clair's adjutant general, angrily attempting to restore some order among the retreating soldiers, heard and remembered the forlorn rattle of their muskets.

THE SOLDIER AS EXPLORER AND BUILDER

In the long view of history, the frontier army's most important peacetime duty was exploration. This began in 1804 when Capt. Meriwether Lewis and Lt. William Clark moved up the Mississippi on an expedition personally planned by Thomas Jefferson to explore the "Louisiana" area just purchased from France. Both officers were experienced Indian fighters, strict disciplinarians, and effective leaders; Lew-is could make scientific observations, Clark was a cartographer. Their one casualty occurred shortly after their departure when a sergeant died of a "Bilious chorlick" (apparently, appendicitis). In late October they reached the friendly Mandan tribes with whom they wintered. The next spring they continued up the Missouri into unknown territory with three sergeants, twenty-three privates, an expert wilderness hunter named George Drouillard, a newly recruited French-Canadian interpreter named Toussaint Charbonneau, Clark's black slave, York, and Charbonneau's young squaw, Sacajawea, with her new baby. (Sacajawea was a brave and useful person, but her historical importance has been sentimentally exaggerated out of all reason.)

Much troubled by hailstorms and "white" (grizzly) bears, they portaged their gear around the falls of the Missouri (now Great Falls, Montana). At the Forks of the Missouri they took the central fork, which they named the Jefferson. Lewis secured horses from the Shoshoni, and they went on through the Bitterroot Valley and the "very bad" Lolo Trail to the hospitable Nez Percé on the Clearwater River in modern Idaho. There they hollowed out log canoes and went down the Clearwater to the Snake River and down the Snake to the Columbia, reaching the Pacific on November 7, 1805. After a wet, uncomfortable winter near present-day Astoria, Oregon, they got back to St. Louis on September 23, 1806, bringing a mass of information concerning the rivers, mountains, Indians, animals, trails, and geography of the West.

The American soldier had been there first; the mountain men—some of them, like John Colter, ex-soldiers—would follow. Meanwhile, in 1805 Wilkinson had sent Lt. Zebulon Pike to explore the headwaters of the Mississippi and assert American sovereignty over the British traders in that area. On Pike's return in 1806, Wilkinson dispatched him up the Osage and Arkansas rivers into what is now eastern Colorado, where he saw—but did not climb—the mountain named for him. Some doubt lingers as to his actual instructions (Wilkinson then was involved in Burr's scheming and may have wanted information concerning the Spanish southwest). Pike next wandered south into Spanish territory, was arrested and carried

into Santa Fe, and finally sent home across Texas in 1807.

The War of 1812 temporarily halted exploration. Afterward, as the army shifted its posts westward, new parties went out. They were numerous and their personnel included botanists, artists, geologists, topographers, and astronomers. Year by year they completed what Lewis and Clark began. Maj. Stephen H. Long made a quick survey trip to the Colorado Rockies, which produced little except the discouraging title of "the Great American Desert" for the valley of the Platte River.

The most celebrated of the army's explorers was John C. Frémont of the Topographical Engineers. After an expedition to the upper Mississippi-Missouri area during 1838–39, he married the daughter of the powerful Senator Thomas H. Benton, by whose patronage he was able to explore the Wind River country (present-day Wyoming) in 1842. A longer expedition of 1843–44 carried him to the Great Salt Lake, Oregon, Nevada, and California. In most of this he was guided by such expert mountain men as Kit Carson and Tom Fitzpatrick; he covered little unknown territory but, with his wife's help, produced interesting and reliable reports of his expeditions which greatly increased public interest in the West.

In 1845—with war with Mexico in the air—Frémont was again on the trail, supposedly to survey the southern Rockies, while Lt. James W. Abert headed across what is now Oklahoma and the Texas Panhandle to map the Commanche and Kiowa country. And Col. Stephen Watts Kearny with part of the 1st Dragoon Regiment was prowling up the Oregon Trail from Fort Leavenworth through Fort Laramie and South Pass, and returning along the eastern slope of the Rockies to Bent's Fort and the Arkansas River—2,200 miles in ninety-nine days, with men and horses still in good condition.

The frontier soldier fought Indians and

Englishmen, but his peacetime duties were sometimes as strenuous as open warfare. He constructed forts, roads, and bridges; cut his own firewood; and frequently raised his own vegetables. (From 1818 to 1833 he even was supposed to raise the wheat for his own flour ration, and enough oats and corn to feed his horse.) Until steamboats became plentiful and reliable, he built and manned the keelboats needed to move troops and supplies along the western lakes and rivers. He carried the mail into the odd corners of the Northwest, and escorted survey parties and dignitaries negotiating Indian treaties.

Post surgeons formed the first U.S. weather service from 1818 to 1890, collecting data on the weather and the topography of their stations. They also furnished emergency medical care to civilians in their vicinity. (Dr. William Beaumont's study on human digestion, the first scientific research on that subject, grew out of his treatment of a young French Canadian who had accidently been shot in the stomach at Fort Mackinac.)

Even more demanding were the army's duties in keeping squatters out of Indian territory, suppressing the liquor traffic, and maintaining law and order between whites and Indians and between Indian tribes. These efforts were deeply resented by local civilians. The American frontiersman wanted land and intended to take it. Men who were honest, honorable, and generous in dealings with their fellow whites—who considered themselves good Christians and law-abiding citizens—could regard the Indian as a species of wild animal and deal with him accordingly. They wanted the Indian driven farther westward or exterminated.

To achieve this, they were willing to risk Indian wars, fully expecting that the army would do any serious fighting and dying that would become necessary. In doing business with the Indians, fur traders, from the powerful American Fur Company to the scruffiest bootlegger, depended upon diluted alcohol to lubricate their dealings. It put the Indian into a frenzy, destroyed his self-control and sense of values, and left him easily swindled. Every move by the army to protect the Indian or to break up this liquor traffic was denounced as unbridled tyranny; officers found themselves sued for doing their legal duty, and obliged to defend themselves in local courts before hostile judges and juries.

The existence of military reservations was also unpopular. Officers establishing posts staked out areas large enough to provide their garrisons with timber and pasture (and also to keep whiskey peddlers at a distance), but soon found civilians demanding that these reservations be opened for settlement—or simply squatting on choice sites and selling liquor. The expulsion of such illegal squatters would be strongly protested as denying free Americans the right to earn an honest living, and might be attended by long legal complications.

It was hard work and thankless, but it was done and mostly well done. In the process the U.S. Army became a thoroughly professional force.

The day is cool, the leaves along the river are turning gold and red. In the autumn of one of the last years of the eighteenth century, a detachment from the Legion of the United States builds a fort that must be ready to shelter them through the coming winter.

They have pitched their tents in precise rows, as directed in Steuben's "Blue Book," a short distance in from the river bank where the long keelboats, "Kentucky" flatboats, and canoes that carried them and their supplies are now securely beached. The cargo has been unloaded and stored in extra tents or brush shelters. Where a reef of rock jabs out into the clear, swift-flowing current, a black kettle steams amid a knot of women—skirts and sleeves tucked up, voices shrilling language that would take the tar out of a marine sergeant's queue—busy with the week's laundry. Almost hidden in the bushes above them, the green binding on his hat proclaiming him a soldier of the 4th Sub-Legion, a sentry watches the river and its banks. North of the Ohio death comes swiftly and silently, and a woman's scalp is no safer than a man's.

In back of the tents other women cluster noisily in the company kitchens, where deer carcasses hang from handy boughs. The day's hunting was good, and there will be venison tonight, with little flour dumplings and boiled bacon. Children and dogs run clamoring among the women, but for all the seeming disorder, the camp is clean and the work progresses with swift efficiency.

On a bank behind the camp, safely above flood level, the fort—a rectangular stockade with projecting blockhouses at its corners—is in full construction. The area has been cleared, the blockhouses begun; between them, rows of cabins for quarters, storehouses, a hospital, and the blacksmith's shop are rising. Spaces between the buildings are filled with "pickets," straight tree trunks between 9 and 12 inches in diameter, and 20 feet long. After being hewed smooth, so that they will fit snugly together, they are planted upright in a trench 3 or 4 feet deep. Inside the main gate an American flag snaps atop a tall pole.

Outside the fort the ground has been cleared for over 100 feet, with the double purpose of securing firewood and leaving no cover for skulking Indians. All stumps have been cut off close to the ground. A shallow drainage ditch has been dug some 3 feet out from the fort's walls to carry away rain water.

Everywhere, work literally is in full cry. Details are bringing in tree trunks from the surrounding woods, sawyers are whipsawing trunks into planks, carpenters are pegging or nailing the planks into buildings. In the open center of the fort a group of masons labor over the stone foundations of a powder magazine; nearby a gardener, limping on an injured foot, tends a vegetable garden and yells at two small boys pursuing a pet raccoon across his seed beds. The steady clangor from the blacksmith's shop is echoed by the chunking of axes in the woods. All of these workmen are soldiers, mostly self-taught through trial and error. Directed by capable officers and non-coms, two companies of them (roughly a hundred and fifty men) can have the fort finished well enough to protect them against Indians and weather before snow flies. They work with their muskets stacked within easy reach and sentries on the alert.

They will spend the winter months strengthening and finishing off their work. A well may be dug inside the fort before the ground freezes to provide a sure water supply. A lightly fortified outwork may be built to hold a smokehouse for preserving meat and a bakery. These forts are very vulnerable to fires and such activities are best kept outside the fort proper. There also will be sheds for the garrison's few oxen and horses, and for the hay, cut along the river bottom, to feed them. The latrines also are outside the fort proper, except for small ones to be used only at night or during sieges.

The day dwindles. At the door of the guardhouse an officer consults his watch and calls out an order. Two red-coated drummers step smartly out into the gateway, poise their drumsticks, and beat "Recall." With a happy yell, soldiers put away their tools. Along the rough track out of the woods come the logging details, followed by the guards who have covered them while they worked. It is time to be soldiers again, to clean up for the "Retreat" parade and roll call, while the flag comes down and the gates are closed for the night.

31. The Second Seminole War, 1835–42. Probably the most difficult campaigning the frontier soldier faced was that against the Seminole Indians in the Florida wilderness—a featureless expanse of swamps, tall grass, and tangled brush infested by venomous insects and reptiles. Here a detachment of Regular infantry listens to the report of an Indian scout. Its officer, in the foreground, shows no insignia of rank except for his faded crimson sash. Some of the enlisted men are in summer uniforms of white cotton; others, the sky-blue winter fatigue uniform. All have the soft leather fatigue cap. They are tired, muddy, and hungry; some are suffering from fever or dysentery. But they will gradually wear out their evasive enemy.

32. Fort Harmar in 1790. Year after year the army's system of forts pushed farther westward. Forts began as isolated stockades, often with hostile war parties prowling the woods' edges about them. They were bases for patrols, surveys, and road building, and refuges for the settlers in times of trouble. Some forts served their purpose and were then left to decay; others within a few years would become the sites of major cities such as Cincinnati. Some, like Fort Leavenworth, still are active military posts. Fort Harmar, built in 1785 and renamed Fort Steuben in 1787, was one of the first American posts to be established in the Ohio Valley.

33. Evening retreat parade inside a fort, 1786. In contrast to the full-dress uniforms of the parading infantrymen, the sentry wears the short blue fatigue jacket used for everyday duties. The officer in the foreground is an artilleryman; his uniform differs from that of the infantry officer at the extreme left in that his coat is lined with scarlet cloth instead of white, and his epaulette, buttons, and sword hilt are gold, in contrast to the infantry's silver.

34. The Treaty of Greenville. Attributed to one of his soldiers, this painting shows Maj. Gen. Anthony Wayne dictating the Treaty of Greenville to the defeated Indians in August 1795. In the background the artist added small details of the daily life of the Legion of the United States. At the lower left an infantry officer confers with a dragoon officer and a frontier scout while a soldier and a woman prepare a meal over a campfire. Beyond them an infantry sentry (almost hidden in the trees) and a dragoon guard the camp.

35. Springfield flintlock musket. At first the new Regular army and many of the militia were armed from the surplus stocks of assorted weapons left over from the Revolution. As these dwindled, the newly established U.S. Armory at Springfield Massachusetts, began turning out the standardized "U.S. Musket, Model of 1795." Very much a copy of the excellent French 1763 Charleville musket, it was an accurate, reliable weapon by contemporary standards. Its caliber was .69, its overall length 59½ inches, and its weight 9 pounds without its bayonet.

36. *Lewis and Clark Meeting Indians at Ross's Hole.* In August 1805, a thousand unknown miles from anywhere, Lewis and Clark at last established contact with the Snake Indians, a branch of the Shoshone, from whom they obtained horses to cross the Rocky Mountains. The two explorers stand at the far right in this painting by C. M. Russell, while their interpreter, George Drouillard, uses "sign talk"—the universal language of western Indians—to put their words into concepts comprehensible to the Snake chief facing him. Just behind them, rifle negligently ready, Clark's servant, York, holds their horses. Her papoose on her back, Sacajawea sits quietly to one side as befits a squaw. Meanwhile, completely shaken by the appearance of such strange beings, the Snake circle like disturbed hornets; one small slip of judgment and they will stampede. In the end Sacajawea—kidnapped out of this same band five years before—will recognize the Snake chief as her brother.

37. Corps of Engineers. Soldiers did much of the army's construction. This scene shows enlisted men so engaged about 1805, wearing the "coarse linen frock and fatigue trousers" issued for such work. One of the nineteen enlisted men (right) added to the Corps of Engineers in 1803 supervises them. Five years later the West Point cadet, here shown in the foreground in his full-dress uniform, would be taking a more active part in the work, Secretary of War William Eustis having decreed that cadets must "labor or at least be near to laborers so as to be able to work if it should be necessary." Soldiers who did manual labor on fortifications, roads, or bridges for sixty days, Sundays not included, were paid ten cents extra a day. If they were artificers (skilled workmen), they got fourteen cents and a "gill of spirits."

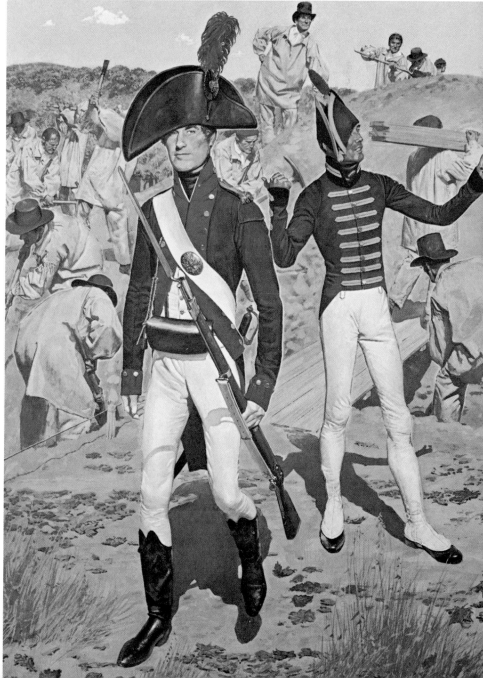

38. Fort Adams. By contrast, most of the work on the massive stone or brick coastal defenses was done by civilian laborers under the direction of Engineer Corps officers. Fort Adams was begun in 1824 on the site of an earlier fort of the same name, to guard the entrance to Narragansett Bay near Newport, Rhode Island. Designed to mount almost five hundred cannon, it was more or less finished in 1842. Normally, such forts were never fully armed or garrisoned. Small caretaker detachments of artillerymen had to labor unceasingly to keep them in some sort of repair against the constant erosions of time and weather.

39. Maj. Gen. Andrew Jackson. "Old Hickory" received all of his formal military education from spare-time study of a translation of French military regulations, but he was a soldier by instinct. Even as a militia general, he insisted that his officers be "Men capable of Command—who will fight and reduce their soldiers to strict obedience." Whatever his shortcomings as a tactician and strategist, his energy, decisiveness, and indomitable pugnacity made him the epitome of the frontier soldier. This portrait is purportedly by John Vanderlyn and was painted in 1819.

40. A Canadian Voltigeur. Some of the enemy regiments engaged along the Canadian frontier from 1812 to 1815 were composed of soldiers born in North America. The officer shown here—uniformed in rifle green with black braid, cuffs, and collar and a red sash—is Adj. John Hebden of the Canadian Voltigeurs, who were largely French Canadians. (For reasons unknown, enlisted Voltigeurs wore gray uniforms, their officers green.)

41. Artillerymen in the Barbary Wars. When Commodore Stephen B. Decatur sailed for the Mediterranean in 1815 to end the seizure of American ships by the Barbary pirate states of North Africa, the U.S. Navy could not provide sufficient Marines for his squadron. Consequently, a company of artillerymen was put aboard the frigates *Macedonia* and *Guerriere,* and took part in the one decisive naval action—the capture of the Algerian frigate *Mashouda.*

42. Battle of Chippewa, July 5, 1814. As Winfield Scott's carefully trained brigade came on against the British line at the Chippewa River, the enemy commander noted their rough gray jackets and mistook them for mere militia. Then—watching their unflinching advance, closing up the gaps made by his artillery's fire—he saluted them with a phrase that would become an American watchword: "Those are Regulars, by God!" Infantry regiments did not carry the "Stars and Stripes" until 1841. Here, the blue flag on the left is the regiment's national color; the yellow on the right its regimental color.

43. Artillery School of Practice, Fort Monroe, Virginia, 1827. Full-dress pomp and circumstance took up a considerable part of the soldier's life. In the background, a detachment follows its red-coated drummers in close-order drill. The foreground figures are an artillery officer (left) and a sergeant of the grenadier company of an infantry regiment. Both men wear dark blue coats and gray trousers; the artilleryman has yellow lace and metal insignia; the infantryman white. At this period the rank of company-grade officers was indicated by chevrons on their upper arm; that of noncommissioned officers by chevrons on their forearm. The tight, long-sleeved coatees and the heavy "tar bucket" shakos, made of jacked leather, were uncomfortable, especially in summer.

44. Inauguration Day, 1841. The military participated in the inauguration of President William Henry Harrison on March 4, 1841, in Washington, D.C. The cavalrymen at the lower left are Regular dragoons. The equally beplumed bandsmen in the center background with their ornate drum major may be from a Regular infantry regiment or from the Marines.

45. Exploration of the West and Indian relations. In 1819 a major conference was held near Council Bluffs, Iowa, between Maj. Stephen Long and other officers and Indian agents and representatives of the Oto, Iowa, and Pawnee. In this contemporary picture, a chief addresses the assembly while an infantryman (lower right) guards against interlopers, Indian or white. Under the U.S. flag at the upper left are some army musicians. The flag in the center is a so-called "Indian treaty flag," with the eagle coat of arms in place of the stars of the national flag.

46. Major Long's camp in 1820. Probably located somewhere in modern Oklahoma, the camp was situated on a bank across from the lodges of a Kiowa village. The Kiowa are fording the river to investigate their white visitors. Long's flag here shows a red and a white hand clasped in friendship; below are a crossed sword and calumet (peace pipe) signifying Long's readiness to either fight or parley.

47. West Point in 1828. After its difficult early years, West Point, founded in 1802, became a high-quality, demanding school. This print by George Catlin shows the Corps of Cadets at artillery drill on the post's central "Plain," now used as its parade ground. Two sets of the officers' quarters at the right of the picture still remain in use. The monument in the right foreground is a memorial to Lt. Col. Eleazer D. Wood, an 1806 graduate of West Point, who was killed in action at Fort Erie, Canada, in 1814.

48. Cadet in quarters, 1842. This sketch by Cadet George H. Derby depicts a cadet studying—apparently just before a parade since his dress shako and musket are conveniently at hand. Until at least 1842, new cadets slept on the floor of their rooms and had to provide many of their own furnishings. Heating came from fireplaces, which also were used for the surreptitious cooking of late-evening "hash" made from mess hall leftovers. The plumbing was outside, and studying was done by candlelight or whale oil lamps.

49. *The Nation's Bulwark.* The common militia was often praised by many political leaders as "the nation's bulwark" and the one sure defender of its freedoms. In this company, sketched in 1829, all the militiamen at least have firearms of a sort, if little of the equipment required by law.

50. The militia ridiculed. While often praised, the militia was also the butt of much ridicule, mostly deserved. This unit makes practically no effort to appear "military," and displays more sticks and umbrellas than muskets. Also, its commander is suffering abject humiliation.

51. An unidentified volunteer militia calvary officer. About 1790 this officer had his portrait painted, probably by a traveling artist of limited skill. Only men of some wealth could belong to a mounted unit since they had to provide their own horse and horse equipment, in addition to their uniform and weapons.

52. New York State Fencibles. Robert W. Weir, professor of drawing at the U.S. Military Academy, did this humorous painting of what must have been "The First Company of New York State Fencibles" sometime between 1840 and 1845. Although a relatively "young" company, the Fencibles were noted for excellence at drill and for their high self-esteem. Here, falling in for drill under the austere eye of a Regular officer (the figure in the central background in a flat-topped cap), their officer has discovered that their colors are in need of further repair.

4

Soldiers of Manifest Destiny

A regiment of regulars in 15 minutes from the evening halt, will have tents pitched & trenched around, besides straw, leaves or bushes for dry sleeping; arms & ammunition well secured & in order for any night attack; fires made, kettles boiling . . . all the men dried, or warmed, & at their comfortable supper, merry as crickets, before the end of the first hour. . . . Volunteers neglect all these points; eat their salt meat raw (if they have saved any at all) or, worse than raw, fried—death to any Christian man the fifth day; lose or waste their clothing; lie down wet, or on wet ground . . . leave arms & ammunition exposed to rain, mud & dews. . . . In a short time the ranks are thinned, the baggage wagons & hospitals filled with the sick & acres of ground with the graves of the dead!

MAJ. GEN. WINFIELD SCOTT[1]

The U.S. Army of 1845 had eight regiments of infantry, four of artillery, two of dragoons, the "corps" of engineers and topographical engineers (consisting of officers only), and a limited number of staff and service personnel. The whole numbered 8,613 on paper and possibly 6,000 in fact, distributed in over one hundred small posts. These were the "Old Regulars," the men who from first to last carried the major weight of the Mexican War. Roughly half of the enlisted men were foreign-born, especially in the infantry. The dragoons had a greater percentage of Americans, but one of them remembered his comrades as including "broken down Lawyers, Actors and men of the world, Soldiers who had served under Napoleon, Polish Lancers, French Cuirassiers, Hungarian Hussars, Irishmen who had left the Queen's service to swear allegiance to Uncle Sam and wear the blue."[2]

Only one company in each artillery regiment was equipped as field artillery, the rest serving either as garrisons for the coastal fortifications or as "red-legged infantry" (so called from the red stripes down the seams of their trousers). One of these four companies was "flying" or "horse" artillery, each man in it having his own individual mount. The other three were "light" or "field" artillery, in which only the officers, noncommissioned officers, and drivers were mounted, the rest of the enlisted men marching on foot or riding the caissons and limbers whenever more rapid movement was necessary.

Expansion for the Mexican War took several forms: Infantry companies were increased from sixty-four to one hundred men; two new companies were added to each artillery regiment; and a "Regiment of Mounted Riflemen" and a "Company of Sappers, Miners, and Pontoniers" were added to the army. A large part of the Regular Army was concentrated on the Mexican frontier where it could practice both drilling and maneuvering by regiment, brigade, and division.

The first clashes of the Mexican War gave evidence that the field artillery companies were an elite arm, capable of maneuvering as swiftly as cavalry and firing with deadly speed and accuracy. Congress therefore authorized an additional light battery in each artillery regiment, but commanders in the field already had formed such units, sometimes using captured Mexican cannon. They were supplemented by a company of Ordnance Department personnel equipped with rockets and mountain howitzers. (For some reason, Ordnance enlisted men were referred to as "men of Ordnance," never as "privates.")

THE "NEW REGULARS" AND THE VOLUNTEERS

The Regular Army had considerable difficulty securing sufficient recruits to serve for five years at $7 a month. Accordingly, after prolonged politicking, in February 1847 Congress authorized the enlistment of ten additional regiments—nine of infantry, one of dragoons—to serve for the duration of the war only, and offered a bonus of 100 acres of land to all soldiers honorably discharged. Haphazardly officered, hustled off to Mexico with little or no training, these "New Regulars" were noticeably unhandy in their first actions. Under Regular Army discipline, however, they soon were trained up to its standards.

In May 1846 Congress had authorized the President to call out 50,000 volunteers to serve either for one year or the duration of the war. (Because of the careless wording of the legislation, the Volunteers were able to request their discharge at the end of one year, which practically all of them did.) Their pay was to be the same as the Regulars', they were to provide their own uniforms and, if cavalry, their own horses but would be reimbursed for both. The Volunteers were raised by the states, almost entirely those of the South and West.

New England was hostile to the war and gave it little support.

The Volunteers were a thorough mixture. Jefferson Davis' well-trained 1st Mississippi Rifles might march in Panama hats and red shirts worn outside their white duck trousers, but they were a "gentleman's regiment." Behind each of their companies marched the privates' black "body servants." The 2nd Mississippi Rifles also wore red shirts, but were a collection of "roughs" from the South, without drill or discipline.

Expert complainers, the 1st Missouri Mounted Volunteers tended to march, camp, and behave much as their momentary fancy pleased. Having both a knack for command and a complete understanding of his fellow citizens, their colonel, Alexander M. Doniphan, ignored their minor misdoings. Serious crimes like rape he punished; when it became something of a traffic problem in El Paso del Norte, he did forbid playing monte in the middle of the main street. He also led, inspired, and damned his Missourians from Fort Leavenworth to Santa Fe, through Navajo country, down to Chihuahua, then south-westward to Saltillo, and finally north again to the Rio Grande port of Reynosa where they took ship for home—some 3,500 miles of marching, with two battles won to boot.

The 2nd Missouri Volunteers were much the same human material, but their colonel, Sterling Price, was accused of playing fast politics to get their regiment. They fought well enough during the Taos Rebellion, but their brutal treatment of the New Mexicans had contributed mightily to bringing on that uprising in the first place. Soldiers and civilians passing through Santa Fe found them a "sweet set of boys.... All do as they please.... The men are about as good as their officers—none have learned enough of military matters to know that they are ignorant." Some of the officers worked as dealers in the Santa Fe gambling halls. A visiting reporter from a St. Louis newspaper concluded that the whole regiment would be "a great accession to our State Penitentiary."[3]

Through 1846 the Volunteers brawled, plagued the natives, and staged an occasional mutiny all the way to the front and along the Rio Grande. The 6th Louisiana pulled the village of Burrita apart. Two companies of the Georgia Volunteers had a private war; a detachment from the 4th Illinois attempted to intervene and was badly cut up. Several men were killed, but no one was punished. An Ohio regiment and the Baltimore Battalion got into a large-scale fight over a catfish. The "Killers"—a "Rowdy Gang" belonging to the 1st Pennsylvania Volunteers—looted their way to war along the Erie Canal: "they just took what they wanted from [the] stores without paying, and if [the owners] spoke of their rights they threatened their lives."[4] With their transport waiting at the Boston docks, one company of the Massachusetts Regiment suddenly decided that they didn't want to leave home; another company with loaded muskets persuaded them to come along anyway. A captain of

the 5th Ohio wrote a friend: "You may imagine faintly what I have to endure by remembering that I have 80 wild, thoughtless, careless boys to look after with as much care as you would look after the members of your family."[5] This state of affairs continued through the war. In 1847 the North Carolina Regiment mutinied against its colonel, with support from neighboring Virginia and Mississippi units. After that was squelched, practically all of the regiment's officers sent the colonel a written invitation to resign his military commission.

Lt. George Gordon Meade of the Topographical Engineers—possibly motivated by having several holes shot in his tent when skylarking Volunteers playfully fired their muskets in camp—delivered himself of a comprehensive assessment:

> Without a modification of the manner in which they are officered, they are almost useless in an offensive war. They are sufficiently well drilled for practical purposes, and are, I believe, brave and will fight as gallantly as any man, but they are a set of Goths and Vandals, without discipline.... They cannot take care of themselves; the hospitals are crowded with them, they die like sheep; they waste their provisions.... They plunder the poor inhabitants of everything they can lay their hands on, and shoot them when they remonstrate, and if one of their number happens to get into a drunken brawl and is killed, they run over the country, killing all the poor innocent people they find in their way, to avenge, as they say, the murder of their brother.[6]

Considered as a whole, the Volunteers were vigorous young men, good citizens by their own lights, always ready for a fight or a frolic, loudly assertive about their "rights," and equally reluctant to admit that anyone was endowed with the right to tell them what to do. Also, though there were men of breeding and education among them, most were from small towns and farms. To be out of their home state was an adventure, and now they were off for Mexico and the Halls of Montezuma, with the recruiting officers' talk of glory, golden Jesuses, plenty of whiskey, and pretty Mexican girls still echoing in their ears. They would eat or drink almost anything, preferably to excess, and regarded orders barring them from red light districts as tyrannical impositions unworthy of the notice of free Americans.

Moreover, except for a sprinkling of Germans in the Illinois and Indiana regiments, the raw Irishmen who filled the so-called Massachusetts Regiment, and the "Dutch, Irish, French, English, Poles, Swedes, Chinese, Indians, etc." who made up five-eighths of the 1st New York, the Volunteers were overwhelmingly native-born citizens and thoroughly convinced of the natural superiority of all things American. The great majority of them were Protestants, brought up to be highly suspicious of all things Catholic. And a tendency toward violence, characteristic of Americans of this period and particularly among those from the frontier states and the slaveholding South, was strong in them. Consequently, they came into Mexico with something of the zealous intolerance of crusaders. To them, Mexicans were inferior beings on the order of Indians or black slaves; they often behaved acccordingly, making free with Mexicans' property and womenfolk and (on at least one occasion) stabling their horses in Catholic churches. They might mellow somewhat after extended service, but it was a slow process.

Volunteer cavalry—some Texas units and the 1st Missouri aside—were almost as great a tribulation to American commanders as to Mexican civilians. Among them, the "Rackensackers" of the 1st Arkansas Regiment were outstanding for their refusal to care for their horses or keep their weapons in serviceable condition. They slept soundly on outpost duty—a habit shared by the 1st Kentucky Cavalry—and evinced a strong distaste for serious fighting and hard work. Fed up with their cruelty and unreliability, an enlisted dragoon wrote them off as dangerous only to "cripples and sick women."

As Meade indicated, what the Volunteers needed, but seldom had, were competent officers who could keep them usefully busy and healthy without blunting their natural combativeness. Zachary Taylor seldom punished their most outrageous behavior, beyond ordering some of the worst individual offenders or units to the rear—a "punishment" he usually was happy to remit on empty promises of due repentance and future good behavior. Partly this was because of his careless good nature, partly because he soon would be seeking the presidency and was unwilling to risk his popularity. The result was that the depredations of his troops stirred up a profound hatred for Americans and lively guerrilla operations wherever his army went. Winfield Scott and John E. Wool managed to keep their volunteer units under tight control, Scott publishing on his own responsibility a general order that gave military courts jurisdiction over crimes against Mexicans.

Another major weakness of the Volunteer system was the short term of service. By the end of its year's enlistment the average Volunteer regiment had been hammered down into an effective unit, with some knowledge of how to take care of itself. But by then the average individual Volunteer had "heard the owl and seen the elephant" and was set on going home. Less than one man out of ten would reenlist. The regiments therefore had to be returned to the United States for demobilization and replaced by newly raised units without training or discipline. This continual shuffling of regiments was always unhandy; in 1847 it put the nation in a dangerous predicament.

Launching an offensive against the Mexican capital, Scott had captured the seaport of Veracruz, wrecked the Mexican field army at Gerro Gordo, and pushed inland to Jalapa. There was no effective enemy force between him and Mexico City. But his Volunteers' enlistments would expire in two months or less, and it was essential that they be sent back immediately, before the yellow fever season ravaged the coastal areas. (It should be remembered that some of them were willing to stay the whole length of their enlistments and risk the yellow fever going home.) Scott, who meanwhile had pushed on to Puebla, three-fourths of the way to Mexico City, sent them off. Then, with approximately six thousand men—almost entirely Regulars—he spent three months in the middle of Mexico awaiting reinforcements. Congressional peanut politics had delayed the formation of the "New Regulars," and Taylor's blunderings in northern Mexico had drawn off all available reinforcements. Fortunately, the Mexicans were even more confused and could not take advantage of Scott's isolation.

Various unusual organizations also were classed as Volunteers. Texas furnished a number of units, some for only a few months' service. Most of these were cavalry and all were generally called "rangers," though that term actually fitted only a few companies of veteran frontiersmen, such as that of Capt. Ben McCulloch. These were the best scouts with Taylor's army in northern Mexico; knowing the country and speaking Mexican-Spanish, they could infiltrate the enemy's camps and pick up vital information. Though many "Texans" were really recent arrivals from other states and sometimes neither good shots nor good horsemen, they usually were competent fighting men, particularly effective in counterguerrilla operations. There was a traditional blood feud between them and Mexico in memory of the Alamo, Goliad, and hundreds of bitterly remembered bandit raids, but their vengeance was both indiscriminate and overflowing. No other Volunteer units treated the Mexican population so ruthlessly.

There also was the small Mormon Battalion, recruited among the Mormon refugees recently driven out of their settlement around Nauvoo, Illinois. Organized at Fort Leavenworth, they marched to San Diego, California, via Santa Fe and northern Mexico. From Santa Fe on they were under Capt. Philip St. George Cooke of the 1st Dragoons, who brought them through canyons and desert despite the fact that they remained more of a migrating stake of the Church of Latter-day Saints than a unit of the U.S. Army. En route Cooke traced out a passable wagon road to California. Later, when the Gadsden Purchase of 1853 had secured enough additional territory from Mexico, their line of march would be the route of the southern transcontinental railroads. (Interestingly, the Mormon Battalion met no enemy, except a stampede of wild cattle somewhere southeast of Tucson.)

The oddest of all Mexican War units was the "California Battalion," also known as the "Navy Battalion of Mounted Riflemen," authorized by Commodore Robert F. Stockton, commander of a naval squadron off the California coast. His authority to do so was dubious at best, but Stockton was an ambitious politician-sailor in search of glory. To command it, he selected Capt. John Frémont of the Topographical Engineers who, with his usual disregard for orders, had wandered into California instead of carrying out his mission to explore the southern Rockies. The second-in-command was a Marine lieutenant of similar instability; the hard core of the battalion was Frémont's original exploring party of certified mountain men and Delaware Indians. The rest were American residents of California (some of them certifiably riffraff), recent immigrants, and assorted local Indians armed with bows and arrows. Stockton also furnished some officers and seamen from his squadron to stiffen it (as well as some navy-style blue flannel shirts by way of uniforms). The battalion did much riding and parading, but no real fighting. However, the glory of it all went to Frémont's head: when Gen. Stephen Kearny arrived from Santa Fe with President James Polk's orders to establish an American government in California, Frémont refused to obey him. (Stockton also would not accept Kearny's authority, but soon was replaced by a more cooperative officer.) Frémont was court-martialed and left the army. A special act of Congress was necessary in order to pay the California Battalion.

One truly useful minor organization was the "Mexican Spy Company," nicknamed "the Forty Thieves." While Scott paused at Puebla awaiting reinforcements, Col. Ethan Allen Hitchcock, then serving as Scott's inspector general, hired a noted retired bandit named Manuel Dominguez as a dispatch rider. After Dominguez proved able and faithful, Hitchcock gradually increased his command to two companies of ex-highwaymen who served the United States loyally as guides, scouts, spies, escorts, couriers, and interpreters. A third company was organized and did good service later as part of the garrison Scott left at Puebla to protect his sick and wounded when he renewed his advance on Mexico City. At the war's end, "Colonel" Dominguez and approximately half of his men considered it wiser to accompany the withdrawing Americans.

This was the first war in which militia played no part. Though Congress gave the President authority to call out militia for six months of active duty, it generally was agreed that militia would not be suited for foreign service. A few units were mobilized early in the war as the quickest way of getting reinforcements to Taylor on the Rio Grande, but saw no action.

OFFICERS

The officers of this period probably were the most assorted lot in American history. Some of the senior Regulars were men of ability and strong character. Winfield Scott remains one of the greatest American generals. Zachary Taylor was a stubborn fighter, amazingly nonchalant under fire, immensely popular with his soldiers. John E. Wool and Stephen Kearny handled independent commands with quiet competence. William E. Worth and David E. Twiggs (known as "Old Davy, the Bengal Tiger") were effective division commanders. But too many of the majors, lieutenant colonels, and colonels were unfit for active service. There was not—and would not be until 1861—any retirement program for officers who were physically disabled or superannuated. Consequently they continued in the service, blocking all promotion of younger men. (Promotion, when it came, was by seniority within each regiment or staff section; except when an epidemic or a bloody little frontier campaign produced unexpected vacancies, it was deathly slow. "Few die, and none resign" was the army's verdict.) Some of these oldsters had entered the army before the War of 1812; a good many were barely literate.

Because most of the army had been scattered by companies in various frontier and seacoast forts, many colonels had not seen their whole regiment together in one place for years and had completely forgotten how to handle it as a unit. Taylor, commanding the American forces on the Rio Grande, could form his army only "in a sort of militia fashion," and was most uncertain as to what he should do with his light artillery, being totally unfamiliar with that arm. More conscientious than most, elderly Col. Josiah H. Vose of the 4th Infantry attempted to accompany his regiment to Mexico, but dropped dead on his first effort to drill it. His successor, huge sixty-five-year-old Col. William Whistler, had been famous for his strength and daring; now he was so consistently and thoroughly drunk that the more-than-easygoing Taylor finally had to get rid of him.

A few of the regimental commanders and many of the junior officers now were West Point graduates. One of them was formidable Lt. Col. Ethan Allen Hitchcock, who read Spinoza's *Ethics* for recreation, corresponded with Henry Wadsworth Longfellow, and, as a mere captain, had unhesitatingly spoken disagreeable truths to an angry President Andrew Jackson. Some of them would become even more famous—captains and lieutenants named Lee, Grant, Sherman, Thomas, Longstreet, Jackson, Pickett, Reynolds, McClellan, Bragg, Hooker, and many more. They were the invaluable staff officers (especially to political generals and doddering Regular colonels), the engineers, the dashing light battery commanders, the company officers of the Old Regular units. Practically all of them proved brave, and most were competent, although some of the foreign-born Regulars, especially English and Scots, thought them unfeeling disciplinarians and over-quick to punish. But Scott hailed their services: "but for our graduated cadets, the war between the United States and Mexico might, and probably would, have lasted some four or five years, with, in its first half, more defeats than victories falling to our share."[7] And Samuel Chamberlain, a harum-scarum private of the 1st Dragoon Regiment who spent a fair proportion of his enlistment in the guardhouse, gave what might be considered a fair summa-

tion: "Our officers were all graduates of West Point, and at the worst, were gentlemen of intelligence and education, often harsh and tyrannical, yet they took pride in having their men well clothed and fed, in making them contented and reconciled to their lot."[8]

The Military Academy, however, was a comparatively minor source of officers. The "New Regulars" were officered by men commissioned directly from civilian life by President Polk, usually as a favor to a fellow Democratic politician. (This proved to be less of a political windfall than anticipated. Polk dourly observed that he could not provide commissions for all the eager applicants and so ended by making fifty enemies for every man he pleased.) Since these new regiments were temporary organizations, there was good reason for giving them equally temporary officers for the most part—so long as a few old hands were included to take care of them. This Polk did not do. The officers he appointed did include some men with previous militia or Regular service, but most were "very young men and men of little general information." Lt. Raphael Semmes of the U.S. Navy (admittedly a censorious person), attached to Scott's army, watched some of them march into Puebla and put them down for "very *hard-looking citizens,* who, apparently, required much drilling . . . to be serviceable. Their uniforms looked as though they had been made by the 'tailor of the village' whence the appointed came; they sat their horses awkwardly, and wore their arms and spurs, like very clever country gentlemen, who might have figured . . . on a race course or at an election, but who had evidently . . . little acquaintance with barracks or battlefield."[9] Hard-boiled Col. William S. Harney was more exact in his estimation of the officers of the new 3rd Dragoon Regiment: They were "nearly all gentlemen" but "perfectly ignorant of everything like military instruction and discipline"—worse, they "appear to possess no pride of profession and pride in their companies."[10]

Officers for the Volunteer regiments were provided according to the militia laws of the states furnishing them. In Missouri and Indiana, for example, the soldiers in each regiment elected their own officers from second lieutenant to colonel; in other states the governor appointed the field grade officers and the company officers were elected. (There were occasional protests that President Polk and various Democratic congressmen interfered to secure the substitution of deserving members of their party.) The results naturally were mixed. The 1st Mississippi Rifle Regiment became the command of Col. Jefferson Davis, an austere product of West Point, who made a very effective regiment of them. The 1st Missouri Cavalry, as rowdy an aggregation of free Americans as ever was mustered into the army, apparently took the precaution of electing officers who knew how to handle them: Alexander M. Doniphan, a militia general of some reputation as colonel; a former officer of the crack 1st Dragoons as lieutenant colonel; and a West Point graduate and veteran of the Seminole Wars as major. But the majority of the Volunteer officers, whether elected or appointed, had no worthwhile military experience. As an extreme example, Archibald Yell, appointed colonel of the 1st Arkansas Cavalry by the special grace of President Polk, had "total ignorance of his duties" and total resolution to so remain. His ignorance got him ignominiously killed at Buena Vista; his undisciplined regiment ran off and left him at the mere approach of Mexican lancers.

Thanks to Scott, the army had standardized drill regulations from which Volunteer officers could learn how to maneuver troops, set up a camp, post guards, and otherwise carry through routine duties. Some studied these conscientiously. A very young officer of the Massachusetts Regiment noted while at sea from Boston to the Brazos: "I am now reading my military books so I will know my duties when I arrive upon the shores of Mexico."[11] Others were less interested, or unwilling to risk their popularity by enforcing discipline or sanitary regulations. Some plainly were afraid of the ruffian element in the units. Comparing them to Regular officers, Private Samuel E. Chamberlain saw that they "would tie up a man one day, drink and play cards with him the next, and excuse their favorites from drill and guard duty."[12] General Wool was more specific: When the officers of his two Illinois regiments did not do their duty, he bluntly told them they "were not worth a damn" and that he would get rid of them if they didn't reform. With much offended protestation, they did.

A final source of officers was promotion from the ranks of enlisted men who had shown outstanding courage or ability. There had been a few such promotions from 1837 on, but President Polk insisted on increasing their number even if newly graduated West Pointers must wait for an assignment.

A larger army required more generals. This need could be met in part by promoting deserving Regular colonels such as Taylor, Worth, Kearny, and Twiggs, but too many such promotions for mere merit would go against the political facts of mid-nineteenth-century America. President Polk could honestly believe that the welfare of the United States and of the Democratic party were one and indivisible. Both Scott and Taylor were members of the opposition Whig party: Scott managed to keep his political affiliation under proper military control during the war, but Taylor soon was actively campaigning for the Whig nomination for the coming election. Polk accordingly squandered much energy in trying to win the war and yet keep his two senior generals from gaining fame or popularity from it. One method was to surround them with general officers appointed from civilian life—naturally all sound Democrats. Some, like William O. Butler, Robert Patterson, and John A. Quitman, had either served in the War of 1812 or had militia experience, and so were capable of routine duties if assisted by a competent staff. (Fortunately, the small size of the American armies permitted the commanding general to keep a close eye on his division commanders.) Patterson was noted for the style in which he lived in the field, with three large four-horse wagons full of personal comforts, including enough "kitchen furniture . . . for a good-sized hotel."[13] One surgeon damned him for having fourteen wagons for his own baggage but none available to serve as ambulances during the advance from Veracruz inland.

There also were new generals such as James Shields and Franklin Pierce, who had no experience whatever but were loyal and energetic, if often awkward in handling their troops in action. Joseph Lane was of the same cut, but showed unexpected ability as a guerrilla eradicator. He also was remembered for engaging in a fist fight with the colonel of the 3rd Indiana in front of the latter's regiment.

The prize specimen of these political generals was one Gideon Pillow, who had been Polk's law partner and remained his pet. A complete incompetent and not exactly a hero, he was characterized as a "third-rate country lawyer," well qualified for the defense of a horse thief, "particularly if the case were a bad one and required dexterous tampering with the witnesses."[14] Pillow nonetheless considered himself a second Napoleon, and had hopes of displacing Scott and even of becoming President on the basis of his war record. Once Mexico City was taken, he began a long intrigue which, with some help from Worth, enabled Polk to recall Scott and hale him before a court of inquiry for assorted alleged misdeeds. So far as there is any indication, the American enlisted men were all on Scott's side, as were most of the company and regimental officers. The guard of. Mounted Riflemen are reliably described as openly weeping as Scott left his Mexico City headquarters for the last time.

REGIMENTAL WOMEN

Once again the regimental women went to the wars. Capt. Ephraim K. Smith's first letter from Texas to his wife, describing his voyage from New Orleans, mentioned that "the first night . . . I was informed that Mrs. Roth (a camp woman of my company) was sick. . . . I gave her my stateroom, and by morning she was delivered of a son. This was the second birth en route. The Mothers are now both well, and doing their regular washing for the men."[15] Once again, these women did more than the washing. In the midst of bloody Buena Vista, "Dutch Mary," a laundress with the 2nd Illinois Volunteers, went along the lines with two camp kettles full of hot coffee. More famous was "The Great Western," an amazon of proven courage who began as a laundress, rose to hospital matron, and then opened an "American House" in Monterrey where she purveyed various types of services, including an officers' laundry.

A few officers' wives joined the armies in Mexico, and were regarded as strange and wondrous beings by both Mexicans and Volunteers long away from home. For contrast, the motley rabble of camp followers included a number of—in the polite circumlocution of the period—"frail but daring fair ones" who plied their ancient trade along the fringes of the army. One captain was blunt enough in reporting that Colonel Harney kept a "vicious & notoriously abandoned prostitute" and diverted "public ambulances and wagons for the transportation of her body & baggage."[16] Most soldiers found any needed feminine comforting among Mexican women. Casual relationships were common enough among the lower classes of Mexican society and, when accompanied by reasonably decent behavior, caused little notice or resentment. Even some girls of better families went astray, dressing in men's clothing and riding with the troops to accompany their beloveds. A few Mexican *queridas* came to strange new homes in the United States, but most had only a few exciting months before their tall "Barbarians of the North" packed up and marched away again. And thereafter they were fortunate if they were not abused, mutilated, or even killed by Mexican soldiers and *rancheros* seeking a cheap and safe revenge for past defeats.

SERVICE ON FOREIGN SOIL

Supplies

The U.S. government had no conception of the problems involved in waging a foreign war. The supply system for its forces in Mexico therefore had to be built from scratch. The staff departments responsible—ordnance (weapons, ammunition, harness), subsistence (food), quartermaster (clothing, equipment saddlery, transportation), and medical—had only a few officers, and they were mostly hidebound from years of undisturbed Washington routine. There were no reserve supplies on hand; American industry needed time to begin production. The army had no wagon trains, and transports could be secured only at exorbitant prices.

It was difficult enough to take care of Taylor's army in northern Mexico. There were very few good seaports on Mexico's east coast, and no good overland route from the Mississippi to the Rio Grande. Kearny's advance into New Mexico followed the well-established Santa Fe Trail, approximately eight hundred miles from Fort Leavenworth to Santa Fe, but his fast-moving column outdistanced its supply trains and had to march on half-rations or less. Doniphan's regiment claimed that it went eleven months without drawing a full ration. In his advance from Veracruz into the interior, Scott was forced to limit his supplies to strict priorities: first were medical supplies, clothing, salt, ammunition, horseshoes, and coffee; second were blankets, hard bread, bacon, and camp kettles. Eventually, he deliberately abandoned his line of communications: taking a great wagon train of essential supplies with him, he marched on Mexico City, securing food and ammunition from the country.

There never were enough wagons and draft animals; teamsters were civilians hired by the quartermaster at $30 a month, working under civilian wagon masters. Many of them were novices who abused and neglected their draft animals and vehicles. The deficiency in wagon trains had to be made up by pack mules, which could cross any sort of ground but were far less efficient: by rough rule of thumb an animal could pull three times as much weight as it could pack. Also, the mules had to be unloaded every night and reloaded the next morning—and the first mules packed would promptly try to get rid of their loads. (One experienced packer said working with mules was like living with your mother-in-law.) These pack trains were handled by Mexican *arrieros* under the supervision of a few American officers; they generally were cheerfully efficient, though apt to be nervous when Mexican cavalry shadowed the column.

Problems were endless. During the summer of 1847 alone, the Comanche raided the Santa Fe Trail, burning 330 supply wagons and running off 6,500 draft animals. "Patriotic" American merchants furnished inferior salt pork, and short weight at that. "Northers" off the Mexican coast wrecked supply ships. Mexican horses proved too light to pull American wagons or carry American dragoons. Medicinal whiskey evaporated strangely in transit. But, somehow, essential supplies did reach the armies in fairly sufficient quantities.

Rations

There had been no major change in the official ration or in the method of cooking it over open campfires. Because of the difficulty of moving large quantities of rations deep into Mexico there was much dependence on local purchase, especially during Scott's advance on Mexico City. Practically all items of the ration could be bought from Mexican sources, though fresh beef largely replaced salt meats. Occasionally fresh mutton was substituted. In some areas the beef was quite "poor" (lean) and soldiers hoarded their issues of salt pork or bacon, using it sparingly to give the beef some flavor. They disliked going without sugar; if insufficient stocks of it were received, quartermasters bought the Mexican *peloncillo* (hard brown sugar) which "does passably well especially when it is boiled with the coffee."[17]

One minor change in the ration was the inclusion of "extra" items such as fresh limes, pickled onions, or sauerkraut to prevent scurvy. These, however, proved hard to procure so cucumber pickles often were substituted. Fresh fruit usually was available, but overindulgence in it frequently caused diarrhea.

Because of the shortage of acceptable flour in northern Mexico, Taylor suggested that the troops be issued small hand mills to grind Indian corn, which was plentiful. Wool tried this, issuing each company one mill and each soldier nine ears of corn per day, but was at once assailed by clamorous protests against his "corn laws." He was a grim enough commander to make his Volunteers shave, but they considered grinding corn too menial and absolutely would not do it.

Most soldiers sampled Mexican cooking when they had spare money. Mexican peddlers came into the camps offering bread, eggs, fruit, and vegetables, which could be put into the mess kettles, and every Mexican town of any size had a public market where foodstuffs of all sorts were sold. Sutlers still followed the armies, selling food, tobacco, and various small necessities. They were forbidden to sell liquor; some of them risked bootlegging, others did an excellent business in brandied fruits. In some districts, hunting and fishing furnished a variety of diet, and there were always unofficial foragers, expert in stealing chickens or livestock, though this was a doubly risky business in Mexico, between prowling *ranchero* cavalry and American patrols. In the more permanent camps, enterprising regimental quartermasters like Lt. Ulysses S. Grant would draw flour instead of the issue hard bread, rent Mexican ovens, hire Mexican bakers, and turn out "soft" bread, which sold well to other regiments. The profits went into the regimental fund to provide various comforts for the men and the upkeep of the regimental band.

Southern officers often brought a slave along to look after their equipment and cook for them; others might hire an American or Mexican servant or a soldier's wife. Soldiers were divided into messes; if they did not have a cook, they might take turns preparing meals or do it cooperatively. On Christmas 1846, Private Chamberlain of the 1st Dragoons noted his mess "had secured a fat Pig, a ten pound Turkey, a dozzen of eggs, and 'Boss' Hastings, a veteran in war and the culinary art, had gotten up a plum pudding." Everything was almost ready, when "Boots and Saddles" blared. Kicking out their fires, the dragoons mounted and rode off, watching Volunteers come running to snatch up their food and cooking utensils. "The strength of discipline was never more forcibly shown!" (The dragoons' first mission—which they executed with great enthusiasm—was to clear a neighboring ranch of Volunteers who had gone on a looting, gang-raping spree. The second was to rescue an outpost of Rackensackers who reported themselves driven back by overwhelming numbers of Mexican cavalry—but proved to have run away from a passing band of wild horses. That night the dragoons ate hard bread and salt pork, but "by next morning [we] had acquired a complete mess kit, and a couple of hams and a dozzen smoked buffalo tongues, and there was some tall swearing by certain volunteer officers."[18]

The Americans paid in hard money for the supplies and services they obtained in Mexico. This policy was not viewed with enthusiasm in Washington, as President Polk and his advisers wanted a cheap war. Completely ignorant of both war and Mexico, they expected their armies to seize whatever they might need—a policy that would have raised all Mexico against them and left them dependent on only the supplies they could bring with them. As it was, by prompt payment the Americans could be certain of getting whatever supplies were available, with local good will thrown in, since Mexican armies had a tendency to simply take what they wanted. At the same time, American commanders could keep their forces concentrated instead of having to scatter them across the country seeking supplies that the Mexicans surely would have removed, hidden, or destroyed.

Uniforms

Contemporary artists usually depicted the Americans battling in full-dress uniforms, complete with tall shakos, plumes, and long-tailed coats. In fact, the Regulars campaigned in their fatigue uniforms—sky blue for the infantry and artillery, dark-blue jackets and sky-blue trousers for the dragoons—with jaunty little dark-blue visored caps. The Volunteers wore uniforms of all sorts, some of them striking, others simply peculiar. In some regiments, no two companies had quite the same uniform; in others, such as the Texas Mounted Volunteers, both officers and enlisted men wore strange assortments of battered civilian dress. Some states left it to the individual Volunteers to clothe themselves properly out of the $21 the federal government allowed them for that purpose. Naturally, many Volunteers promptly squandered the money on whiskey, women, or pistols—and then screamed loudly when they had to endure rain and cold in insufficient clothing. When the Volunteers' uniforms wore out they resented having to put on the Regulars' sky blue.

Finally the supply of clothing for Scott's command simply collapsed. The "New Regulars" and the Volunteers coming in had not been completely uniformed before leaving the United States. At the same time, clothing already issued was wearing out, there was a shortage of blankets, and some soldiers were barefoot. Since there was no hope of help from home, Scott bought shoes and blankets. A large stock of captured Mexican uniforms was issued. Once Mexico City was taken, Scott's quartermaster general soon had a thousand Mexicans making new uniforms from locally manufactured cloth. Its quality left something to be desired, and some of the colors were not regulation, but at least the ragged soldier was properly clothed once more. Spurs and horseshoes were hammered out from the barrels of captured muskets.

The U.S. armies in Mexico undoubtedly were the hairiest in American history. Contemporary pictures show an endless assortment of beards, mustaches, and whiskers. Probably the hairiest of the hairy were the 2nd Dragoon Regiment: "hair hanging down their backs, immense mustaches, and beards six or eight inches long." Possibly this affectation began during the war's earlier stages when it often was difficult to find enough water for drinking, let alone shaving. When thickly coated with dust after a hard march, Americans "lost all resemblance to humanity and presented an appearance at once grotesque and horrible," which must have shaken the less hirsute Mexicans.[19] Wool tried to keep his command clean-shaven and properly shorn, as did various garrison commanders, in the interest of military hygiene, but mustaches and whiskers remained—if possibly more neatly trimmed.

Medical Care

Disease was the major killer in the Mexican War. Better than six men died of disease for every one killed in action or dead from wounds, and three or four more were discharged for disability resulting from sickness.

Volunteers and recruits for the Regulars were likely to run through an initial visitation of mumps and measles. Upon arrival in Mexico, diarrhea and dysentery (known as the "Mexican sickness" or "Montezuma's revenge") became a problem because of contaminated drinking water. Typhoid was fairly common. Venereal disease was always present, especially around Santa Fe where "the sensual habits of promiscuous sexual indulgence ... would scarcely be credited.[20] Yellow fever (also called "yel-low jack," "black vomit," or *vomito*) was an especially dreaded disease that ravaged the semitropical coastal area around Veracruz every summer. Scott made every effort, with considerable success, to keep his soldiers—except for the necessary garrison and supply personnel in Veracruz itself—out of the area during the danger period, but the latter suffered considerably. There was no known cure for the disease, but doctors tried to keep the patients' strength up by careful nursing.

One minor factor the troops found troublesome was the prevalence of lice and fleas, whether in abandoned Mexican buildings or on the persons of charming young ladies who "like all Mexicans raised large stocks ... not only for home consumption, but for distribution among their friends."[21] (The New York Volunteers, however, were unhappily lousy before they embarked for Mexico, the lack of recruits having led their officers to accept a well-populated contingent of jailbirds and tramps.)

The armies did not have enough medical officers, and some of those who accompanied the Volunteers were young and inexperienced. There also was a great need for competent enlisted or civilian assistants in the hospitals. Doctors were surprised at the number of Volunteers who were in poor physical condition when they enlisted—and learned that many had joined the army in the hope of restoring their health! They also noted that Volunteers from the Ohio Valley tended to fall ill easily, their constitutions having been weakened by having had the "ague" since birth. Surgeons were particularly troubled that many wounds would not heal properly, and that it was almost impossible to keep flies from laying eggs on open wounds. Some use was made of a recently developed sodium hypochlorite "disinfecting fluid," and great attention was given to the cleanliness of the troops' quarters and kitchens: the walls were whitewashed, and chloride of lime was applied to latrines and garbage pits. Possibly the most important medical innovation was the use of ether as an anesthetic during operations, though it is difficult to tell how frequently this was done. In the field, many medical officers put their trust in "blue mass," a powerful cathartic, even for cases of diarrhea.

"A Peculiar Campaign"

By modern standards it was peculiar campaigning. The armies were followed everywhere by enterprising American citizens who set up eating places, saloons, and gambling dens to fleece the troops, and various mercantile establishments to tempt the Mexicans. Oddly enough, these businesses seemed to have little trouble finding transportation, at times when army quartermasters were desperate over the lack of shipping, wagons, and mules. There were wandering theatrical companies, and newspaper publishers, complete with editors, reporters, and printers. An American circus that turned up in Puebla and later followed on to Mexico City was very popular. There were small gangs of "speculators" who seem to have been interested principally in gambling and bootlegging, with some theft and dealing in stolen property on the side; and there were traveling brothels. Since the army had no military police and barely enough mounted men for the most essential patrols, these people could not be properly supervised, and were sometimes guilty of crimes against soldiers and Mexicans alike. After the major fighting was over, the armies made an effort to clear their rear areas of dubious civilians, deserters, and discharged soldiers—the last group being especially notorious in northern Mexico for looting, rape, and murder as they supposedly made their way home.

Desertion plagued the armies in Mexico. Even before open hostilities began, Mexican authorities smuggled leaflets into Tay-

lor's camp across the Rio Grande, calling on the foreign-born—and especially the Catholic—soldiers to "Separate yourselves from the Yankees." Numbers of them—undoubtedly far more interested in women, fun, and an escape from the severe American discipline than in religious considerations—did desert. They were put into a small, frequently reorganized unit officially titled the "Legion of Foreigners," but often termed the "Battalion of St. Patrick." The best information available indicates that the greater part of this unit were neither deserters nor Irish, but miscellaneous foreigners picked up around Mexico. There was a similar attempt to get Scott's troops to desert during the wait at Puebla; a Belgian and a German were arrested as the agents responsible. Most of the Legion was captured after desperate fighting (in which tradition says the Mexican Spy Company participated) at Churubusco in the battles around Mexico City; fifty-one of them who had deserted in time of war were hanged; those who had deserted before the declaration of war were whipped, branded with a "D," and later drummed out of the service. By one of history's little ironies, this Legion of Foreigners (built up again by later American deserters) formed one of the few reliable units that protected the Mexican government from the rest of its rebellious army while it signed the peace treaty with the United States.

Developing technology aided the army in this war. Back in the United States railroads could be used for short hauls to move troops and supplies, and the "electric" telegraph was helpful in transmitting orders, though sometimes it malfunctioned. Steam transports and warships were becoming common. As the war went on, the smoothbore flintlock musket was progressively replaced by the Model 1842 percussion musket, which was more reliable in bad weather. Mounted Riflemen and the Mississippi Rifle Regiment were armed with the Model 1841 rifle—a far more accurate weapon. Dragoons had the breech-loading Hall carbine, and all mounted units were beginning to receive the 1847 "Walker" Colt revolver. "India rubber" equipment came into use—sacks for perishable foodstuffs, rain cloaks, and canteens (the last gave their contents a foul taste and soon were discarded).

Extraordinary Victory

The American soldier had fought—and won—his first foreign war. Mexico had been a new place, of utter strangeness. Americans had made an uncomfortable acquaintance with chaparral, mesquite, and cactus in all their hostile forms. Snakes in profusion were stirred up around the camps, a lieutenant of the "flying artillery" solemnly recording a rattlesnake of "twenty-seven feet and three inches long." A Georgian wrote: "Everything you touch has a spider on it. . . . We never dare draw on a boot or put on a hat or garment without a close search for some poisonous reptile or insect crouching in their folds . . . [a scorpion had crawled up the inside of his trouser leg while he was having a stand-up breakfast]. Besides these we have centipedes, hordes of flies, and everything else that crawls, flies, bites, and makes a noise."[22] Roads were ankle-deep in sand, dust, or mud and usually bad. Water either was totally lacking, available only in small puddles that were "offensive to every sense," or a foot deep in the soldiers' tents after a sudden storm. Freezing nights following blistering days.

The little American armies had advanced into almost unmapped country. The roads before and behind them, the country to either flank, were haunted by the *rancheros* and *salteadores* of the Mexican irregular cavalry. "Woe to the unfortunate soldier who straggled behind. He was lassoed, stripped naked, and dragged through clumps of cactus until his body was full of needle-like thorns; then, his privates cut off and crammed into his mouth, he was left to die in the solitude of the chapperal or to be eaten alive by vultures and coyotes."[23]

But there also had been high, cool country with mountain streams brawling down off the snowy peaks. In the towns where was the sonorous clangor of church bells, the passing and repassing of religious processions, the colorful markets. Life had a pleasant languorousness. There were good wines, strange things to see, and laughing, accommodating women. Lonely soldiers of proper conduct and good presence might find hospitality and even friendship with upper-class Mexicans and carry on conventional flirtations with their daughters. Mexican girls of good family were graceful and exotic; they rode "astraddle" like men, smoked *cigarritos* with polite deftness, and carried on intimate conversations with their dark eyes and fans alone. Even dour Lt. Thomas J. Jackson (later most unsuitably nicknamed "Stonewall") brought home the habit of using Spanish terms of endearment. And when the war was won, dozens of enlisted men asked for their discharges in Mexico, or simply deserted to remain with women and a way of life they had come to love.

At the beginning of 1845 the United States had been a minor nation, not even supreme in North America. Europe considered it "without an army and without credit" and definitely inferior to Mexico in military prowess.[24] In 1848, all this was changed. American armies had formed almost overnight; had campaigned across a hostile vastness of desert, mountain, and swamp; had taken Mexico's strongest cities from garrisons outnumbering them two to one; and had fed, clothed, and equipped themselves from the enemy's own resources. Against all odds of men, guns, fortifications, terrain, and weather they had won every battle and almost every skirmish. Scott had achieved a victory that Europe's first general, the Duke of Wellington, had declared impossible. The United States stretched undisputed from the Atlantic to the Pacific.

The war ended, the Volunteers returned home to heroes' welcomes, the "New Regulars" were disbanded. The old regiments went back to their seacoast garrisons or fanned out across the newly won western territory. Companies of dragoons took the trail to California "dressed in bright red flannel shirts and black broad brim felt hats." The "Great Western," with three big wagons loaded with merchandise, arranged to go along as a laundress. Army professional talk would always carry a salting of Mexican-Spanish terms.

Always innocent of military understanding, President Polk believed that no further increase in the Regular Army would be necessary. But in occupying the Southwest, the United States had inherited the ancient wars between hapless New Mexicans and the raiding Apache, Comanche, Kiowa, and Ute. There were Indian troubles in California, Washington, and Oregon, and a final Seminole outbreak in Florida. Friendly tribes had to be protected from local gangs of whites eager to steal their land and livestock, or from regiments of "volunteers," raised by ambitious territorial governors who thought extermination the best solution to the Indian conflict. Between 1850 and 1860 there were twenty-two Indian "wars"; in 1857, thirty-seven different expeditions were in the field against hostile tribes. On the whole, they were conducted with a professional competence not always noticeable in the Indian campaigns that followed the Civil War.

Also through 1857–58, much of the army was involved in the bloodless Utah Expedition that nailed down federal authority among the stubborn Mormons. Thereafter, troops were dispatched to "Bleeding" Kansas to halt the murderous brawling between pro-slavery "Border Ruffians" and antislavery "Free Soilers."

Meanwhile the Topographical Engineers continued their frequently hazardous explorations and mappings. New posts were constructed to protect the emigrant movements to California and Oregon, and through the winter of 1849–50, the military government in California was busy rescuing straggling parties of emigrants caught in the mountains. The occupation of California gave the army a set of new troubles. Getting troops there was only the beginning, but bad enough. The Fourth Infantry sailed from New York in 1852 with approximately seven hundred officers and men and some one hundred women and children. The regimental quartermaster, First Lieutenant Grant (whose own wife was pregnant and must stay behind), had difficulty fitting them into an already overloaded steamship. Landing at Aspinwall, Panama, they crossed the Isthmus by railroad, dugout canoes, and marching to board ship again at Panama City on the west coast. En route, cholera and malaria broke out; over a hundred men died and half the rest were invalids when they reached California. Once in California, there was the problem of large-scale desertions by soldiers eager to get rich in the goldfields. Lt. William T. Sherman and three other officers once ran down and captured twenty-seven armed deserters. For the most part, this passed as it became evident that few miners ever struck it rich, but for a while the commanding officer in California had to do his own cooking.

The army grew again; two regiments of cavalry and two of infantry were added in 1855. That same year a highly effective "rifled musket" was adopted. It could fire the new "Minie ball" and so be loaded as rapidly as the old smoothbore musket, but was accurate to 600 yards' range, in place of the smoothbore's 200. The army got an increase in pay, with a private receiving $11 a month. There was a promising experiment in the use of camels in the Southeast. Scott established an Army Asylum for disabled enlisted men. In 1859 he went out to the Pacific coast on the last of those quasi-diplomatic missions at which he excelled and cleared up a teapot squabble with the British over the ownership of San Juan Island.

But it still was a small army, its upper grades still clogged with aged, crotchety senior officers. Officers in isolated little western posts found life too rough and the cost of living too high to bring out their families. Some found comfort in whiskey, many resigned and sought civilian employment—to prosper like Henry W. Halleck and George B. McClellan, or to be rawly buffeted like Grant and Sherman. At first unnoticed, the southern states were rebuilding their militia and drawing on the federal government for weapons to arm them. As this became more open, northern interest in militia also revived. In the years 1859–60 a touring drill team from Chicago, Elmer E. Ellsworth's "Zouave Cadets," became almost a national sensation with the showy uniforms and drill it had copied from the French North African Zouave regiments. At West Point there were increasing clashes between northern- and southern-born cadets. Then, in late 1860, cadets from South Carolina, Mississippi, and Alabama began resigning.

March 2, 1847. Out of a clear, high sunset the 1st Missouri Mounted Volunteers ride into Chihuahua City. Most of its population watches cautiously, prepared to be complaisantly submissive but also ready to bolt and hide—these barbarian heretics have just destroyed a Mexican army at the crossing of the Sacramento River. Its dazed, bloodied survivors babbled of hordes of long-haired giants who slew terribly with cannon, rifle, saber, pistol, and caught-up rocks and could not be killed.

Tall, lanky riders swaggering in their saddles, dusty hair and beards blowing about their sun-blistered faces, the 1st Missouri is not a reassuring sight. They have a band of sorts, making a valiant effort to play "Washington's March." Their officers have coaxed and cursed them into something resembling normal military order, but they still have a hungry, wolfish look. They wear every sort of headgear; their dress is a mixture of worn buckskins and tattered remnants of clothing picked up along their line of march. The only things clean about most of them are their weapons. The greater part ride tough little mustangs, as uncurried and neglected-looking as their riders. Only here and there one of them—usually an officer—bestrides a tall American blood horse he has nursed across the broken miles from Fort Leavenworth.

In their midst rides Col. Alexander Doniphan—six foot four, solidly built, big hands and feet, bristly reddish hair—and his small staff, mostly in semi-uniform. Then the hoof-clatter in the streets is underscored by the grinding of iron-shod wheels, and the guns of the Missouri Volunteer Artillery go by, with captured Mexican pieces trundling behind them. The artillerymen are almost as ragged as their comrades, but with more discipline about them.

Whips crash and the housefronts echo back expert profanity in several tongues. The streets fill with the looming dirty-gray canvas tops of giant Santa Fe Trail wagons, their beds some 16 feet long and 6 feet high, rear wheels 7 feet in diameter, tugged along by four or five teams of gaunt oxen or mules. These belong to American traders who followed Doniphan's column from New Mexico, and whom he had formed, wagons and all, into a provisional battalion that fought gallantly at the Sacramento. With them are Doniphan's few supply wagons, sick and wounded soldiers jumbled in with camp kettles, tents, and barrels of salt pork. Almost involuntarily a murmur of *"Pobrecitos. Los Pobrecitos"* runs among the watching Mexicans. Two girls dart out with bottles of wine and bits of food. A frowsy rear guard closes the column.

The Missourians parade on into the central plaza, where the city officials wait to offer a formal submission. A long wolf-yell of triumph surges along the column; the band swings into "Yankee Doodle"; the column halts; and Doniphan dismounts to receive the surrender. One soldier notes that he struts somewhat like a gander, but he has reason enough for pride. Ceremonies done with, he remounts; orders ring out and the Missourians parade on through the town to halt on a ridge beyond it. Evening is no time to let this regiment loose in a still unreconnoitered city.

Amid disgusted clamor the stained tents go up, more or less in line. The artillery fires a "national salute" of thirteen guns in honor of their achievement. Details steal enough firewood from the outlying houses to cook their supper. By one campfire's flicker a nineteen-year-old private enters the day's doings in his diary, concluding "and went to bed as usual among the rocks."

53. The light artillery, 1855. Nothing better exemplified the new professional self-confidence and pride of American soldiers during this period than the dash and efficiency of their light artillery. Here a battery comes forward at a fast trot while its first sergeant (left foreground) speaks briefly with an officer of the Quartermaster Corps. Their dress uniforms are the model adopted in 1851, simpler, more comfortable, and—to the officers' great relief—considerably less expensive than the style they replaced.

54. The Mexican War (1846–48). The war with Mexico was one of long, wearying marches. This painting has caught their spirit—a resistless flow of infantry under the gleam of their musket barrels; detachments of high-chinned dragoons; long lines of white-topped wagons; a dog that joined the army. The men are wearing their overcoats, since autumn mornings in the valley of Mexico often are chilly. A few have replaced their forage caps with Mexican sombreros; the mounted officer at right is wearing a locally procured poncho.

55. Uniforms during the Mexican campaigns. The American infantry officers' field uniform worn during the Mexican War consisted of long dark blue coats, sky-blue trousers, and crimson sashes. These stood out conspicuously against their men's short sky-blue jackets. The dragoon's yellow cap band places him as a trooper of the 2nd Dragoon Regiment.

56. Winfield Scott (1787–1866). Scott first saw action as a lance corporal of the Virginia militia cavalry during the *Chesapeake-Leopard* incident of 1807, when he captured a foraging party that had landed from the British warship *Leopard*. The next year he was given a direct commission as a captain in the new Regiment of Light Artillery. Proud, sometimes petulant, occasionally petty—but always in the end a great gentleman—he served the United States with courage, intelligence, and devotion until 1861. Then, as he wrote President Lincoln, "being broken down by many particular hurts, besides the general infirmities of age," he requested retirement. He had been commanding general of the U.S. Army for twenty years, and few officers have shown such deep concern for the welfare of its soldiers.

57. *Landing at Veracruz.* The landing north of Veracruz in March 1847 by Scott's army of 13,000 was the first large-scale amphibious operation carried out by American soldiers. Although most of Scott's requisitions for necessary equipment had been disregarded by authorities in Washington, the operation was carried out with amazing dash and precision through the skilled aid of Commodore David Conner's squadron of the U.S. Navy.

58. Samuel E. Chamberlain. Few American soldiers had as many adventures in Mexico as Samuel E. Chamberlain, scapegrace private of the 1st Dragoons. In his later years he wrote them down as he remembered them, and illustrated them profusely. Here he fights an impromptu duel, saber against machete, with a Mexican whom he surprised in bed with two of his lady friends. (The Mexican has wrapped a blanket around his arm to serve as a shield.) The ladies urge their compatriot to dispose of Chamberlain quickly and rejoin them.

59. Chamberlain battling guerrillas. In this painting, Chamberlain, surprised in a saloon by a gang of guerrillas, holds them at bay with the breechblock from his Hall carbine. (Although not intended for such use, the breechblock could be taken out of the carbine and used as a pocket pistol.) Chamberlain got out of this scrape by defeating one of the guerrillas in single combat.

60. *The "Great Western" as Landlady.* Chamberlain's depiction of the "Great Western" ejecting a Mexican would-be customer from her "American House" in Monterrey is a more accurate portrayal of soldiers' off-duty amusements—the traditional women, wine, and cards.

61. The storming of Chapultepec. Standing in wagons, with their hands and feet tied and nooses around their necks, condemned deserters, who had served in the Legion of Saint Patrick against their former comrades, watched for two hours as the Americans stormed the castle of Chapultepec, the final key to Mexico City, knowing that they would be hanged the moment the American flag rose above the castle. When it appeared, witnesses remembered, they gave a forlorn cheer.

62. *The Emigrant Soldier and His Family, Scene in New Mexico.* While contemporary pictures of American soldiers became more common during this period, many of them were highly inaccurate. This "emigrant soldier" apparently was intended to represent the Mormon Battalion, which had no uniforms whatever and had to leave their families behind. (Brigham Young, the Mormon leader, commandeered most of their clothing allowance and pay to finance his peoples' migration to Utah.)

63. *The California Guard.* Properly Stevenson's (or the 7th) Regiment of New York Volunteers, the California Guard was raised for service in California. The uniform shown here bears only a vague resemblance to that actually worn by the New Yorkers, and it seems probable that the artist simply touched up an existing plate showing some other organization, possibly even a European regiment.

64. *Perilous Ferriage of the Missouri.* River crossings could be a major difficulty in western travel. Quicksand was troublesome, but caused little danger if you kept moving; swift currents and tricky streambeds could be risky. The greatest peril was a sudden flood, or freshet, often caused by storms miles away upstream and out of all sight and hearing, which carried along uprooted trees. Here, a ferry struggles through a welter of them, near the present site of Nebraska City.

65. Fort Bridger. One famous frontier post of this period was Fort Bridger, in the extreme southwest corner of modern Wyoming, at Black's Fork on the Green River. Built by the famous mountain man and scout Jim Bridger in 1843, it originally was a small wooden structure as shown here. In 1853 Bridger was forced out by the Mormons, who enlarged and strengthened the fort, but burned it down four years later as U.S. troops approached during the "Mormon War." The army then occupied it until 1890.

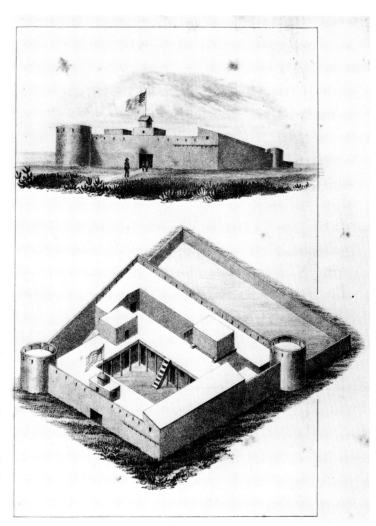

66. Bent's Fort. Built in 1828–34 by William Bent and his three brothers, Bent's Fort was an impressive adobe structure on the Arkansas River in eastern Colorado. A major frontier rendezvous until its owners destroyed it in 1849, it served as an advance base for several military expeditions but was never an army post.

67. Camels in the West. In 1854, Secretary of War Jefferson Davis managed to convince Congress that camels would be useful for transporting army supplies through the barren areas of the Southwest. Accordingly, some seventy-five of them were purchased, and several Turk, Greek, and Armenian camel drivers were hired to tend them. The camels reached the United States in 1856, and proved quite efficient, though their scent and appearance occasionally stampeded mules and horses. Few soldiers developed an affection for them. When the Civil War ended this experiment, and the extension of the railroads made them unnecessary, most were sold—although a few escaped to become the inspiration of several legends.

68a and 68b. Poet and artist at West Point. Among West Point's more unusual cadets were Edgar Allan Poe and James McNeill Whistler. Poe was a Regular Army sergeant, who was appointed in 1830 but simply went away without completing his first year. Before leaving, however, with the encouragement of Col. Sylvanus Thayer and money subscribed by his fellow cadets, he published his second book of poems. Whistler was a cadet from 1851 to 1853. Though from a military family, he had neither aptitude nor interest in a soldier's life, yet seems to have enjoyed his cadet days. His budding artistic talent produced several drawings like these, which are part of a set of four showing the progressive collapse of a cadet on guard duty during a hot summer day.

69. _Review of the Regiment._ Many volunteer militia units copied the uniform and precision of drill of the Corps of Cadets. This illustration shows the socially impeccable New York 7th Regiment passing in review in Washington Square, New York City, in 1852.

70. Light Guard of New York. Outstanding volunteer militia organizations included the scarlet-coated Light Guard of New York, which is now a National Guard unit.

71. The red-uniformed National Lancers. Formed in 1836, the Lancers retained their unusual weapons and uniform for over sixty years. They were the pride of Boston and are now also a National Guard unit.

72. Unknown militiaman. Many volunteer militia organizations that were once well known have vanished, leaving only a few bits of insignia or an occasional portrait—like that of this gray-clad officer—as possible clues to their identity.

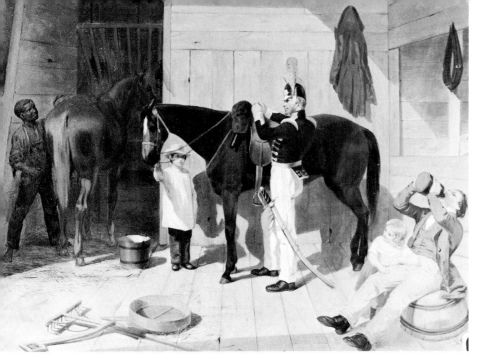

73. Militia cavalryman. Much to the admiration of two boys, a volunteer militia cavalryman prepares to mount and ride forth. Probably he will join a Fourth of July parade or similar holiday affair. (Certainly the thirsty citizen in the right foreground considers it an occasion for celebrating.)

74. Astor Place Riot, 1849. The militia also had grim duties, including the preservation of law and order. A classic example was the 1849 Astor Place Riot in New York City. Beginning as a quarrel between supporters of the visiting English tragedian William Charles Macready and those of his American rival, Edwin Forrest, the riot rapidly got beyond control of the police. The militia (dimly visible through the smoke in front of the opera house) then fired on the mob. Twenty-two people were killed and thirty-six were wounded.

5

Soldiers of the Civil War

Be a man never so much a man, his importance and conceit dwindle when he crawls into an unteaseled shirt, trousers too short and very baggy behind, coat too long at both ends, shoes with soles like firkin covers, and a cap as shapeless as a feed bag. Let me recall how our private looked to me ... in the ranks, a position he chose from pure patriotism. ... He is just in front of me trying to keep his balance and his temper, as he spews from a dry mouth the infernally fine soil of Virginia, and with his hands—he hasn't a handkerchief—wipes the streaks of dirty sweat that makes furrows down his unshaven face. No friend of civilian days would recognize him in this most unattractive and disreputable-looking fellow, bowed under fifty-eight pounds of army essentials.

PRIVATE ABNER SMALL, 16th Maine Volunteer Infantry Regiment, after three years of campaigning[1]

On January 1, 1861, the U.S. Army numbered 1,098 officers and 15,304 enlisted men, distributed throughout the country from New York across three thousand miles to San Francisco, and from Pensacola, Florida, to Seattle. Most of it was engaged hunting hostile Indians out of wilderness outposts on the edge of nowhere. One such place was blistering Fort Yuma on the Gila River at the southeasternmost corner of California. A soldier died there, so averred an old army tale, and went to hell: The next night his ghost was back, asking for his overcoat and blankets.

In February, breakaway southern states declared themselves the independent Confederate States of America. In Texas, old Gen. David E. Twiggs happily surrendered the U.S. forces there to the state authorities, and thereafter accepted a Confederate commission. Most of his troops withdrew successfully and somewhat belligerently. Warned to slip quietly around San Antonio to avoid irking its citizenry, the 3rd Infantry Regiment donned its full-dress uniforms and marched through the town "with everything we possessed flying, floating, and beating ... band playing,

[the] drum-major nearly turning himself inside out with his baton, and every man and officer as fine as brass and bullion could make him."[2]

THE REGULARS

Except for the 5th and 9th Infantry and 3rd Artillery regiments, which remained stationed in the Far West, the Regulars were brought back east of the Mississippi. It was slow work and considerable reorganization was necessary. Within a few months, 313 Regular officers resigned their commissions to "go south." They included former Capt. Pierre Gustave Toutant Beauregard, who was very offended that he had not been allowed to continue as Superintendent of the Military Academy just because he had announced that his primary loyalty was to Louisiana and not the United States. Shortly thereafter he was in command of the Confederate forces besieging Fort Sumter—and still demanding that the army pay him the $165 that travel from West Point home to Louisiana had cost him. But, aside from Twiggs and one or two others, these departing officers meticulously observed contemporary standards of professional honor, formally submitting their resignations and accounting for all government property and funds in their keeping before their departure. Fewer than thirty enlisted men followed them.

Because of its dispersion, the Regular Army played only a limited part in the first clashes of the Civil War. In several crises, however, its intervention was decisive; isolated units saved St. Louis, Fort Monroe, and Fort Pickens, which commanded the Pensacola naval base. Even more important were the eight companies of Regulars that Lt. Gen. Winfield Scott was able to scrape together to ensure the safety of Washington, D.C., and the inauguration of President Abraham Lincoln. At the first Battle of Bull Run, the single battalion of Regular infantry present dealt very roughly with several Confederate regiments and covered the retreat of the federal army, aided by one company of Regular cavalry.

In 1861, a few months after the surrender of Fort Sumter, the Regular Army was increased to nineteen regiments of infantry, six of cavalry, five of artillery, a battalion of engineers, and various service and administrative troops. The 1st and 2nd Dragoons and the Mounted Riflemen became respectively the 1st, 2nd, and 3rd Cavalry regiments; the 1st and 2nd Cavalry regiments were renumbered the 4th and 5th. All were to have cavalry yellow as their distinctive color. The former dragoons and riflemen were not flattered; they especially disliked giving up their distinctive facings of orange for dragoons, green for riflemen. In keeping with immemorial army policy, however, they were to wear out their old uniforms before drawing new ones; two years later there was comment on the "marvelous durability of orange facings."

During the period 1861–63 a small Regular infantry division stiffened the Army of the Potomac, and a brigade served with the Army of the Cumberland. Regular cavalry regiments and artillery batteries were distributed throughout the various armies, the latter being particularly effective both in themselves and in the example they set volunteer artillery units. Unfortunately, because of its stricter discipline, longer term of enlistment, and lower enlistment bounties, recruiting for the Regular Army was difficult. Some of the new infantry regiments never could be fully activated. Since they frequently were thrust in to cover a retreat or plug a gap, as at both battles of Bull Run and at Gettysburg, their casualties were heavy. In November 1864, the infantry regiments with the Army of the Potomac were so reduced that their survivors had to be taken out of the line.

THE VOLUNTEERS

As a first source of additional troops, President Lincoln naturally turned to the volunteer militia of the loyal states, requesting 75,000 men for three months of service. Some 92,000 men responded. Not all of them were properly armed or equipped and some regiments—hastily assembled from separate companies, each with its own uniform—presented a most variegated appearance. Such units behaved well enough at the first Battle of Bull Run (July 21, 1861), though an infantry regiment and a battery of artillery insisted on leaving the army just before the battle because their enlistments were up. Thereafter Volunteers replaced militia as combat troops. The militia continued in existence and was useful for internal security duties, such as escorting prisoners, dealing with draft riots, and meeting local emergencies like the Minnesota Sioux Rebellion of 1862. Its strength dwindled because of the demand for men for the Volunteers. In 1863 some Pennsylvania units called out to oppose Gen. Robert E. Lee's invasion of the North remained true to old militia tradition by refusing to cross their state boundary into Maryland. Ohio and several other states thereafter reorganized and strengthened their militia, which did good service during the final Confederate offensives in 1864.

The Volunteers were the fighting strength of the federal armies. The President would request a specific number of troops for a given period of service; the secretary of war would assign each state a quota, according to its population, specifying the type of units required; and the state governors would then supervise the enrollment of their respective units. (Additional Volunteers were raised among loyal citizens of Alabama, Arkansas, Florida, Georgia, Louisiana, Mississippi, North Carolina, and Texas as the war went on.) Enlistment normally was for three years, but some units were accepted for terms as short as nine months.

During mid-1864 the enlistments of most of the Volunteers expired. In order to keep as many as possible of these veteran regiments in the service, the federal government authorized a special $400 bounty, a thirty-day furlough, and free transportation home to every Volunteer who would reenlist. If three-fourths of a regiment reenlisted, its officers retained their commissions. Most states added a smaller additional bounty. In one of the proudest episodes of U.S. military history, well over half of these soldiers did reenlist as "veteran volunteers" and brought large numbers of new recruits back to camp with them.

The problem of keeping Volunteer regiments up to strength never was satisfactorily solved. At first, each regiment kept a small recruiting party operating in its home state, but Secretary of War Edwin McM. Stanton abolished these in 1862 for reasons known only to his erratic mind. Heavy casualties later that year made it necessary for the states to raise more regiments, which came green and awkwardly into the field while veteran regiments dwindled down, often to less than half their original strength. The recruiting system was restored, but the governors had found the creation of new regiments a cheap and effective political tool and so new regiments continued to get most of the available recruits.

To stimulate enlistment, the federal, state, and local governments offered increasingly large bonuses to recruits; by the last years of the war these might total as much as $1,000. This produced the endless corruptions of "bounty jumpers"—men who would enlist, draw their bounty, desert, and then enlist in another regiment. One individual claimed to have done this thirty-two times. Another solution was the draft, as embodied in the Enrollment Act of March 1863. This was a poor piece of legislation, which permitted a drafted man to hire a substitute or to buy exemption for $300, and was valuable chiefly as a stimulant to volunteering. A class of "substitute" or "bounty" brokers soon developed, literal traders in human flesh who, for a consideration, would find a substitute for a drafted man. Some brought in Europeans, unable to speak a word of English, under pretense of finding them employment, and got hold of all or most of their bounties after getting them enlisted.

Conscripts might make useful soldiers, but most of the substitutes and the bounty jumpers literally made the veterans weep. The 13th Massachusetts received 186 of them in August 1863, mostly "thieves and roughs," more than half of them under assumed names, "and it frequently happened at subsequent roll calls that some . . . were unable to remember the names under which they enlisted."[3] Many were foreigners, and three were Confederate deserters. Forty of them deserted that night. These "dregs of every nation" were more trouble than they were worth. In combat, they promptly ran away; in camp, they stole from other soldiers; on outpost duty, they deserted to the enemy. (Optimistically, the Confederates tried to use such deserters as factory hands or soldiers and quickly found them treacherous and

worthless.) Possibly one man in three could be pounded into something resembling a soldier by application of grim Regular-style discipline.

The Volunteer regiments came to the war in an astounding variety of uniforms, discipline, and character. Out of New York State alone came such differing units as the 5th Infantry—Duryee's Zouaves—in full Zouave dress, so steady and disciplined under fire they were considered fit to serve with Regulars; the 44th Infantry, which called itself "Ellsworth's Avengers" and accepted only unmarried men of proven moral character; the cantankerous 79th, which consisted mostly of Scots and wore kilts in full dress; the Irish 69th, with their green flags; the gray-uniformed pug-uglies of the 11th Regiment, recruited from New York City's volunteer firemen and so called the "Fire Zouaves"; and finally the *"Enfants Perdus,"* an incomplete regiment of foreign-born "roughscuff of New York City" who could be trusted to do little except desert.

There were other proud organizations. The brigade made up of the 19th Indiana and the 2nd, 6th, and 7th Wisconsin regiments was drilled, disciplined, and trained by exacting Brig. Gen. John Gibbon to Regular Army standards. Since Gibbon got them the short white leggings and stiff high hats the Regulars wore in full dress, the army named them the "Black Hat Brigade." Their first fight was at Groveton, Virginia, in August 1862; attacked by almost twice their number of Confederates under the dreaded Maj. Gen. Thomas J. "Stonewall" Jackson himself, they lost 750 out of their 2,000 men in a slam-bang, stand-up fight—and gave Jackson a complete bellyful. From then on they were called the Iron Brigade. By contrast, the 109th and 128th Illinois were so crippled by desertions and disorders sparked by agents of the traitorous pro-Confederate "Knights of the Golden Circle" that they had to be completely reorganized.

Foreign-born soldiers made up almost a fourth of the federal armies. There were brigades of Irishmen, many of them fresh from Erin, with an unusually pugnacious lot of chaplains. Excellent shock troops, cheerful, fond of hard liquor and brawling, they tended to regard their American service as practice for the forthcoming liberation of Ireland. Germans were even more numerous; in several of their regiments orders were given in "undefiled high Dutch" and drill and maneuvers were those of some German principality. Various observers thought American discipline was too loose to bring out the Germans' best qualities, but the Americans could be stubborn fighters, and their bands were superb.

The 15th Wisconsin was made up mostly of Norwegians, with some Danes and Swedes; its mail call must have been perplexing with five "Ole Olsens" in a single company. The Garibaldi Guard, otherwise the 39th New York, was a real foreign legion, including Hungarians, Russians, Croats, and Italians; its uniform was modeled on that of the Italian light infantry, and its colonel ended up in Sing Sing in 1863 for an assortment of crimes. The 15th Missouri called themselves the Swiss Guards; the 58th New York was also the Polish Legion. There were Spanish-speaking soldiers in the New Mexican regiments and in California's "Native Cavalry Battalion," which wore Mexican *vaquero* dress and was armed with lances.

Three regiments of Indian Home Guards were raised for service in the Indian Territory. They drew regulation uniforms but modified them by cutting the seats out of their trousers for greater convenience, and donned war paint and feathers for action. And finally there were the black regiments, some 152 of them altogether, which formed whole divisions in 1864. They varied greatly in efficiency: Those raised in Massachusetts and Con-

necticut from free blacks and another recruited in Louisiana from "free men of color" (mostly old French/Spanish Creole families and often white men to all outward appearances) seem to have been the most efficient. The rest were almost entirely former slaves; few could read or write, so it was hard to find useful noncommissioned officers among them. Some sixty of their regiments saw actual combat, several performing very well. Full of good nature and fond of display, they took readily to drill and discipline, and reportedly were less prone to drunkenness than their white comrades.

The most singular troops were the men of the six regiments of U.S. Volunteers, also known as "Galvanized Rebs." They were Confederate prisoners of war, who volunteered for service against hostile Indians in the West rather than spend the rest of the war in prison camps. (Some of them probably had been forced into the Confederate service against their personal convictions.) On the whole, they served well and faithfully.

Volunteers as a group, especially those enlisted during 1861 and 1862, were splendid military material, definitely superior to the average Regular recruits. At the same time, roughly one out of every four was actually unfit for military service, being either too young or too old, or too sickly. Preliminary medical examinations often were farcical, if not entirely lacking. During the last years of the war, substitute brokers sometimes managed to get actual cripples or half-wits accepted long enough to obtain their bounties. A number of women managed to enlist, and at least one of them served a three-year enlistment without being discovered!

The Civil War Volunteer was a true descendant of the Volunteers who served against Mexico. An overwhelming number of officers and men alike knew next to nothing about taking care of themselves in camp or in the field. Even in comfortable, well-supplied camps they could become incredibly slovenly: latrines were not properly kept up or not used; filth was allowed to pile up in and around the tents; men neither bathed nor changed underwear. In 1862 the colonel of the 70th New York took advantage of the leisure of the short coastal voyage from Washington to Fort Monroe to have his men's hair cut short, and found "the pile of dirt disclosed beneath the earlocks of some must have been accumulating all winter and ... 'would grow a hill of corn.' "[4]

In sad fact, much of the war was waged in a negligent fashion. Orders were mislaid or ignored, horses were unfed and uncared for, wounded were neglected in dirty, freezing hospitals. As an army moved into battle, amazing numbers of men would slip out of the ranks. (Common excuses were a "call of nature," a broken shoelace, or sudden stomach cramps.) Thereafter, they would go skulking as "coffee boilers" just behind the fighting, robbing civilians, pilfering food from supply trains, and boiling coffee over their little fires to kill time. If discovered by a passing officer they would "rise ... and ask innocently, 'Lieutenant, can you tell us where the Umsteenth Regiment is?' " and then make a pretext of moving off to rejoin it, but would be back at their fire as soon as he was out of sight.[5] Once the fighting was over, they would get their precious hides back to their units to draw rations and pick up their mail. Some of them would make money peddling stolen goods. More men would attempt to sneak to the rear during combat, often pretending to be wounded. "Helping" a wounded comrade was another favored dodge—a wounded man still able to walk might have half-a-dozen cowards around him pretending to bring him to the surgeon.

Too often there was no real effort to keep such men with their units. The army still had no real military police. Most of the field armies had some units detached to serve as "Provost Guards," which were supposed to gather up stragglers, guard prisoners, and generally maintain order, but these troops never were specifically trained or organized for such duties. When there was extensive skulking during a battle, the stricter generals might organize "recruiting parties" of cavalry and staff officers to drive the runaways back into line. Such details made free use of the flat—and sometimes the point—of their sabers, skulkers being considered somewhat subhuman.

Another major fault with Volunteers was their increasing tendency to strip the countryside of edibles, even when they were issued full rations, and to steal horses. Naturally, cavalrymen seem to have been preeminent in these maraudings since they were able to "ride around loose and get things."[6] This often progressed from stealing chickens and shooting pigs to plundering smokehouses and cellars, and then to plain robbery.

Relatively few regimental officers seem to have been concerned or to have enforced orders against looting. The leaky discipline that characterized many Volunteer regiments is well exemplified by an exchange of messages between Maj. General Henry Halleck and Maj. Gen. Ulysses S. Grant in 1862. Halleck scolded Grant because some of Grant's regimental commanders had been giving perfectly healthy men two or three months of sick leave because of favoritism or some other improper motive. Grant replied that he had issued strict orders against such actions, then made a personal investigation, found that his orders had been ignored, and put several officers under arrest. At the same time he reported that he was court-martialing the colonel of the 21st Missouri Volunteers, which had just arrived by river steamboat, for having allowed his men to take pot shots at civilians along the river banks.

Some generals did little to curb such disorders, and some even encouraged them, tacitly or openly. Brig. Gen. John B. Turchin (formally Col. Ivan Vasilovitch Turchinoff of the czar's Imperial Guard) was court-martialed for applying typical Russian occupation policies in Alabama, but later was reinstated. General William Tecumseh Sherman wearied of attempts to maintain discipline and decided not "to quarrel with our own men about such minor things" because "the rebels deserved all they got and *more*."[7] On his march across Georgia he kept his regular foraging parties under a certain control, but did nothing whatever to curb the hundreds of "bummers" (armed stragglers) who ravaged the countryside around his army like professional bandits. And, shortly after Grant (newly promoted to lieutenant general) arrived to accompany the Army of the Potomac on its 1864 campaign, that army's provost marshal, God-fearing Maj. Gen. Marsena Patrick, was outraged to find that some soldiers he had caught stealing chickens and sheep had been detailed to do just that by officers of Grant's personal staff!

OFFICERS

It was obvious that the quality of the Volunteers would depend on the officers, and most of them were as green as the proverbial gourd. There were only some 440 Regular officers on active duty, and only two ever had held independent commands of any size—Lt. Gen. Winfield Scott and Brig. Gen. John Wool. Scott was seventy-four; Wool, seventy-seven. Both had received serious wounds during the War of 1812; Scott, moreover, suffered from dropsy and a leg wound received in Mexico, and could no longer either mount a horse or walk any distance without help. Nevertheless, the proud, irascible old soldier was magnificent. Though clogged by President James Buchanan's timidity, Secretary of War John B. Floyd's open efforts to aid the South, and a disorganized general staff (both the Adjutant General and the Quartermaster General joined the Confederates), he drove himself through twelve to seventeen hours of labor every day and seldom, if ever, missed one of those gourmet meals in which he delighted. When Scott asked for retirement in late 1861, he had seen Lincoln firmly installed as President, met the first crises from Washington to Missouri, practically completed the organization of the federal armies, and roughed out the basic plan by which the war eventually would be won. Wool remained on duty until 1863, his fiftieth year of service—to the last a reliable, devoted soldier.

Most of the other Regular officers were competent enough in the grades they held, but had much to learn about generalship. The army had no advanced schools for officers—any military education they received after graduation from West Point had to come from individual study in their off-duty hours. In the fourteen years since the Mexican War, daring young officers of great promise had gradually become stiff martinets, their fighting edge worn away by long peacetime routine and paperwork. Others were aggressive, successful Indian fighters, who knew everything about commanding fifty dragoons but had had no opportunity to handle larger units. A few were too accustomed to drowning their frustrations in bite-'em-back commissary whiskey; others were notable only for "grumbling at and trying to get around whatever order they may receive."[8] And some, unfortunately, were competent and energetic yet had no knack for commanding Volunteers or getting along with politically potent Volunteer officers.

Undoubtedly, the majority of Regular officers had at least an occasional feeling that their army had gone to hell, but did their duty to the best of their abilities. One advantage they all had—knowledge of the system by which the army was fed, clothed, equipped, and paid. Those who did not develop into effective generals could thus still be useful in administrative assignments.

Approximately five hundred Regular officers who had left the army after the Mexican War returned to active duty, four-fifths of them going into Volunteer regiments, where they were invaluable. The process produced some startling promotions. Two former captains—George B. McClellan and Henry W. Halleck—returned as major generals and shortly became commanding generals of the army. (Halleck replaced McClellan.) Sherman had left the army in 1853 as a not-particularly-distinguished lieutenant, Grant in 1854 under something of a cloud as a captain. Neither was a success as a civilian. In 1861 both reentered the army as colonels and soon became brigadier generals, thanks to influential relatives and friends. Both, being men of some conscience, were surprised and somewhat uncomfortable to find themselves senior to Brig. Gen. Charles F. Smith, who had been a captain and Commandant of Cadets at West Point when they both were cadets, and who had remained in the army.

Smith might be taken as an exemplar of the Regular officers' service to the nation in the years 1861–62. A Regular's Regular and a gifted soldier, he served Grant loyally and intelligently as a subordinate. He also knew how to make soldiers out of raw Volunteers, "with the least jar on their previous habits of life" but found the process counter to all his experience and his temper.[9] Envious Volunteer officers and excitable small-bore politicians charged him with disloyalty. Then, on a freezing February 14, 1862, with Grant's offensive against Fort Donelson teetering on the edge of failure, Smith took his division in against the Confederate earthworks, riding slowly at its head, sword in hand, long white mustache blowing in the wind. "Come on, you volunteers, come on! . . . You volunteered to be killed for love of your country and now you can be!"[10] Their assault broke into the fort, and the Confederate command went into something of a panic. For a few weeks Smith seemed destined for a great military career. But he injured a leg, infection developed, and he died that April. Grant wrote Smith's wife a heartfelt letter of regret, but it was a Volunteer who had followed him into Fort Donelson who penned a fitting epitaph for the old Regular: "by his presence and heroic conduct he led green men to do things that no other man could have done."[11]

Volunteer officers were raised in the traditional ways. One common method was for the governor to appoint the colonel; the soldiers then elected the lieutenants and captains; and the captains elected the majors and lieutenant colonel. Naturally there was considerable finagling; in some regiments the privates got to vote for nothing higher than a lieutenant. In other cases the colonel, too, was elected, or might receive his commission from the governor as a reward for getting enough men to enlist to form a regiment. (In the latter case, the would-be colonel normally subdivided his recruiting task by offering a captain's commission to anyone bringing in enough men to form a company.) Whatever the faults of this system, it had been used in America since colonial days; also, it really was the one possible method when many officers were needed in a hurry.

Only in a very few cases would officers and noncommissioned officers be given any training in advance—usually officers and men started out equally ignorant.

However, there was a sprinkling of former Regular, Volunteer Militia, or foreign officers, and enlisted men as well, who at least knew the rudiments of drill and discipline. Some governors, duly concerned for the welfare of their constituents-in-uniform, worked at getting Regular officers transferred to the regiments they were raising—a move quite popular with the Regulars in question since it meant quick promotion. The enlisted men and some junior officers also seem to have favored this—although Regular officers might be strict disciplinarians, they knew how to take care of their men.

In electing their officers, the enlisted men often were judicious enough, choosing comrades of intelligence and character. The major weakness of the system was that officers and men, coming from the same locality and often from the same families, were too much akin for effective discipline.

Most were from small towns, villages, and farms where daily life went on in a "sleepy, slipshod way." An exacting Volunteer colonel of artillery wrote: "I have not come across more than half a dozen [officers] who can get fairly wakened up. Their orders come out slow and drawling, and then they wait patiently to see them half-obeyed in a laggard manner."[12] Hard service would give surviving officers more self-confidence and authority, but the educational process was expensive.

As in the American Revolution, a crowd of foreign officers appeared to offer their services. One American general muttered that there was a tendency to make a colonel out of anyone who claimed to have seen Garibaldi, that flamboyant Italian patriot being popular at the time. John Frémont, made a major general early in the war for political reasons, surrounded himself with a staff of gold-braided central Europeans whose average incompetence was matched only by their ignorance of the English language. A few foreign officers, however, were skilled European professionals who had come over to enjoy a good war and get in some practical experience. "Leatherbreeches" Hubert Digler, captain of Battery I, 1st Regiment Ohio Volunteer Light Artillery, was an outstanding example. His combat uniform was a white shirt, spotless doeskin breeches, and tall boots. He rode a big white horse, and he was famous for taking his 12-pounder "Napoleons" forward into the infantry skirmish lines and dueling down any number of Confederate guns. His men swore by him: When his horse was shot from under him during a fighting withdrawal at Chancellorsville, one of them rode practically into the onrushing Confederate infantry to pick him up.

The competent foreign-born officer, whether a naturalized American citizen or soldier of fortune, had to face a pervasive American "anti-foreigner" attitude. No matter how patriotic or able, he was often passed over for promotion and given the less-attractive assignments. Digler was constantly praised, but ended the war a captain, as he began it.

Two innovations improved the quality of the army's officers. The first, in July 1861, was the institution of examining boards to screen out the obviously incapable volunteer officers. These included men of little education, who worked hard but could not read well enough to comprehend army regulations, or write and spell sufficiently to produce a coherent report—and also well-educated officers "of good social standing" who simply would not bother to study. A good many marginal officers resigned, rather than face a board. The second innovation was an act of Congress that August, allowing any officer of the armed forces with forty years of service to retire with appropriate pay and allowances. This cleared away many aged and disabled officers.

Officer losses were heavy. The Civil War enlisted man expected his officers to set an example of bravery under fire, and improved weapons made such gallantry far riskier than it had been in earlier wars. Officer replacements were either appointed by state authorities or promoted out of the ranks. In the latter case they usually were tried veterans, but there always were failures like "Jonathan Slick" of the 12th Connecticut. "Jonathan" was found by his brigade commander sitting on a barrel and eating an apple while talking with a sentry (the latter being against orders since it would distract the sentry); his uniform was a nonregulation red shirt, trousers, and bare feet. He remained seated as the general approached, though he did salute—with the apple core still in his hand! Sometime thereafter he was found guilty of cowardice in action.

General officers were appointed by the federal goverment. Their number included a considerable proportion of "political generals," ambitious civilians with little or no military experience. President Lincoln has been much blamed for this, but the situation facing him was by no means as simple as some righteous military historians have assumed. Many of these new generals were "War Democrats"— men who broke long-time political associations to support the Union at a time when 313 Regular officers were going over to the enemy. They were political and community leaders; often they were effective orators who could raise regiments practically overnight. Their commissioning was simple acknowledgment of their contribu-

tion to national unity and the war effort. Like Benjamin F. Butler and Frémont, some of them left sorry military records, but, in their own fashion, during the war's first desperate months, most of them rendered services that no Regular officer could have performed. Others, such as John A. Logan and Francis P. Blair, did as much, and also became excellent combat officers. They may have lacked understanding of logistics and strategy, and might have found it necessary to go home on awkward occasions to mend their political fences, but they could lead men in battle with zeal and determination.

Because the number of Regular officers in each grade was limited by law, a good many Regulars were given higher commissions in the Volunteers for the duration of the war. A twenty-two-year-old lieutenant might serve as a Volunteer lieutenant colonel, "the disciplinarian and drillmaster of his regiment," under a Volunteer colonel with no knack for either task. And captains might be Volunteer brigadier or major generals.[13] This dual status was further complicated by the award of "brevet" promotions, both in the Regulars and Volunteers. (Having no system of honors or awards, from the Revolutionary War on the army had given honorary promotions, or "brevets" for outstanding service, or to officers detailed to certain staff positions. The results were a fine confusion as to which officer really ranked which, hurt feelings, and occasional squabbles which did nothing to help preserve the Union.)

WOMEN OF THE CIVIL WAR

Once more women followed the drums, but the times were changing. Some regiments mustered complete with laundress; the "admirably equipped" 2nd New Hampshire Volunteer Militia came into Washington in 1861 complete with uni-

formed nurses. Some regiments, especially the Zouaves, followed French custom and had *vivandières,* sprightly young women in feminized uniforms who carried little kegs of liquid refreshment slung over their shoulders. Supposedly they all had husbands in their respective regiments; however, two of the Garibaldi Guard's *vivandières* proved to be runaway juvenile delinquents.

Mary Tebe, *vivandière* to the Collis Zouaves (114th Pennsylvania), was thoroughly respectable, and reputedly a dead shot with her revolver. "Gentle Anna" Etheridge went to the wars with the laundress contingent of the 3rd Michigan, and stayed when the hardships of field service sent the others home. Her courage as a surgeon's helper caught the eye of Maj. Gen. Phil Kearny, who had seen enough fighting in both the American and French armies to know the real article; he ordered that she be made a sergeant cook in his headquarters mess and found her a horse. Thereafter, wearing a black riding habit with sergeant's chevrons and a pistol in her belt, she brought meals forward under fire to generals in hot corners, rallied downhearted units, and continued to help with the wounded. Both she and Mary Tebe received the Kearny Cross, a decoration instituted by Kearny's old division after he fell fighting at Chantilly, Virginia, in September 1862. All agreed that she was attractive, a perfect lady, and absolutely without fear. She served through the whole war, had one very slight wound, and then apparently vanished into some government office.

Kady Brownell of Rhode Island, daughter of a British soldier, went into action at the first Battle of Bull Run beside her sergeant husband. Bridget Divers, better known as "Irish Bridget," joined the 1st Michigan Cavalry with her husband, serving as a nurse and general rabble-rouser (there is a story of her rallying defeated cavalrymen with a yell of "Arragh, go in, b'ys!"). She had several horses killed under her, loved the army, and went off to fight Indians as a regimental laundress when the war was over.

But there also were ladies of a different sort, with no interest in the excitement and color of battle. Amy M. Bradley entered the war with the 3rd Maine, but turned to nursing and became an expert on hospital ships and convalescent camps. Clara Barton, a shy spinster clerk in the Patent Office, collected food and hospital supplies, gained the support of overworked Quartermaster General Montgomery C. Meigs, and got wagonloads of her supplies to the wounded. (After the second Battle of Bull Run in 1862, her supplies running low, she mixed what remained together and served a concoction of crumbled hardtack, wine, whiskey, brown sugar, and water.) Crossing a pontoon bridge at Fredericksburg that same year, she lost part of her skirt to a Confederate cannon shot. After the war Lincoln appointed her to handle correspondence concerning missing Union soldiers; she would become an international figure and the first president of the American Red Cross. "Mother" (properly Mary Ann Ball) Bickerdyke did the same sort of work with the western armies, moving with Sherman on his campaign across Georgia and through the Carolinas.

Other women worked directly with the army's hospitals. Dorothea L. Dix, a lady known for good works in workhouses, asylums, and prisons, was made Superintendent of Nurses in 1861. She wanted steady, plain women over thirty, strong enough to "turn a full-grown man around in bed" and not afraid of hard, dirty work. Louisa M. Alcott, later the author of *Little Women*, was one of them until her health broke. Despite the example of Florence Nightingale, many medical officers did not want female nurses and their lot sometimes could be thoroughly disagreeable. (In fact, the nursing service never was really organized; several different groups and various temporary volunteers were involved.) Mary E. Walker was another woman who could not be discouraged. One of the very few female doctors in the United States, in 1861 she requested an appointment as an assistant surgeon. Refused, she worked in various army hospitals without pay, proving her competence. In early 1864, she was appointed a contract surgeon. Captured later in the year, she was exchanged for a Confederate surgeon—the only female–male exchange during the war. After being discharged in 1865, she was presented with the Medal of Honor.

Both the Union and Confederate armies—but especially the latter—had a surplus of "beautiful girl spies" offering their services. (A glance at their surviving photographs brings the unchivalrous thought that most of them really looked more like neglected mud fences.) One exception was "Major" Pauline Cushman, the clever New Orleans-born actress who served the Union as counterintelligence agent and spy. Eventually, she "went to the well" once too often: captured in Tennessee, she was sentenced to hang, but the confusion caused by a federal offensive enabled her to escape. By contrast, the men of the 1st Wisconsin Heavy Artillery elected Ella Hobart Gibson their regimental chaplain in 1864 despite the War Department's disapproval.

A good many officers' wives spent time with their husbands, especially when the armies rested in winter quarters. Grant was most eager to have his wife with him whenever possible. Some wives came along even into the field. Mrs. James B. Ricketts, whose often-wounded husband began the war as a Regular captain and retired in 1867 as a major general, "from the time she was married . . . always made out his Muster Rolls & Reports."[14] In the Confederate Army of Northern Virginia, pretty Mrs. John B. Gordon kept her specially fitted wagon so close behind her husband's division that she was almost captured at Winchester, Virginia, in 1864, trying to rally fugitives from it. Crabbed Lt. Gen. Jubal A. Early, the Confederate commander and thorough misogamist, expressed regret the Yankees hadn't bagged her. These wives could be a nuisance in more ways than one. Gen. Marsena R. Patrick recorded that three of them had joined in looting a Virginia home.

As always, there were the unmarried "fair but frail," the "cyprians" and "soiled doves" who settled in vast numbers in Washington, Richmond, Norfolk, Memphis, and New Orleans and sometimes appeared more of a threat than the enemy's weapons to the soldiers' health. Mobile brothels followed the armies into the field—rumor claimed that one maintained a degree of exclusiveness by imposing a graduated set of fees, lowest for general officers, highest for privates.

LIFE IN THE FIELD

Rations

The army's eating habits began to change during the Civil War, though the ration remained much as it had been since the beginning of the century: pork or beef, flour or hard bread, smaller amounts of sugar, coffee, salt, and vinegar, plus the usual soap and candles. With this the soldier could expect 2½ ounces of dried beans or peas, and a smaller amount of rice or hominy. Newer items were black pepper, molasses, yeast powder, and ¼ pound of fresh potatoes or other vegetables "when practicable." When fresh vegetables were not available, "desiccated vegetables" (a mix of shredded carrots, beets, onions, string beans, and other vegetables, dehydrated and compressed into sheets—termed "baled hay" or "desecrated vegetables" by the soldiers) might be substituted. Dried apples were popular when they were available. Hard liquor could be issued when bad weather or unusually hard service might make it necessary to "preserve the soldiers' health"; wise commanders were duly attentive to such matters.

As the regiments formed, they were provided with regulation rations, mess kettles, and other utensils, and instructed to form their men into messes and be about feeding themselves in established army fashion. The results varied from regiment to regiment, depending largely on the quality and experience of their officers. The average American male was somewhat helpless, if not quite hopeless, in such matters. A few regiments, especially those made up largely of Germans or French, might possess a sufficiency of professional cooks. The red-trousered Frenchmen of the 55th New York Volunteers were as notable for their food as for their fighting—though their habit of supplementing official rations with bullfrogs and even snakes (some had served in French armies in Africa) was neither much appreciated nor imitated. In the camps around Washington during the war's first months, one or two wealthy colonels reputedly solved their immediate problem by hiring caterers to feed their regiments. And the very fancy 7th New York Militia Regiment simply took its three meals a day in Washington's best hotels.

Competent colonels got company kitchens organized, saw that they were kept clean, established regimental bakeries to provide soft bread, and kept a hard eye on their commissary officer. Other colonels established themselves at the bar of the nearest comfortable hotel and let things go. In their regiments, food was poorly cooked under increasingly filthy conditions, with the result that much of it went to waste. Given unappetizing food and too little of that, soldiers flocked to sutlers'

booths advertising "pies and cakes" and similar junk foods, or slipped away from camp to steal chickens. (The sutlers' offerings became known as "pi-zan cakes," irate medical officers swearing that these pies had cardboard crusts and unmentionable fillings.) Soldiers got indigestion, then diarrhea and dysentery; the sick lists lengthened and morale declined.

Companies in the same regiment might fare very differently. The green-uniformed 1st U.S. Sharpshooters admitted that their Company A had the lowest sick rate in the regiment—its captain, a Swiss veteran of European wars, forbade his men to fry their rations and enforced strict cleanliness. There were generals who took an abiding interest in how their men were fed. As a brigadier general waging successful amphibious operations along the Carolina coastal islands, Ambrose E. Burnside was a good provider and personally checked the food his soldiers were served. The same was said of one-armed Philip Kearny, whom Winfield Scott described as "the bravest man I ever knew, and a perfect soldier."

Though the epitome of desk-bound commanders, Maj. Gen. Henry Halleck, during his one brief venture as an army commander in the field in mid-1862, also showed that he had a strong streak of common sense. One look at his army's sick list sent him through its kitchens, tasting the food they produced. Upset in more ways than one, he ordered that an officer in each company must—as had been the Regulars' prewar tradition—inspect each meal; senior officers and medical officers were to see that all necessary corrective action was taken.

The first general improvement was to replace the small messes with a company mess. Two or three men were detailed as cooks. Soldiers swore that such cooks were selected because they were too stupid and slovenly to drill properly—and that accusation probably was true in many cases. Poor cooks, however, were only the last stage of the problem. Again and again, careful commanders found that their men were not receiving the full ration. Some commissary officers were inefficient, some were embezzlers who sold rations to local civilians for their own profit and concealed such transactions by a "singular entry" form of bookkeeping.

Joseph Hooker began his command of the Army of the Potomac in early 1863 with a rough-handed reform of the whole commissary system, from its senior staff to the company cooks. About that same time in Tennessee, Maj. Gen. William S. Rosecrans found that enlisted men of his Army of the Cumberland were coming down with scurvy despite the issue of fresh vegetables. Investigation showed that most of these vegetables were being diverted to the staff officers (some of whom had their families visiting them) of various headquarters. Shortly thereafter, a number of comfortable military careers were abruptly dislocated.

The marching ration, issued to the troops when supply trains would not be able to keep up, was 1 pound of hardtack (a hard-baked saltless cracker, roughly 3 inches square and ⅜ inch thick), either ¾ pound of salt pork or 1¼ pounds of fresh meat, and coffee, sugar, and salt. Soldiers could pack five days or more of these rations in their "odorous haversack," a gray canvas bag carried on the left hip and supported by a canvas sling over the right shoulder, which was designed to carry rations and served as a general catchall. (There always were some shiftless characters who, rather than carry a full haversack, would either throw most of their rations away or eat the whole lot in one or two meals, and then steal or beg food until the next issue.)

Even though they had to carry their salt pork ration, the soldiers seem to have pre-

ferred it to fresh beef, which usually came from cattle herds driven along with the army and slaughtered as required. There seldom was time to let the carcasses bleed and cool, and the meat had to be cooked promptly before it became fly-blown. Bacon tasted better than salt pork, but its fat would dissolve in hot weather and soak through the haversack. Salt beef (called "salt horse" or "old bull") was issued occasionally, but even occasionally was too often for the soldiers' taste. If properly preserved, it was too salty to eat without preliminary soaking; if not, it usually was tainted.

In the field, the soldiers might cook by messes or individually. No individual cooking or eating equipment was issued, but each soldier soon learned to furnish himself with a knife and a big tin cup or an empty tin can with an improvised wire bail. Half a canteen made an all-purpose utensil which could be used as a plate, frying pan, and entrenching tool. A mess would "pick up" a coffee pot, frying pan, and hatchet and take turns carrying them. At short halts, soldiers would broil their salt pork at the end of a forked stick, and boil coffee in their cups or cans. Seasoned campaigners might crumble their hardtack into their coffee. If there were weevils in the hardtack (a not uncommon occurrence), they would be skimmed off easily, without affecting the coffee's taste. Hardtack soaked in water and then fried in pork fat was "skillygalee." If crushed (which sometimes required a heavy blunt instrument) and soaked in water, it was "hellfire stew." "Lobscouse" was a soup or stew made with salt pork, crushed hardtack, and whatever else might be handy. Coffee was consumed in great quantities and whenever possible. Some soldiers carried their coffee and sugar mixed in a cloth bag in their haversack, all ready to boil. (In 1862, an "essence" of coffee—coffee extract mixed with sugar and dried milk—

was issued, but its taste repelled even veteran coffee boilers.)

When flour or corn meal was issued in place of hardtack, it might be made into flapjacks or, more commonly, mixed with water to form a stiff dough and then baked on a hot rock (hoe cake) or in a ball on the end of a ramrod. One soldier described it as consisting of alternate layers of soot and paste. When there was time, some soldiers would concoct soups or stews. A favorite dish when available was beans: boiled over the evening campfire, then put in a covered container with a piece of salt pork and buried under the fire to bake overnight and be eaten for breakfast. When there was no time for cooking, or storms put out the fires, veterans would make sandwiches of their hardtack and salt pork; epicureans among them would sprinkle sugar on the pork. To "wash" his cooking/eating utensils, the soldier scoured them with dirt.

One awkward feature of feeding troops in the field was that officers were not issued rations. They could buy them from the nearest commissary officer, but that gentry normally operated well to the rear. Also, they could not buy from him on credit—and their pay frequently was several months in arrears. When they did have money, they might find that the commissary officer was demanding fifty cents for an item that was only fifteen cents on the official price list. The result was that regimental officers might go hungry for days unless their men shared their food with them or their black servants (if they had them) found something to steal. Either alternative was bad for discipline, but a starving officer could hardly keep up with his regiment and do his duty otherwise.

"Living off the country" was the usual remedy for short rations. Much of it was individual or gang pilfering, which increased as the war went on. However, it might be done on an orderly basis by regularly detailed foraging parties. This began

on a major scale during Grant's 1863 campaign against Vicksburg, and reached its height during Sherman's march across Georgia. The army would carry an emergency supply with it; for example, five days' bacon, twenty days' bread, and thirty days' salt, sugar, and coffee. Every day each regiment or brigade would send out a party of one or two officers and from twenty to fifty men, mounted on commandeered horses, to gather supplies and livestock from the farms along the line of march. On occasion they might use plantation gristmills to grind the grain they seized into flour. Vehicles and draft animals of all sorts were impressed to haul the foodstuffs back to the column. Official foraging parties normally were forbidden to enter houses, but this prohibition seems to have been almost routinely disregarded by troops eager to get at pantries and wine cellars. In farm country like central Georgia, if it timed its advance to coincide with the ripening of the crops, an invading army could live high on smoked hams and fresh chicken, duck, goose, turkey, pork, beef, and mutton, with peanuts, honey, molasses, yams, preserves, and garden vegetables for trimmings. Immense amounts of food were wasted—in Sherman's case purposely—to deny it to the Confederates. Once an area had been "foraged" in this fashion, there was little or nothing left for the inhabitants, let alone another army.

Horses

For a Civil War army the supply of forage (hay and grain) for its horses and mules was as important as rations. Hay was heavy and bulky to transport; many of the mountain or pine woods regions produced little forage of any sort. Animals receiving only reduced allowances of grain rapidly lost weight and strength; they were worked to death by the thousands along the primitive, muddy roads and in hurried cavalry raids. As in many other things, it took the army at least two years to get its supply and handling of its animals properly systematized. Many cavalrymen, teamsters, and drivers neglected or abused their animals, sometimes deliberately in the hope of disabling them so as to be sent to the rear out of danger. It was difficult to teach the average young American cavalryman that he must take better care of his horse than he did of himself, or the average teamster to use his brains and not just his whip when bogged in a mud hole. Relatively few northern boys were good horsemen when they joined the army, but cavalrymen were needed, and regiments of untrained men on untrained horses were sent into action. They suffered frequent humiliation during the first year of the war but they learned rapidly, and by the autumn of 1862 they were winning more fights than they lost. Their equipment was lightened and they were issued breech-loading carbines that gave them a much faster rate of fire. Just as important, they learned how to care for their horses; if a horse developed a sore back, strict officers would make its rider walk and lead the animal.

Many of the horses purchased for the army were unfit for hard service. Others were half-broken or not broken at all. Considering the horse dealers who provided them, one federal officer lamented that "Men otherwise known to be of the staunchest integrity seem to lose all sense of the equity of things when it comes to selling or swapping horses."[15] As for breaking in the three mule teams used to haul each supply wagon and training them to pull together, it was agreed that no man ever did that without "breaking his Christian character."

Clothing

The United States never before had raised so many troops. Possibly 100,000 men served during the Mexican War (records are unclear); the Civil War saw 2,128,948 men enter the armies. Feeding them was problem enough, but that was simple beside the problem of clothing them. The volunteer militia turned out in their stylish uniforms, but some new recruits began their service in whatever clothes they were wearing when they enlisted. Many northern regiments wore gray in 1861, as there was plenty of available cloth in that color, which had been a favorite of militia units for many years. Since a good many Confederate regiments mustered in wearing the traditional American blue, some of the early battles were greatly confused affairs.

Initially, there was a severe shortage of essential garments. During the first months of the war, shocked civilians saw soldiers mounting guard around Washington in their drawers, for lack of trousers. A great deal of inferior clothing was purchased, sometimes through the ignorance or corruption of the purchasing agent, but often because nothing else was available. Much of it was "shoddy," a material made out of scraps and ravelings that had been glued, rolled, and shaped to look like sound cloth, but would dissolve under a light rain. At Fort Monroe in August 1861 the 10th New York (or "National Zouaves") had worn out their dark brown uniforms and their requisitions for replacements had been long unfilled. By way of calling their predicament forcefully to the attention of higher authority, their Company A "fell out for afternoon parade in clean underwear only" under their first sergeant, whose "sash, belt, and sword [were] rather too clearly defined against the ground of white."[16]

The first years saw a considerable number of regiments in zouave and semi-zouave uniforms, which were smart, but somewhat conspicuous. As these wore out, they often were replaced with the ordinary fatigue uniform of dark blue blouse and sky-blue trousers, but a good many regiments kept their full zouave dress throughout the war. Also, a number of new zouave regiments were raised, and some existing regiments were put into zouave uniforms. (The Quartermaster Department would either manufacture such special outfits or import them from France.) A surprising number of organizations wore somewhat specialized uniforms, probably the most conspicuous being the two regiments of U.S. Sharpshooters, in dark green.

One major complaint concerning the Civil War uniform was that it was too hot for summer service in the South. Otherwise, the army was well clothed by any standard, though most of its regiments never could be cured of the carefree American habit of throwing away their overcoats or anything else that began to feel heavy on a long march.

Medical Care

In 1861, the senior officers of the Army Medical Department were too old and routine-bound to meet the war emergency, and the doctors who came into the service with the Volunteer regiments might be capable enough in civilian life but knew pitifully little about taking care of soldiers in the field. There still was no comprehension of the causes of most diseases, or of the role of infected insects, water, and food in transmitting them. Surgeons used chloroform, or sometimes ether, but few of them would bother to wash their hands or their instruments between operations. In fact, there may have been some backsliding in standards of medical cleanliness since the beginning of the century.

The soldier's usual contact with medical attention came at the morning "sick call," when those feeling ill (and those pretending sick in the hope of dodging work or drill) lined up before the regimental surgeon. He looked them over, ordering the serious cases to the hospital, administering appropriate treatment to minor cases, and sending those capable of working back to duty. His "treatment" was usually calomel

or blue mass for bowel troubles, quinine for fevers, and an occasional jolt of wine or brandy as a stimulant for a run-down condition. Opium and laudanum were used as sedatives, the former also being prescribed for bad cases of dysentery. Some medical officers prescribed castor oil in place of calomel, which had unpleasant side effects and finally was dropped. When the "fever season" began in the spring, it was customary to issue everyone a ration of whiskey and quinine, which would suppress malaria but was useless against typhoid. One odd fact soon became apparent—units of big, tough farmers and lumberjacks tended to have far more sickness than those of comparatively runty city boys. The former seldom had been exposed to many contagious diseases and so had not built-up immunity; they also were much more careless about their food and the cleanliness of their camps.

If wounded during the first years of the war, the soldier would be lucky to escape a prolonged period of suffering. Casualties usually were heavy. The Civil War soldier tended to fight "all out" and regiments might sustain from 50 to 80 percent casualties in a matter of hours. These vast numbers of wounded swamped the surgeons, and it was difficult to find shelter for them. Evacuation of the wounded to the base hospitals was the responsibility of the quartermasters, who might neglect it. Consequently, wounded men might lie for days with little or no care before they were moved off in supply wagons or railroad cars.

Hospitals had to be improvised in any available buildings, often dirty and ill-ventilated. Ambulance drivers, as a class, were referred to as "sneaks"—a term of considerable more derision then than now, indicating a worthless soldier. Testimony that they robbed the wounded, pilfered hospital stores, neglected their horses, and were arrant cowards was practically unanimous. Fortunately, several able young medical officers were able to institute a number of reforms from late 1862 on: proper hospitals were built, Medical Department ambulance units were organized, and effective systems of supply and evacuation were developed. By the end of the war the army's medical organization was a model of its kind and amazingly efficient.

Civilian Relief Groups and Purveyors

These improvements were powerfully supported by civilian pressure. The war was fought on American soil and every American family was touched by it. Alarmed by reports of sickness and suffering in training camps and hospitals, public-spirited citizens offered their services. Individual citizens acted as volunteer nurses or helped prepare bandages. Ladies' "relief societies" began collecting food and clothing. Then prominent physicians, ministers, philanthropists, and businessmen combined to organize the U.S. Sanitary Commission, which in fact had to do most of the moribund Medical Department's work during the first year of the war. Profiting by the lessons of the recent Crimean War, the Sanitary Commission accumulated "sanitary stores," provided smallpox vaccine when the Medical Department's supply ran out, made "sanitary" inspections of camps, and provided information on the latest medical and surgical techniques. It mobilized doctors, nurses, and hospital attendants in emergencies, provided hospital ships and hospital trains, set up kitchens and rest homes where sick or wounded men on furlough could be fed and sheltered. Its representatives moved with the armies in the field, shepherding wagonloads of medical supplies and special foods for the wounded. One particular service the Commission offered was aid for soldiers in getting their service records in order. Beyond all this, the Sanitary Commission had the prestige and political influence to force improvements in the Medical Department, which it did without any hesitation.

Somewhat smaller but just as hard-working was the U.S. Christian Commission. As its name implied, it interested itself primarily in the mental and moral welfare of the soldier, but its chiefs were canny enough to know that such efforts could be helped along by physical comforts. They did distribute Bibles and religious works, but they also set up reading rooms in every good-sized camp, with newspapers from the soldiers' home states and free stationery and postage stamps. Moreover, they helped soldiers' families and black refugees. The ministers they sent into the hospitals may not have been properly appreciated, but their nurses were.

Altogether, these and other civilian agencies were invaluable, although there were two valid complaints concerning their work. First, some of the smaller agencies were organized on a state basis and would aid only soldiers from their state's regiments. Sherman refused to let them operate with his army in Georgia unless they gave aid to all. Second, the agencies' civilian doctors and nurses were too easily imposed on by deserters and malingerers, who would fake wounds or illness to get away from the front and were happy to receive tender loving care while they were about it.

A host of less charitable civilians hung on the army's outskirts, especially when it went into winter quarters. Some were useful, such as the "newsboys" who brought in newspapers; the photographers who recorded the war and its soldiers so graphically; and the "express companies" that delivered packages of food, clothing, and sundries from home. (Those packages needed checking to halt the shipment of liquor to industrious soldiers who were setting themselves up as regimental bootleggers, or of civilian clothing, which would facilitate desertion.) Express companies

watch over the doings of their respective enemies. In plain fact, they are fraternizing, exchanging mild insults and professional opinions on the shortcomings of army life. At one narrow stretch inventive soldiers have taken advantage of the evening breeze and a trick of the current to float makeshift little boats back and forth, swapping northern coffee for southern tobacco. When the Confederates begin asking for newspapers a passing officer breaks up the traffic, amid protests from both parties. Regardless of the possible cost in casualties, northern newspapers insist on printing all sorts of military information that southern generals would find useful, and there is no point in helping them obtain it.

Somewhere a soldier begins singing in a strong, resonant voice:

> *Our Johnny has gone for to live in a tent,*
> *They've grafted him into the army!*
> *He finally puckered up courage and went,*
> *When they grafted him into the army,*
> *I told them the child was too young, alas!* ...

Others join in. A jew's-harp twangs and picks up the tune. A Yank with an abundant mustache and a heavy German pipe produces a small accordion:

> *He looks kinder sickish—begins to cry—*
> *A big volunteer standing right in his eye.* ....

The song ends. Out of the laughter from the south bank a mellow voice begins:

> *The years creep slowly by, Lorena,*
> *The snow is on the grass again.* ...

Others from both sides catch it up and take it through all six flowery verses. Then comes:

> *... When this cruel war is over,*
> *Praying that we meet again.* ....

More men have sauntered down from the camps. Little fires leap and flicker. The songs go on: "Just Before the Battle, Mother" and "Tenting Tonight." Then down the north bank through the dusk, brass instruments glinting faintly, marches a brigade band. While the darkness gathers, and the first stars glitter, it plays. The songs are sad, sentimental, filled with resignation—"Auld Lang Syne" and "The Vacant Chair"—and the two armies sing with it.

There is a pause. Then in the starlight the bandmaster swings his stick, and drums and trumpets roar to "John Brown's Body" and "We Are Coming, Father Abraham." Northern voices shout the verses. Another pause, and from the far bank voices call, "Play one of ours." And the band swings into "The Bonnie Blue Flag" and "The Yellow Rose of Texas" and "Dixie," while the falsetto Rebel yell reechoes.

The music fades, the instruments click as bandsmen shift them and catch their breath. The bandmaster raps out four short words. Down the dark valley go the notes:

> *Midst pleasures and palaces*
> *Though we may roam—*
> *Be it ever so humble*
> *There's no place like home. . . .*

Men start singing. Some choke and cannot. The music ends; the band slings its instruments and marches back to camp to the tiny tapping of a single drum. The sentries shake themselves and take up their beats.

In another week the roads will be dry enough for marching; the men who sang together will be at each others' throats.

75. The American soldier, 1863. Guided by a cavalry first sergeant, an ordnance officer brings his ammunition train forward at a gallop. Such trains had the right of way in emergencies; normally, their canvas tops were marked to indicate the division to which they belonged. The service stripe on the sergeant's left forearm indicates five years of faithful service.

STANTON LEGION
W. H. ALLEN, COMMANDER.

TO PRESERVE THE UNION!

RESPOND

TO YOUR COUNTRY'S CALL!

$25 Bounty as soon as mustered in service.
25 Government Bounty 48 hours after being sworn in.
25 State Bounty as soon as the Regiment is completed.
50 Bounty from Common Council before leaving the State.
One Month's pay in advance as soon as the Co. is mustered in

This Regiment is being formed under the special orders of His Excellency GOV. E. D. MORGAN, and will, as soon as completed, be placed in active service.

In the formation of the Regiment great care will be taken to admit none but competent, able and experienced Officers,—the Governor as well as the Commander being desirous that men enlisting in it shall have every guarantee that they will not only BE WELL OFFICERED, but their health, comfort, and efficiency properly provided and cared for.

The vacancies occurring while in the field, in the rank of Company Officers, will be filled by deserving non-commissioned Officers. The deserving rank and file will also be promoted to non-commissioned Officers, and thus on to the highest grade of Company Officers.

The Regiment is now stationed at Camp New Dorp, S. I., in good and clean Barracks.

Good Rations, Clothing, and elegant Uniforms of the latest United States pattern, will be issued at once.
An excellent Regimental Band is formed and will be in attendance daily. The Sunday Dress Parades will be open to the friends of all members of the Regiment and the public.

1st Lieut., FRANK WELLINGTON.
2d Lieut., A. CLARKSON MERRITT. **Capt. HENRY T. FROST.**

Recruiting Office. 194 Canal Street.

BAKER & GODWIN, Printers, Printing-House Square, Opposite City Hall, New York.

76. "To preserve the Union!" The early volunteers joined the army out of a mixture of patriotism and excitement. Federal enlistment bounties were small—$25 for nine months' service or $100 for three years.

77. Recruiting for the war. By 1863 larger incentives were needed to recruit soldiers, and larger numbers of "volunteers" were foreigners, down-and-outers, and riff-raff. One of the latter is being helped to the recruiting station by a friendly policeman.

78. Drafted. The introduction of the draft in 1863 was not welcomed, as this cartoon of the period depicts.

79. Hiring a substitute. A citizen who was drafted, but did not wish to serve, could hire a substitute to take his place. Here one such patriot visits a "substitute broker" who advertises a "supply of ablebodied men allways on hand" but keeps the flap of his holster unfastened while displaying his stock.

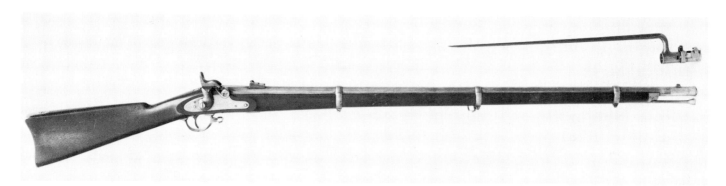

80. Percussion musket. The standard weapon of the Civil War infantryman was this model 1861 muzzle-loading "rifle musket," caliber .58, 56 inches long (without bayonet), and weighing almost 9 pounds. Its percussion lock (which the army had begun using in place of the flintlock in 1841–42) would function even in bad weather—which always had made the flintlock useless, except as a long handle for its bayonet. A hard-hitting weapon with an effective range of 500 to 600 yards, the "rifled musket" fired the new "Minie ball," which was both accurate and easy to load. A fresh, well-trained soldier could fire three rounds a minute, but two rounds was a good average for sustained firing.

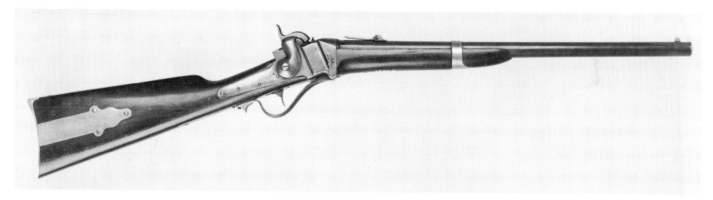

81. Sharps carbine. The caliber .52 Sharps, considered the best of the single-shot breechloaders used during the Civil War, was manufactured both as the short cavalry carbine shown here and as a longer weapon for infantrymen. In the longer form its accuracy made it the chosen weapon of the two regiments of U.S. Sharpshooters.

82. Garibaldi Guards. The soldiers who mustered around Washington, D.C., in 1861 were often a decorative lot. Here the officers and men of the 39th New York Volunteer Infantry Regiment, self-styled the "Garibaldi Guards," pose for a photographer.

83. Volunteers at drill. A contemporary painter has shown an unidentified regiment in dark blue overcoats and scarlet trousers maneuvering itself into impossibly perfect alignment. Note that the officers carry light packs—a custom soon abandoned.

"Detail from "Reported for duty""

Teaching a Baltimore Secesh manners

"Our guard duty at Hampton, was very severe, some of us being on post all the time" Extract from a letter of a Yankee Volunteer

84a, 84b, and 84c. Whimsical sketches by Samuel E. Chamberlain. These three sketches provide a down-to-earth picture of the 3rd Massachusetts Militia Regiment in 1861. The colonel in the top picture obviously likes his drink. In the center, a southern sympathizer has been "bucked and gagged" for insulting a sentry. At the bottom, another guard detail lavishes attention on a comely mother while two Zouaves (far right) disturb the peace.

85. After a year of campaigning. Active service in the field gave soldiers of both armies a rough and ready appearance. An understrength company of the 24th Michigan Volunteer Infantry Regiment stands ready for inspection. Some wear long frock coats, others the short fatigue blouse. Most retain the black dress hats, however battered, that mark them as men of the Iron Brigade. (The 24th was assigned to the brigade in late 1862 and had a difficult apprenticeship before being fully accepted.) The small leather pouches on their belts hold percussion caps for their rifles.

86. Jackson in the Shenandoah Valley. Often poorly supplied and frequently careless of what clothing they had, Confederates had an even more irregular look than Union soldiers. Here Stonewall Jackson's men pass their commander during one of their forced marches along the Shenandoah Valley. (The artist has somewhat "prettied up" both Jackson and his horse.) One Confederate explained, "All Old Jackson gave us was a musket, a hundred rounds and a gum blanket, and he druv us like hell."[19]

87. Marching in all seasons and all weathers. Battling the elements was the Civil War soldiers' common lot. Here a storm-pelted column fords an icy stream, its officers riding with the rear ranks to keep it well closed up.

88. Foraging. Even while the main armies marched or camped in relative safety, their patrols and foraging parties led a risky and exciting life. A group of Sherman's "bummers," equipped with horses and saddles they have picked up as they went along, have glimpsed another party through the pines. "They're Johnnies as sure as you're born, boys!"

89. Sharpshooter on duty. Outpost duties between the armies could amount to a constant small war of raiding and sniping. This sharpshooter is using a special target rifle with a long telescopic sight. Veteran soldiers on such service, however, often arranged informal truces.

90. Interior guard duty. Throughout the army there was always interior guard duty, such as that served here by black infantrymen.

91. Artillerymen on duty. During sieges, even when the infantry up front were having a reasonably quiet day, artillerymen like these manning a mortar battery had work to do.

92. Camping—something of an art. The ideal campsite was a well-drained area with enough trees for partial shade and good water and firewood handy. If troops occupied the same camp for any length of time, they usually built "arbors" of branches for extra shade and shelter.

93. Camp entertainment. Much of the routine work in camp was done by black camp followers. Here one of them entertains Union troops by dancing around a campfire to another's fiddling. (There may very well be a pot of beans baking underneath the campfire to be ready for breakfast.) Card playing and reading—when there was anything to read—were favorite camp pastimes.

94. Reveille on a winter morning. Snow and cold made tent camps unpleasant, as illustrated in this picture by Henry Bacon of a morning's roll call.

95. Coffee call. Coffee "strong enough to float an iron wedge" was an important aid to the soldiers' morale. Usually, Union troops were well supplied with it, much to the envy of the Confederates. Here soldiers line up for coffee call; the man at the right wears the crossed-axes insignia of the pioneers—selected soldiers who performed the duties of modern combat engineers.

96. Doing the laundry. Cleanliness was difficult, but soldiers sometimes found time and means to do their laundry.

97. Log company kitchens. In winter camps, log kitchens replaced the open cooking fires, and "corduroy" walks were put down to keep men out of the mud. Many Americans were experts with an ax, and such work was done quickly and efficiently.

98. Winter quarters in Virginia. In winter camps between campaigns, soldiers built up the sides of their tents with logs or boards and added improvised fireplaces and furnishings, as in this view of the inside of an officer's hut, with its pensive occupant and his orderly array of equipment. Provident cavalry and artillery officers put up shelters for their horses, and every regimental camp became a small military town.

99. Headquarters of the First Brigade of the Horse Artillery, Brandy Station, Virginia, in 1864. The brigade's headquarters were well-built, with chimneys of salvaged brick. A barrel with its ends removed has been placed on top of the nearer one to improve the chimney's draft. The horse artillery was a dashing arm; as shown here, the officers had a tendency to design their own uniforms.

100. Amphibious operations. Army-navy cooperation in amphibious operations was normally effective, as in the clearing of Hatteras Inlet in 1861. Such operations were common along the Atlantic and Gulf coasts and the western rivers.

101. The Ellet Ram Fleet. The army also had its own private navy, the Ellet Ram Fleet, shown here breaking through the line of Confederate gunboats (foreground) at Memphis. Ram service required courageous soldiers, as the rams had neither guns nor armor, but possessed only speed and sharp prows.

102. Desertion "in the face of the enemy." Desertion plagued the armies, and occasionally a soldier who deserted would be ceremoniously shot as an object lesson. This sketch records one such occasion. The deserter, "W. W. Lunt, private of the 9th Maine Vols," stands blindfolded at the left, his coffin at his feet. Next is an officer, holding a handkerchief at arm's length: He will drop it as the signal to fire. Then comes the firing squad. Beyond them waits a wagon to carry the body to the grave. In the background is a line of infantry regiments and a general with his staff; "reporters and artists" wait at the lower right.

103. Signal communications. The U.S. Army's system of semaphore signal communications, developed by Assistant Surgeon Albert J. Myer, later first chief of the new Signal Corps, was undoubtedly the world's best. Signalers used a single flag by day, a torch by night. Transmissions averaged three words a minute; their maximum effective range was approximately 10 miles.

104. The army telegraph. The electric telegraph was first used by armies in the field in 1862. After much bureaucratic squabbling the Military Telegraph Service took it over in 1864, restricting the Signal Corps to semaphone communications only. Though most of its personnel were civilians, the Military Telegraph Service was tightly disciplined. Through 1864–65 it laid and took up an average of 200 miles of wire a day, keeping the various Union armies in contact with Washington and with each other. Its "battery wagons" were mobile telegraph offices. These new means of communication required soldiers with the technical aptitude to understand and handle them.

105. The 50th New York Engineers. The American soldier was handy with pick, shovel, ax, or any other tool. Whatever he needed, he usually could make or fix. The 50th New York Engineer Regiment is shown cutting a new road up the south bank of the North Anna River in 1864. Behind them is a pontoon bridge other engineers have put into place across the river.

106. Seven Days Bridge. Bridges improvised out of local materials across the swampy Chickahominy River saved the Army of the Potomac in 1861.

107. Petersburg fortifications. The maze of Confederate fortifications around Petersburg successfully blocked Union attacks for almost a year.

108. *The Surgeon at Work at the Rear During an Engagement.* Medical attention on the battlefield was at best hasty and painful. There were no effective antiseptics, and often the only anesthetic available was a slug of whiskey. This illustration by Winslow Homer shows a surgeon taking bandages from the special pack carried by his enlisted assistant. The two-wheeled ambulance behind them proved uncomfortable and was replaced by a four-wheeled model.

109. Ambulance corps. This Zouave ambulance detachment is demonstrating the method of removal of wounded soldiers from the field.

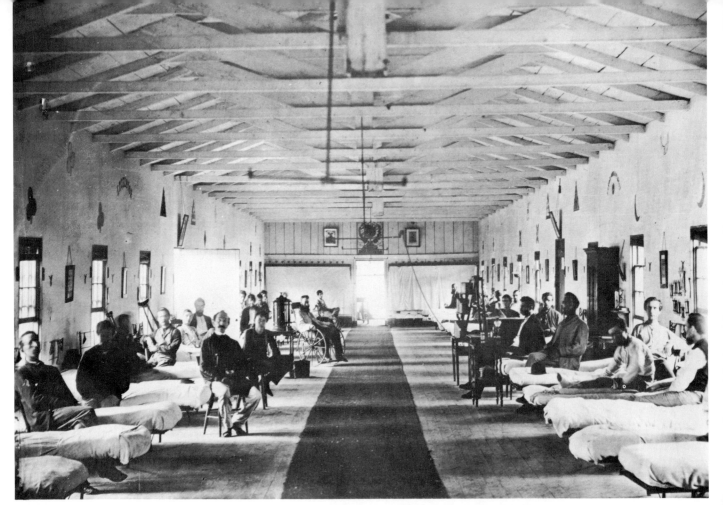

110. Armory Square Hospital. The clean, airy Ward "K" of Armory Square Hospital in Washington, D.C., is an example of the great improvements made in medical care during the Civil War.

111. The regimental chaplain. The ideal chaplain was cheerful, sincere in his faith, helpful with the soldiers' personal troubles, assiduous in his religious services, and ready to share hardship and danger. The chaplain of the 2nd U.S. Sharpshooters was one of the best shots in the regiment and always had a respectful congregation. Unfortunately, many chaplains were failures, and some could not even be trusted to look after their regiment's mail.

112. Fraternizing. As savagely as they fought one another, veteran soldiers frequently fraternized between battles. Here a Yankee Zouave and a Johnny Reb swap newspapers while their comrades share a kettle of coffee.

113. Prisoners of war. Prisoners on both sides endured much unnecessary suffering—more because of insufficient supplies, unfamiliar climates, and the negligence and incompetence of their keepers than from intentional malice. Veterans often sympathized with the men they guarded, as shown in this illustration: A Union sentry allows Confederate prisoners to buy pies from a black vendor.

114. Burying the dead. After the battles the dead were buried as decently as time and tools permitted. A Union detail begins this work at Bloody Antietam in 1862.

115. *The Return of the Flags.* Soldiers came home in 1865 to become civilians and everyday citizens once again. Glad as they were to be safely out of the army and the war, there still was a seriousness about them. They had given their youth to the dangers and the comradeship of famous armies; they would go back to small and quiet things and places, to pick up half-forgotten occupations or find new ones. *The Return of the Flags* by Thomas Waterman Wood catches that mood: A New York Volunteer infantry regiment with its riddled flags watches as their transport eases into New York harbor. With them is a waif, picked up somewhere down south and brought along.

116. *Furling the Flags.* For the Confederate veterans there were the added burdens of defeat and the knowledge that war had left many of them little to return to. *Furling the Flags* by Richard Norris Brooke catches, however crudely, the despair of men who had done their best, but all in vain.

CHAPTER

6

The Indian-fighting Soldier, 1866-97

The great war was over, and the Volunteers wanted to go home. But west of the Mississippi, from the Rio Grande to the Canadian line, there still was war, battle, and sudden death.

In far Wyoming, the little garrison of Kansas cavalry at Platte Bridge Station knew that the surrounding hills were filling with hostile Indians, and that an approaching wagon train would soon need help. But the Kansas officers had only a short time left to serve and would not accept the obvious risk of such a mission.

First Lt. Caspar W. Collins of the 11th Ohio Cavalry, passing through with a detachment escorting the U.S. mail, volunteered. Knowing the risk, possibly fey, he rode out in his newly purchased full-dress uniform with twenty-odd Kansas troopers at his back. Half a mile beyond the Platte, hundreds of warriors swarmed from ravines and engulfed them. Collins coolly swung his men into line, checked the rush momentarily with a carbine volley, and wheeled for the bridge. Warriors and troopers galloping neck-and-neck, revolvers blazing against painted chests, sabers licking through jabbing lances and swinging tomahawks, they broke clear. Four men dropped in the rush; though wounded himself, Collins reined in to help one of them. An arrow took him in the forehead; a swirl of warriors pulled him down. When his body was found later, his heart had been cut out and one hand and one foot hacked off. Powder had been crammed into his mouth and ignited, blowing off his face—possibly before he was dead.

Over a hundred miles back down the trail at Fort Laramie, hard-nosed Brig. Gen. Patrick E. Connor, once Private Connor of the old 1st Dragoons, was struggling to organize an expedition to halt such raiding. Many of his Volunteers had served out their enlistments and had to be discharged; the rest did their duty grudgingly. Ordered to march, the 16th Kansas Cavalry refused, protesting that their enlistments might expire before the expedition returned. Connor confronted them with two howitzers and some tough and unsympathetic California troopers; the 16th Kansas reconsidered and moved out as ordered.

THE POSTWAR ARMY

Most of the Regular regiments were ghosts. Of the Army of the Potomac's "Regular Division" their general said, "I left half of them [at Gettysburg] and buried the rest in the Wilderness." Troops were urgently needed to preserve law and order in the South; more had to be concentrated in Texas to put military muscle behind the U.S. diplomatic request that France get its army of occupation out of Mexico. The Fenian Brotherhood had to be checked in its somewhat comic-opera attempts to launch invading "armies" (mostly Irish veterans of the Civil War) into Canada from the United States. Assorted bandits and raiders were loose along the Mexican border, and several Indian campaigns were dragging to frustrated endings as swivel-chair quartermaster officers and conniving civilian contractors fouled up their supply system, weather turned bad, Volunteers were discharged or simply deserted, and Washington increasingly protested over their expense.

Meanwhile Congress dithered. It was July 28, 1866 (Robert E. Lee had surrendered at Appomattox on April 9, 1865), before the postwar army was officially organized. On paper, it would be 54,302 officers and men. There would be the five prewar regiments of artillery, but the cavalry was increased to ten regiments, and the infantry to forty-five. Enlistment of up to 1,000. Indian scouts was authorized. Two cavalry (the 9th and 10th) and four infantry regiments were to have black enlisted men and white officers. Four more of the infantry regiments were to consist of officers and men from the Veterans Reserve Corps (an organization—originally called the Invalid Corps and formed in 1863—of soldiers unfit for combat duty but capable of limited service as guards, escorts, and hospital staffs). The engineer battalion was retained, but the artillery went back to its prewar status, with only two completely equipped "light batteries" per regiment, the others serving as infantry or coast artillery. (In fact, only one such light battery seems to have been activated per regiment, for reasons of economy.) The awkward result was that there seldom were any artillerymen around when needed during the Indian wars, and details of doughboys or cavalrymen had to be given hasty instruction on whatever sort of "wagon gun" (Indian term for a fieldpiece) was available and sent forth to battle.

While Congress so labored, it rewarded itself with a 100 percent pay increase, but slashed the army's pay back to prewar levels, even though inflation meanwhile had cut deeply into the dollar's value. In 1867, however, it did grant a moderate increase.

This army was not popular in Washington. Many congressmen considered it far too large and too expensive. One New York representative (a Confederate sympathizer during the war) proposed simply abolishing it until the next war, if any, meanwhile turning its peacetime functions over to the Department of the Interior. Some Democrats resented the employment of troops to maintain order during elections in the South. Also, Congress now was full of former Volunteer generals, a good many of whom felt that their valor and abilities never had been properly acknowledged by cruel Regular Army superiors. Consequently, abolition of the Military Academy was repeatedly proposed.

In 1869, Congress abruptly cut the infantry from forty-five regiments to twenty-five, and reduced the ten brigadier generals allowed the army to eight. (In this slash, the four black infantry regiments were reduced to two—the 24th and 25th.) No further enlistments, promotions, or commissions were allowed until this reduction was complete. Then, from 1870 to 1874, further legislation restricted the army's strength to 25,000 enlisted men and slightly over 2,000 officers.

By way of a climax, in March 1877 Congress adjourned without passing an army appropriations bill. From July 1 on, the army therefore received no pay. Enlisted men were fed and clothed since these supplies could be obtained on credit, but most officers had to borrow money to feed their families. (One or two public-spirited bankers advanced them money at little or no interest; more seized the opportunity to charge extra.) Some married enlisted men were in considerable trouble. Nevertheless, the army continued to function normally; reportedly the rate of desertion actually declined. Finally President Rutherford B. Hayes called a special session of Congress which, after weeks of further wrangling, passed an appropriations measure in mid-November. The same thing happened in 1879, but this time the payless interval was shorter. There was little money for better weapons, uniforms, and equipment. Vast surplus stocks, often of poor quality, were left over from the Civil War and had to be used up, even if not particularly suited to Indian campaigning.

All of this might have sufficed for a peacetime army, but the United States was not at peace. From 1865 to 1891 the army waged ten major campaigns and over nine hundred engagements against hostile Indians, not to mention various civil disturbances in the South and East, and bandit raids in the West. Casualties, desertion, sickness, and necessary details reduced the army's effective strength. Companies often had only a single officer and a dozen men available for duty, sometimes less. Putting such understrength units into the field was sending a boy to do a man's job—they might be able to catch a hostile war party, but also might come off second-best when they did. Indians who would have submitted peacefully if confronted with a veteran regiment were perfectly willing to try their luck against a couple of weak companies. There is a story (variously told) of a captain, grown gray in frontier service, who received a telegram from Lt. Gen. Philip Sheridan, ordering him to take his company and bring in several hundred hostile warriors who had broken loose from their reservation and gone on the warpath. Suddenly fed up, the captain wired back: "Captain ———'s respects, general—and how does one do that with seven cavalrymen?"

During this period there really were two armies, divided by the Mississippi River.

Neither of them resembled anything now depicted in films and on television. East of the Mississippi there were green parade grounds and well-established posts with big brick barracks and roomy officers' quarters, where a captain could settle his wife, a posse of children, and a maiden aunt—with a small room or rooms at the back for a maid or a married enlisted man and his wife who helped around the house. (Today, such accommodations are known as "maidless rooms.") Except in the rare cases of natural calamity or civil disturbances too rough for the militia to handle, life was leisurely. As one lieutenant remembered, "full-dress uniform, lavish expenditures for kid gloves, bouquets, and Lublin's extracts were matters of daily fact."[1]

Officers of War Department staff bureaus—the adjutant general, quartermaster general, commissary general, inspector general, judge advocate general, surgeon general, paymaster general, and chief of ordnance—made themselves comfortable in Washington and the major headquarters, cultivated their political connections, and increasingly consulted their own conveniences before the needs of the troops in the field. Their appointments were permanent, there being no exchange of officers between the staff and the combat troops. Their enlisted assistants found life safe and easy.

Of course, not everything east of the Mississippi was as soft as the Indian-fighting end of the army thought. Fort Mackinac, set on an island in the strait between Lake Michigan and Lake Huron, was practically isolated in winter, with only irregular mail delivery. Some of the outlying coast-defense fortifications could be miserable places during winter storms: Fort Warren on George's Island in Boston harbor even had a resident ghost, "The Lady in Black," who—so veterans told recruits—liked to slip up behind a shivering sentry on pitch-dark, windy nights.

In all fairness, some of the despised—*and* envied—staff sections did go West and make themselves useful on occasion. Paymasters ran appreciable risks from both Indians and white bandits on their trips to isolated posts; there were not a few instances of their being ambushed and their small escorts shot up. One of them somehow won a reputation for his courage, intelligence, and skill in leading Indian and halfbreed scouts. A number of quartermaster officers found themselves with the major columns in the field, far from the sheltering wings of the quartermaster general. Very few of them ever really saw a hostile Indian, although they did experience certain horrors of war: "hauled over the coals by the general commanding, growled at by the battalion commanders, sneered at by the captains and damned by the lieutenants."[2]

West from the Mississippi the army was still that of the frontier soldier. It was a different country, one of long distances, rough terrain, few and crude roads, violent extremes of climate, and sudden shifts of weather. A military column moved out into it like a ship putting to sea, carrying its supplies with it. Wild game and native grasses might supplement these, but neither game nor grass was a certain resource. Water might be scarce, especially in late summer and autumn; on the high prairies there was no wood for campfires, and soldiers used "buffalo chips" (sun-dried buffalo droppings) for cooking. There were quicksands in the river crossings; a dry creek bed might suddenly become a cresting torrent from a thunderstorm miles upstream. Troops marched when the temperature was at "thirty below, with a blizzard blowing"; Col. Ranald S. Mackenzie took a column across eastern Wyoming in December 1876 when the thermometers froze. Soldiers pursuing Geronimo through blistering Mexican canyons stripped to their underwear and improvised moccasins to replace their worn-out shoes.

There were few big fights, but these were deadly. Indians took no prisoners, except for the pleasures of finishing them off by torture, at which the Comanche and Apache were supremely skilled. Surround-ed, without hope of escape, veterans saved their last shot for themselves. There was no place to leave sick or wounded men in safety; consequently, they had to be carried along in wagons or Indian "travois," and even a few of them slowed down the march of a column.

THE WESTERN FORT

To keep the tribes under observation and to serve as bases for any necessary campaign against them, the army built a network of forts and rough roads throughout the Indian country. Along the Missouri River, the Yellowstone, the Columbia, and the lower Colorado, shallow-draft river steamboats (said to be able to float on a heavy dew) helped supply the forts when the water wasn't too low or frozen.

Most of these forts were temporary affairs, constructed of whatever materials were available in their vicinity—quadrangles of low buildings around a dusty parade ground, with a flagpole standing tall in front of the headquarters. Very few forts were palisaded or fortified in any fashion. Indians might try to run off horses or cattle grazing near a fort, but their theory of warfare held that it should be exciting and profitable, and that it was time to go elsewhere when there clearly would be more casualties than loot. From 1860 on, there were less than a half-dozen occasions when Indians risked an attack on a military post. All were failures.

Some of these forts were almost as primitive as a prairie dog town. At Cantonment Reno on the Powder River in Wyoming, "officers and men were living in holes excavated in the faces of clay-banks."[3] Some forts could offer no better shelter than tents, even in winter. In many of them the buildings were run up hurriedly from green timber and roofed with poles and dirt. Floors often were dirt, packed down, but dusty in dry weather, and muddy when the roof leaked. Winds blew through unchinked crevices in the walls, and ceilings slobbered mud after heavy rains. On occasion a tent might have to be pitched inside such a building to protect bedridden sick. Soldiers slept two to a bunk on straw ticks. (The man who shared your bunk was your "bunkey.") Interiors were crowded and poorly lighted; if fleas, lice, or bedbugs got established they were almost impossible to eradicate. In winter, the potbellied barracks stoves seldom could warm more than the center of the room. There was little comfort, and basic cleanliness required infinite effort.

These forts had to be built almost entirely by their garrisons, as Congress refused any appropriation to hire civilian labor. Once again, resentful soldiers complained of being made jacks-of-all-trades, with haymaking and ice-cutting details thrown in. At Fort Custer, Montana, which was established in 1877, a soldier of the 11th Infantry recalled:

I drove a mule to grind the clay to make the bricks with which the fort was built, and soldiers dug the clay, moulded the bricks and set them in the kilns, and tended the fires that burned the bricks.... I helped to burn the lime.... carried a hod for the plasterer.... worked at the sawmill getting out lumber from the logs brought to Fort Custer by log trains. The drivers of those . . . log trains were soldiers. The logs were cut in the timber by soldiers. The doors and the shutters were made by soldiers and so on all down the line.

Another wrote, "we are so busy every day of the week that we have to do our drilling on Sunday."[4]

This work took time needed for training, and also hurt morale. A soldier who had been on fatigue duty all through a hot day "cuts a sorry figure . . . at dress parade in the evening. He may have found time to wash his face, but the chances are that his toilet on the whole is incomplete. He is no credit to himself. . . . he loses pride, and after a little he is neither soldier or laborer."[5] Unfortunately, the work had to be done, and there was no one but the soldier to do it.

During the late 1880s, as the fighting dwindled and the troops could be concentrated in the larger forts, living conditions improved. Fort Fetterman in eastern Wyoming had been established in 1867; by late 1876 it was regarded "in a mild kind of a way as a Mecca," with its neatly painted adobe barracks, officers' quarters, magazines, storehouses, stables, corrals, theatre, icehouse, root cellar, granary, bakery, a fifteen-bed hospital, sawmill, saddlers' and blacksmiths' shops, a paint shop, laundresses' quarters, and a "steam engine for pumping water from the North Platte River."[6] Some forts had stone or brick buildings; lawns and trees were planted and water pipes and even sewers installed. Soldiers received individual cots—which they still called "bunks"—with "spring mattresses, linen sheets, and feather pillows." But just a little way beyond the target range and the corrals, the land reached open and empty toward the mountains, and the guard of the grazing horse herd rode warily with loaded carbines.

In these isolated posts life followed a strict routine, regulated by the schedule of "calls" from "Reveille" to "Taps." (Varying from post to post, the first might be from 4:40 to 5:30 A.M.; the latter between 9:00 and 10:00 P.M.) In cavalry units the trumpeters sounded these calls; infantry used the fife and drum or, in small posts, the bugle. Immediately after "Reveille" roll call, "Stables" sounded in the cavalry, and troopers spent an hour or so grooming their horses and cleaning the stables before breakfast. (In some regiments these activities were reversed, on the theory that a soldier did a better job if he were fed first.) Thereafter, there was guard mount as the new guard detail relieved the old one. "Adjutant's Call" brought the officers to the post headquarters for a short briefing; for the enlisted men there was "Sick Call" and then drill or fatigue duties until dinner. After that there was more drill and fatigue until around 4:00 P.M., which brought "Evening Stables." Horses brought in from pasture by the herd guard were groomed and watered. Supper was followed by a full-dress "Retreat" parade at sundown. Then there was free time until "Tattoo" and the final roll call of the day. A quarter-hour later "Taps" sounded, lights went out in the barracks, and another day was done.

Sunday was a holiday, except for a full-dress inspection. If the post had a chaplain there would be "Church Call" and religious services. This, however, was infrequent since the army had only thirty post chaplains and over one hundred forts west of the Mississippi. (The regimental chaplains, authorized during the Civil War, had not been on the whole either effective or respected, and the office had been abolished except for four chaplains who served with the black regiments.) Some post chaplains were energetic killjoys, and opposed soldiers' efforts to hold post dances on holidays.

The companies were managed by their first sergeants (known also as "top-kicks" and a variety of other nicknames, many of them unprintable), under the Olympian supervision of their captains. Lieutenants, especially new ones, were supposed to observe, learn, and keep out from underfoot.

> Sez the captain, "All we want yez to do
> Is turn out for Reveille!
> And after that, remember the top-kick runs
>   the company!"[7]

No enlisted man might speak to the company commander without the topkick's permission, and for all practical purposes the captain's word was law. Discipline was always strict; depending on the officer and the situation, it might be harsh. The problem of keeping tough men in hand under prolonged hardship, monotony, and danger was not easy, but a good first sergeant, backed by a cadre of veteran sergeants and corporals, could handle it. Much of their work was informal: recruits were given good advice, trouble-makers were taken behind the stables and thoroughly walloped. Even official punishments tended to be informal and outside the Articles of War—with so much work do do, there was no sense allowing a culprit to sit idly in the guardhouse. Instead, he usually was given extra fatigue; in more extreme cases, the old punishments of being tied up by the thumbs or carrying a heavy weight for long periods were employed.

Frontier Soldiers

As before the Civil War, the soldiers of this new army were drawn from odds and ends of American manhood. There were veterans from North and South to whom the army was home, boys who wanted adventure, and good men who somehow lacked the secret of success in a commercial society. But there also were larger numbers of the illiterate, the down-and-out, men on the dodge from a woman or a lawsuit, and plain criminals who had enlisted at a judge's suggestion.

> Oh we had our choice of signin' up
> Or bein' sint to jail . . .

There were "snow birds" who enlisted to have shelter and food through the winter, intending to desert in the spring. Others joined to secure free transportation to the western mining districts, intending to desert there and make their fortunes. Approximately half of them were foreign born, and almost half of these were Irish, with Germans next. A few Italians appeared, usually as bandsmen. Many of these immigrants could not speak English, very few could read or write it. But numbers of them had served in European armies, and some became excellent noncommissioned officers.

On the whole, they were a tough lot, fond of liquor and gambling, contentious, often lazy and careless. Discipline and training could make useful soldiers out of most of them, but officers and noncommissioned officers had to be firm and unhesitating in the process. Hard times back East could bring in a better class of recruit as skilled workmen lost their jobs. Sometimes the weather cooperated; one army saying held that "A hard winter is the best recruiting sergeant."

With such unpromising material, desertion was all too common. Between 1867 and 1891 almost one-third of all enlisted men deserted, often with horses, weapons, and equipment. The 7th Cavalry was one of the worst sufferers, noncommissioned officers and privates going off in large groups and sometimes shooting their way out of camp. For differing reasons a good many men enlisted under names other than their own. Human memory being imperfect, there were awkward moments at roll calls, paydays, and musters when recruits failed to remember their new identities. Wise sergeants would warn beforehand, "Remember your army names!"

Few recruits could ride, and not too

many were familiar with firearms. Not until 1881 did they get any preliminary training at recruit depots before joining their regiment. Once with the regiment they were put to work, receiving only minimal training in most cases. Consequently, cavalry regiments went into the field with a high percentage of raw soldiers who were poor horsemen, poor shots, and likely to panic. At the Little Big Horn at least a third—possibly more—of the 7th Cavalry were these amateur soldiers.

The black regiments took several years to develop. Most of their men were former slaves and wholly illiterate. Comparatively few white officers wanted to serve with these regiments; of those assigned, a good many understood nothing of the character of their men. There were incidents. For example, a first sergeant in the 9th Cavalry led a small-scale mutiny in which he and a lieutenant were killed, and two other lieutenants wounded. Constant service and good leadership steadied them, and the black soldier proved cheerful and enduring if somewhat lacking in initiative and self-reliance. He was less given to drunkenness and desertion than the white soldier, and more likely to reenlist. Consequently the black regiments soon contained a high proportion of steady veterans. They came to be called "buffalo soldiers," supposedly so identified by Indians because their hair resembled a buffalo's coat; but the 9th Cavalry was also known as "Henry's Brunettes," from the name of their scar-faced commander.

Indian scouts had a valuable part in the army's campaigning. They generally were enlisted for six months and received uniforms, rations, and a cavalryman's pay, plus forty cents a day extra if they provided their own horses and horse equipment. Some units were very well known, probably the most famous being the well-organized battalion of Pawnee Scouts led by the North brothers, Major Frank and Captain Luther. They went into action with

their medicine men riding at their head, playing a "weird croon" on their sacred flageolets.

Along the Mexican border a small contingent of Seminole-Negro scouts (descendants of exiles from Florida) and Tonkawa proved effective. In Arizona, Gen. George Crook raised loyal scout companies from among the wildest of the Apache, including warriors recently in arms against him. Other scouts were recruited from the Osage, Omaha, and Arikara (usually called "Ree"). Crow and Shoshoni served both as scouts and as auxiliaries under their own chiefs. In 1876–77 Crook even recruited Sioux, Cheyenne, Arapahoe, and Bannock scouts to serve against those elements of their tribes that still were hostile. With one exception—the mutiny of some White Mountain Apache scouts at Cibicu Creek in 1881 following the arrest of a popular prophet—the Indian gave loyal service as a scout, tracker, and fighting man.

The Indians needed expert leadership from officers who understood their ways and psychology. Usually these were young men of rare character and courage, such as Capt. Emmet Crawford, Lt. Charles B. Gatewood, and Lt. William P. Clark, whom his Cheyenne friends called "White Hat." Unfortunately, many officers, up to and including Sheridan, distrusted them. Some of Crook's most trustworthy scouts, who had assisted in the capture of Geronimo, were sent off to Florida as prisoners with the hostile Apache they had helped to catch.

In addition to the Indian scouts, there were a few white men and halfbreeds whose knowledge of western geography and Indian language and ways made them almost indispensable as guides, interpreters, and advisers. The first were surviving mountain men, such as the famous Jim Bridger and the Delaware Black Beaver. Then came Frank Grouard, Baptiste Pouvier and Baptiste Garnier (known as "Big Bat" and "Little Bat"), Al Sieber, Tom

Horn, "Lonesome Charley" Reynolds, Mitch Bouyer. Later, the title of "scout" would be claimed by men whose major service had been as couriers or at most as "guides" through known territory. William Cody derived a lifetime of publicity as "Buffalo Bill" from such service.

As important in their own way as these scouts were the civilian employees in charge of the pack mules and wagon trains. If carefully selected and intelligently employed, they served as devotedly as any soldier; if picked up haphazardly, they would clog and delay any operation. Crook was famous for the study and skill he applied to the organization of his trains of pack mules. Quite a few of his packers were Chileans, Peruvians, or Mexicans—hardy, cheerful men who sang sad Spanish love songs, were excellent cooks, and called their mules horrifying names in dulcet tones. Most mule skinners (teamsters) were native Americans who did their cursing at full pitch, punctuated by cracks of their long "black-snake" whips.

Frontier Officers

The officers were veterans. Most had served through the Civil War, and many of the "Old Regulars" had years of service before that. A good many carried one or more wounds—some as many as six. In its 1866 reorganization of the army, Congress decreed that its higher grades were to be divided equally among Regular and Volunteer officers, all of whom must have at least two years' creditable service. Vacancies in the grade of lieutenant were to be filled with Volunteer officers. Meanwhile all Regular officers reverted to their permanent grades, a painful experience by which a Regular captain, serving temporarily as a major general of Volunteers, could find himself again a captain overnight. All Volunteers had to pass an examining board, but it is quite probable that backing from general officers or influential

politicians was given more weight than the test results.

The new 7th Cavalry Regiment offers a good example of the scramble made of the army's officers. (It is ironic that so much detailed information is readily available on the 7th, which never was a first-class combat outfit like the 5th or 6th, let alone Ranald Mackenzie's 4th Cavalry.) Its first colonel was Andrew Jackson Smith, an 1833 West Point graduate and thoroughly competent; when he retired in 1869 his successor was Samuel D. Sturgis, who was a "West Pointer" of no visible competence whatever. Both men usually were on detached service, leaving the actual command of the 7th to Lt. Col. George A. Custer. Very brave, tireless, an expert showman, spectacularly lucky, Custer had been the "goat" (lowest man) in the West Point class of June 1861. In 1863, at age twenty-three, he was jumped· directly from first lieutenant to brigadier general of Volunteers and fought his way up to major general. He had much ambition and few scruples, but lacked the steadiness of character to command a regiment.

The senior of the three majors, Alfred Gibbs, known as "General Etiquette," was also a West Point graduate; partially disabled by a wound from an Apache lance in 1857, he did the work of organizing the regiment, but died suddenly in 1869. Wickliffe Cooper, the second, had been a Volunteer colonel with an excellent record; he committed suicide during an attack of delirium tremens in 1867. Joel H. Elliot also had been a Volunteer colonel, who had come up out of the ranks through intelligence, courage, and dedication. He was younger than most of the captains and possibly too eager for honors. Pursuing fleeing Indians with a small detachment at the Washita fight in 1868, he was surrounded and killed. Custer made no effort to look for him, thereby further turning his regiment against him.

Most of the twelve captains had been

Volunteer colonels. Frederick W. Benteen, the senior, was a first-rate soldier; he hated Custer and could face him down before the assembled officers of the regiment. Miles Keogh was a gallant Irish soldier of fortune and a consistent off-duty drunkard; he turned his pay over to his orderly, who managed his daily life for him. Edward Myers, a hot-tempered, slow-witted German who had come up out of the ranks of the old 1st Dragoons, was court-martialed and almost expelled from the service in 1867. Lee P. Gillette was another hopeless alcoholic; in 1868 his fellow officers got up a purse of $1,500 to persuade him to resign. Robert M. West began well after brilliant Civil War service, but drink also got the better of him and he resigned in 1869.

Of the lieutenants, Charles Brewster resigned rather than face charges that he was "constitutionally inefficient." Frank Y. Commagere was thoroughly unqualified and resigned hurriedly in 1867. James T. Leavy was retired that same year for insanity. Samuel M. Robbins was cast from the service in 1871 for repeated public drunkenness, public cohabitation, and assault and battery (his great political pull enabled him to resign). H. Walworth ("Salt") Smith was usually under arrest; in 1871 he embezzled $1,200 and deserted. David W. Wallingford had mighty Kansas political backing despite a disgraceful Civil War career; after much misconduct, his open association with a "notorious prostitute" resulted in his explusion. One story is that he thereafter turned horse thief and died in the Kansas penitentiary.

The proportion of foreign-born officers is surprising. Besides Keogh and Myers, there were two former English officers who served quietly and competently. Lt. William W. Cooke, later the regiment's adjutant, was a Canadian, and another lieutenant—acknowledged the 7th's most accomplished curser—was French.

SERVICE ON THE FRONTIER

Officers' wives followed their husbands into the frontier. Gently reared girls found themselves living in tents, two-room adobe huts, or lean-to shanties. They raised children; conjured up party menus out of tough beef, bacon, beans, flour, rice, coffee, sugar, and dried apples; and created furniture out of odd crates and barrels, disguised with a little calico or muslin. Officially, they were "camp followers"; in fact, they were members of their regiment. They picked up head lice while visiting Indian families (the cure: shampoo thoroughly with a strong tobacco solution, and massage the scalp with lard); a rabid wolf might interrupt an evening gathering on their front porch; curious Indians wandered into their quarters while they were taking an improvised bath; and their offspring came home with resounding new expressions learned while watching a teamster break in a six-mule hitch. But (a few faint hearts excepted) they flourished, and found visits to old homes and families in the East increasingly unsatisfactory. But there always was the waiting when the troops went into the field, and the desolation that might follow. The famous scout officer, Charles Gatewood, died still a lieutenant, the honor due him for securing Geronimo's final surrender stolen by over-ambitious Brig. Gen. Nelson A. Miles. For Gatewood, there was a grateful republic's usual reward: "a free plot of ground in Arlington Cemetery, and to his widow a tawdry seventeen dollars a month."[8] His son became a soldier after him.

Officers and their families lived in constant apprehension of what Congress might do next to them. The 1869–74 reductions forced almost nine hundred officers out of the service. A good many whom the "Benzine Boards" (apparently so called because they "cleaned" the officers' list) screened out were definitely good riddance, but enough good men were shoved out with them to unsettle those who remained. Stagnated promotion, the constant threat of drastic cuts in their pay and allowances, years of constant warfare and hardship, the everlasting necessity to make do with insufficient forces and inferior weapons, and the perpetual cross hauling between eastern do-gooders who saw the Indian as an innocent, abused child of nature and westerners who wanted him exterminated convinced many of them that their government and fellow countrymen were somewhat beyond normal comprehension. Many turned inward; the army was their life and everything outside it was hostile wilderness. They took pride in not voting, and officer and enlisted man alike considered "politician" a cuss word.

Nonetheless, their professional efficiency increased. In 1881 William T. Sherman, then commanding the army, opened the "School of Application for Infantry and Cavalry" at Fort Leavenworth to train officers in the handling of large units. As an example of its necessity, when the 21st Infantry Regiment was assembled for field maneuvers in 1889, it was the first time the entire organization had been in one place in twenty years. A school of instruction for cavalry and light artillery units was set up at Fort Riley in 1892, and several professional associations, such as the Military Service Institution of the United States, took up the study of military history and theory.

Rations

The army's rations were those of the Civil War (sometimes in more ways than one, since there was war-surplus hardtack that had to be used up). Clever captains could rig up a field oven to bake fresh bread, which both pleased their men and saved money for their company fund. In some times and places hunting and fishing were excellent; a captain in the 7th Cavalry had raccoon for breakfast and roast wild turkey for dinner, with sage hen and fat buffalo meat for other meals. There were wild plums and berries. But there also were long marches on quarter-rations and little water, and occasions when troopers ate the flesh of played-out horses—sometimes raw when there was too much rain or danger to light a fire. In such times it was noted that General Crook would eat only what his men ate, even when his scouts brought in game.

In garrison, breakfast was substantial, if hurried—coffee, hash or beans, and bread. Dinner, at noon, was the main meal, with stew or roast meat. Supper was light, sometimes consisting of only coffee and bread. All of these meals were gradually improved, either by hunting or, especially after the institution of the post canteen, by extra items purchased out of the company fund. Post gardens when successful added fresh vegetables in season. Fresh vegetables or fruits, sent by wagon to isolated posts, could be protected against freezing by heating large rocks in a fire, packing them in around the shipment, and covering the whole with tarpaulins. Some posts, isolated by winter and hostile tribes, might suffer from scurvy until spring brought the first wild onions.

Tobacco was almost as important as food. When Crook's command captured a small Indian village at Slim Buttes, after the Battle of the Little Big Horn, the almost-starving soldiers ransacked its lodges first for dried meat and then for tobacco.

In the field, tobacco frequently was chewed rather than smoked. Chewing required no matches (frequently a scarce item) and involved no risky flares of light at night. Moreover, a veteran "chewer" could indulge himself while on sentry duty and other occasions when smoking was a major offense. Veterans could go through formal guard mount or retreat parade with a massive quid tucked comfortably alongside a rear molar and scarcely twitch a cheek muscle until the formation was dismissed. Some of the soldiers who did smoke adopted the Indian custom of using "kinnikinnick," a mixture of bark, dried leaves, and tobacco.

Feeding the army's horses and mules frequently was a problem, especially during winter campaigns. Prairie grass was nutritious, although it took eastern-raised horses a year or so to become accustomed to it, as well as hardened to campaigning. But in winter, few horses would paw through snow to get at the grass underneath; when other feed failed, they were given cottonwood leaves if those were available.

Uniforms

Cursed with a surplus of poor-quality Civil War uniforms, which seemed to be cut to fit only "goose necked and pot bellied men," and boots and shoes apparently designed for flat or splay feet, the army was hard put to present a respectable appearance and to keep from freezing in winter. Various forms of headgear, designed by noncombatants, were tried and found wanting. By the 1870s, practical winter clothing finally came into use—much of it made up by the reigments in the field. Muskrat-skin caps and gloves, buffalo-skin coats and leggings, and "snow excluders" (overshoes) kept the soldier warm. In the South, British-style sun helmets and white duck uniforms were officially introduced in the 1880s. Meanwhile, officers and soldiers uniformed themselves at the post traders, buying blue flannel shirts, good hats, and other practical items for wear in the field. High-cut moccasins might replace boots. The effect could be picturesque, but it certainly was not regulation. In southern posts officers and men wore stiff-brimmed straw "boaters" in summer. In 1872 a showy new dress uniform was introduced, modeled somewhat on that of the Prussian Army, which had just won the Franco-Prussian War.

Weapons

The soldier's weapons were indicative of the low value the nation placed upon his life. At the end of the Civil War, practically all infantrymen still were armed with the muzzle-loading Springfield caliber .58 rifle-musket. Cavalry had a variety of breech-loading carbines, some of them effective repeaters like the 7-shot Spencer. With thousands of surplus Springfields on hand, and Congress unwilling to provide funds for new weapons, the army set about converting the Springfields to breechloaders. The result was the "trap-door" (so called from the design of its breechblock) caliber .45–70 Springfield, which used the new center-fire metallic cartridge. The infantry version, sometimes called the "Long Tom," was a single-shot, hard-hitting rifle with a long-range accuracy that hostile Indians found unsettling. The changeover to this new weapon took some time; meanwhile, infantrymen trudged off to the frontier with the old muzzle-loading rifle-musket, which could not be reloaded fast enough to stop Indians swarming from ambush.

The cavalry found its Spencer repeating carbines highly effective for several years, cavalry actions frequently being brief, violent affairs in which rapid fire power was essential. (Cavalrymen also carried a caliber .45 revolver, but—fond American legends to the contrary—hitting anything but a pointblank target with a revolver during a mounted engagement took much practice. Recruits were far more likely to shoot their horses, their comrades, or themselves.) However, a short carbine version of the trap-door Springfield was more-or-less thrust upon them in the early 1870s. At least one disgruntled officer pronounced a single-shot carbine less effective in a mounted skirmish than an Indian's bow and arrow, which was just as accurate at short range and could be discharged far more rapidly. The odds became more unsettling when a fair number of Indians secured Henry or Winchester repeating rifles by theft, purchase, or capture—and occasionally as gifts from their "Great White Father." When Colonel Mackenzie wanted his crack 4th Cavalry Regiment rearmed with Winchesters, the chief of ordnance (safe and far away from vulgar frontier scufflings) gave him nothing but a lecture on comparative ballistics. The army tested a good many weapons, both single-shot and repeaters, but not until 1892 was the Springfield replaced by a modern rifle. For this, it had to turn to Denmark for the design of its Krag-Jorgensen magazine rifle, an effective caliber .308 weapon that fired smokeless-powder cartridges.

Whatever his weapons, the soldier got little effective training in their use until 1879, when a comprehensive system of target practice was introduced (according to some cynics because the Nez Percé War in 1877 had proved that the average recruit couldn't hit the side of a box canyon, let alone a moving Indian, while the Nez Percé picked off soldiers right and left). Target practice was popular and officers and men worked hard at it, many becoming dead shots at ranges up to 600 yards. Matches between the best shots of neighboring posts (for the Fort Custer team that meant Fort Keogh, 125 miles as the crow flies to the northeast) were major events.

Since there seldom was any opportunity to use them, sabers and bayonets were more and more left behind when troops went into the field. But officer and enlisted man, trooper and doughboy alike provided themselves with heavy sheath knives that functioned as eating utensil, toothpick, weapon, and all-purpose tool. Similarly, the soldier solved the problem of how to carry his ammunition. Ordnance issued pouches in which the cartridges rattled loudly every time the soldier moved. The soldier's solution—apparently discovered by different men in different places—was a canvas waist belt with loops into which individual cartridges could be thrust.

Amenities and the Post Exchange

The soldier might not be well paid, clothed, armed, fed, or housed, but his morals were the object of much tender solicitude. Originally the post sutler was allowed to sell wine or beer to enlisted men, who also could buy whiskey on occasion with the approval of their company commander. Since the officers usually got their own liquor from the same source, it was at least potable. Any soldier who managed to get drunk would be taken in hand by his comrades. Unfortunately, President Rutherford B. Hayes was an idealist who would not serve liquor at White House dinners; in 1881 he ended its sale on military reservations. This sent the thirsty soldier who wanted a drink back to the hog ranches, with a resultant increase of drunkenness, indiscipline, and disease.

Another "reform" during the years 1878 to 1883 denied the company laundresses the quarters and rations to which they had been entitled for over a century. Since most were married to noncommissioned officers, this made little difference in the matter of quarters, but considerably more as to what they could put on their table. For the rest, their labors were essential and—new regulations and virtues notwithstanding—post commanders tended to make their lot as easy as possible. Most of them seem to have been Irish, full of fun or fury, great battlers with tongue, fist, and chunks of firewood, and given to loud lamentations over real or supposed misfortunes. It was a soldier's point of honor to pay his laundry bill, even if he could pay nothing else. Considering the ladies involved, such procedure undoubtedly was also the safest.

The institution of the civilian post trader (a term that replaced "sutler") came under increasing criticism. Some were honest men who tried to please their customers, but all of them expected to profit as much as possible from their stores. In 1880, officers of the 21st Infantry Regiment at Vancouver Barracks established a cooperative store (called a "canteen" after British institutions of the same type) for their regiment. It was so successful, both financially and in building up unit morale, that other regiments copied it. This effort achieved a certain degree of uniformity in 1892, and the name was changed from "canteen" to "post exchange." Enlisted men could get "canteen checks" (small folders of detachable coupons) good for purchases there on credit, to be paid for at the next payday. Profits were used to build up the canteen, or put into post and company funds for buying athletic equipment, extras for the company messes, and furniture for "day rooms" (small lounges that began appearing in the newer barracks). The canteen would purchase billiard and pool tables and charge five cents or so a game for their use. A reading room would offer magazines and newspapers (the *Police Gazette* was a favorite) and games such as checkers and dominoes. There would be a bar dispensing wines and beer at prices no hog ranch could match. Many had a lunch room; at lonesome Fort Mackinac the favorite item was a sandwich of "imported Swiss cheese, ham, and French mustard." Later on there would be a soda fountain.

But all this was for permanent posts, and not too many Indian-fighting soldiers saw one. Even in the best posts payday night was a howler for lots of soldiers. If the commanding officer had good relations with the local civilian authorities, he could pick up his more energetic sinners at the local jail the next morning. If relations were poor, local magistrates might fatten their purses by levying heavy fines, and sooner or later there would come a time of reckoning, as the American soldier studied appropriate vengeance.

TWO LITTLE-KNOWN MISSIONS

Through this period the army carried out two little-known missions. Beginning in 1870, the Signal Corps developed an effective nationwide weather service, including a storm and flood warning system and the experimental use of balloons to study unusual atmospheric conditions. Its efficiency attracted international attention and led to the exchange of weather data with other nations. In 1881, two Signal Corps detachments participated in the First Polar Year, an international study of the Arctic. Its expedition to Point Barrow, Alaska, was highly successful, but the one under Lt. Adolphus W. Greely to Ellesmere Island (west of northern Greenland) was trapped for almost three years when ice blocked the navy ships sent to pick them up. Only seven of the twenty-five officers and men survived, but they saved all their scientific records. In 1891, Congress ordered this weather service transferred to the Department of Agriculture.

Meanwhile, the Department of the Interior had found itself unable to manage Yellowstone Park, the first of our national parks, and requested that the army take over. Other national parks also came under army protection as they were created. Soldiers built roads, fought forest fires, stopped illegal lumbering, caught poachers (in Yellowstone Park elk were killed solely for their teeth, which were used for jewelry), handled visitors, and generally developed the methods of park operation used today. The National Park Service, which was created in 1916, took over a going concern.

"What do you want here, you _____?"

Big-eyed, half-terrified, but very much the man and protector of his womenfolk, the four-year-old boy glares at the two horsemen halted in front of his family's quarters. Unconsciously, one hand has locked on the skirts of his mother, standing primly tall behind him.

The foremost horseman is daunting enough—a ragged mass of gray-streaked, dusty beard hides most of his face; his eyes are reddened and his lips are cracked from alkali dust. A dirty bandage, splotched with dark brown, comes from under his ragged hat to cover one ear. His once-jaunty blue flannel shirt is full of tears and rents, some patched clumsily with coarse white thread, and covered with a catalog of stains and spots; his buckskin britches are in shreds, and the worn-out feet of his boots have been replaced by moccasins. One stirrup has been broken and mended with wire; gaunt and leg-weary, his dusty roan horse is trying to nibble bits of greenery projecting through the front fence.

The patrol has come home after months chasing Cheyenne "dog soldiers" on the loose. At the post hospital across the parade ground, orderlies lift wounded men from travois, improvised from captured lodge poles and buffalo robes. A clamorous keening echoes from "Soapsuds Row" as laundresses lament other men left buried somewhere below a canyon rim.

Jauntily, the horseman tugs off his tattered hat and addresses the mother, "Hullo, old lady."

One hand slipped deftly across her son's mouth, the mother stares across the first horseman's shoulder at the even more disreputable figure behind him.

"Clancy, is *that* really my husband?"

Private Clancy straightens in his battered saddle and gives her a salute fit to gladden the heart of a major general.

"Indade, ma'm. 'Tis him."

"Very well, Clancy. Now take him down to the creek and *scrub* him!"

117. Army dress uniform in 1872. The uniforms adopted at this time were colorful and striking.
Shown here are those of a Signal Corps sergeant (left foreground) and an officer and black troopers of the 9th Cavalry Regiment. All wear a black felt helmet, dark blue coat, and sky-blue trousers; the cavalrymen's plumes, cords, and facings are yellow, the sergeant's bright orange. The
fork-tailed version of the Stars and Stripes is a cavalry company's guidon.

118. "**Bucking for orderly.**" It was "Old Army" custom for the smartest soldier of a new guard detail to be selected "Orderly for the Commanding Officer." It was a choice assignment—nothing to do except carry messages for the C.O. Your duty ended when he went home to his quarters that evening, and you probably got a two-day pass to boot. Competition for it—"bucking for orderly" in army talk—was keen, and every top sergeant wanted one of his men to win. Consequently, preparation in a cavalry company (later "troop") was a cooperative effort. The most alert and soldierly of the men it furnished the guard would get himself up immaculately, and review the general and special orders, the serial numbers of his weapons, and other military minutiae. Under the "top kick's" unsparing eye, his comrades would groom a selected horse and clean and polish his equipment. They would lift him bodily into the saddle, dust off the soles of his boots, and smooth every wrinkle out of his uniform. And they—and the top kick—would be hard to live with if he didn't make orderly.

119. "**We're on the trail of Sitting Bull, / And this is the way we go— / Forty miles a day on beans and hay / In the Regular Army, oh!**" A column of infantrymen—"walk-a-heaps" the Indians called them—and their mule-drawn supply wagons move across the Dakota prairie through December weather.

120. Saturday morning inspection. Another "Old Army" custom was the inspection of the enlisted men's barracks each Saturday. Bare, shabby-clean, with every object in perfect order, this "squad room" nevertheless is far more comfortable than the mud-and-pole shanties of many frontier forts.

121. Enlisted men, 1888. Noncommissioned officers could be identified by chevrons, which indicated their grade and duty. Here, a quartermaster sergeant (left) confers with a saddler sergeant. The privates in the background wear the light canvas "stable frock" and "overalls" issued for the fatigue details.

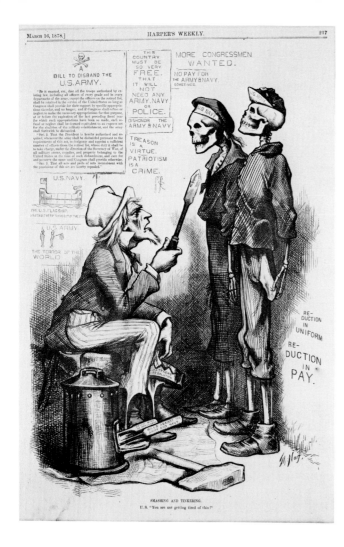

SMASHING AND TINKERING.
U. S. "You are not getting tired of this?"

122. *Smashing and Tinkering.* During this period of neglect and poverty the army and navy had a champion in the famous cartoonist Thomas Nast, who depicted them as valiant skeletons in *Harper's Weekly*, March 16, 1878.

123. Fort Bowie. Originally Camp Bowie (1867–79), the fort was established in 1892 to guard an important spring at the eastern end of Apache Pass in Arizona Territory. Constructed largely of adobe, it was occupied until 1894.

124. Fort Washakie, Wyoming. Originally Camp Augur, then Camp Brown, the fort was built in 1870. Eight years later it was renamed "Washakie" after the chief of the eastern Shoshone, a firm friend to the whites and an able protector of his own people. The fort was abandoned in 1909.

125. Miles's battle against Crazy Horse. The Indian fighters had to endure and overcome extremes of weather and a vast, rugged country. Indians being most vulnerable when deep winter had immobilized their villages, soldiers made long subzero marches through storms that blew "splinters off the North Pole," to end in desperate fights, as depicted in Frederic Remington's painting of Lt. Col. Nelson A. Miles's defeat of Crazy Horse at Wolf Mountain in 1877.

126. *Hunting for Hostiles.* Patrolling the Southwest meant blistering days, chilled nights, and dry camps, as shown in this Remington painting. But expert Indian fighters held to one grim rule—once the trail of a hostile war party was discovered, it "must be stuck to and never lost."

127. *Two Small Bullet Holes.* Soldiers were constantly aware of the chance of sudden death from ambush, as depicted here by Remington.

128. Putting a horse out of its misery. No excuse was to be accepted for leaving a trail; if horses played out, the enemy had to be followed on foot. A soldier puts an exhausted horse out of its misery during the "Mud March" in pursuit of the Sioux after the Battle of Little Big Horn. Its meat fed hungry soldiers.

129. Care of the wounded while following an Indian trail. A casualty from the Battle of Slim Buttes in Dakota Territory travels in comparative comfort in a litter slung between two mules. Often the only available means of transport was a travois dragged behind a single animal.

130. Burning the Evans-Gordon train. The army also had the mission—generally overlooked and most unappreciated—to protect the Indians. Whites attempting to settle on Indian territory were often expelled. This sketch by M. B. Brubacher shows the wagons and equipment of a wagon train at Wounded Knee Creek near the north boundary of Nebraska being destroyed.

131. *An Evening with Old Nis-Su Kai-Yo.* Professional soldier and Indian warrior shared certain common values—courage, physical hardihood, and loyalty. Here American cowboy artist Charles M. Russell has painted an officer and an elderly chief exchanging tall stories across a campfire in Montana in 1880.

132. Gen. George Crook. There were a number of soldiers who understood and sympathized with the Indian and who learned his customs and his way of thought. Outstanding among them was George Crook, a man whom many tribes remembered as unrelenting in war, but humane, just, and patient in peace. An Apache chief told him, "Whenever you said a thing we knew that it was true and we kept it in our minds."

133. "The long-nosed captain." Lt. Charles B. Gatewood, one of George Crook's specially picked officers who led his Apache scouts, was dubbed "the long-nosed captain" by the Indians.

134. Frank Grouard. Most of the real frontier scouts were quiet men who made little outward show. Their virtues were courage, honesty, common sense, resourcefulness, a thorough knowledge of the country and its Indians, and the ability to find and follow a trail under any conditions. Frank Grouard was one of the most famous during the 1870s and 1890s. He might wear a buckskin coat on campaign, but regarded the theatrical "long-haired scouts" of the Buffalo Bill–type with some contempt.

135. Buffalo Bill. William F. Cody enlisted in the army in 1864 as a private in the 7th Kansas Volunteer Cavalry. After the war he worked irregularly as a scout and guide until he was hired by Lt. Gen. Philip H. Sheridan as chief of scouts for the 5th U.S. Cavalry. Cody's continuous employment (1868–72) as a scout was exceptional, since most were hired by the month or for a specific expedition.

136. Packing. Getting a mule to carry as much as possible without damage to either the mule or the load required both natural aptitude and considerable experience. A mule—"the only animal Noah didn't take into the Ark"—could carry up to 300 pounds over rough country for 30 miles a day. Mules were hardier than horses and needed less food, but had a perversity all their own.

137. Cheyenne scouts. This company of neatly uniformed Cheyenne Scouts was photographed en route to Pine Ridge Agency, South Dakota, in 1890 during the Ghost Dance troubles. The group included warriors who had fought bitterly against the army until 1879. Their commander, Lt. Edward W. Casey, was later shot from behind by a Sioux buck while he was parleying with another one during a reconnaissance.

138. Apache scouts. When recruiting Apache Scouts, Gen. George Crook followed his principle that "To polish a diamond there is nothing like its own dust." He took the "wildest" he could secure, considering them best qualified for hunting down other Apaches. His scouts included tribesmen and even relatives of the hostile Apaches, yet they served faithfully and effectively where very few white soldiers could have endured.

139. Keeping the peace. The militia's inefficiency became all too apparent during major labor troubles from 1877 to 1894. These nattily dressed Kansas militiamen put their Gatling gun into position—and then discovered that the crank used to fire it was "Either lost, strayed, or stolen."

140. Camp sports. Soldiers of the 16th Regiment, Pennsylvania National Guard, box during off-duty time at their summer training camp in 1894.

141. From the barracks to the hospital. As the nineteenth century drew to a close, more and more aging veterans of the Civil War entered the various branches of the National Home for Disabled Soldiers, created by Congress in 1865–66 to provide shelter, medical treatment, and hospital care.

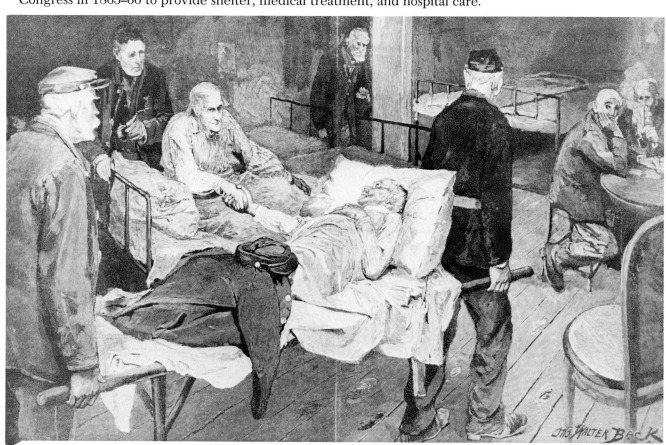

142. Mounted drill at West Point. Following the Civil War, the U.S. Military Academy failed to keep its course of instruction up to date in either military or scientific subjects. Change was opposed: It sufficed that the academy's traditional system had produced the leading generals of both the Union and Confederate armies. Its professors showed no interest in the lessons of the Franco-Prussian War of 1870; Indian warfare was completely ignored; and even practical developments from the Civil War itself might be brusquely disregarded if they contradicted approved textbooks. At least the cadets received considerable training in equitation, including a sort of mounted wrestling.

7

Soldiers of Empire, 1898-1916

Washington officialdom was impatient. The U.S. V Corps, which included the greater part of the Regular Army, was embarking at Port Tampa, Florida, for the invasion of Cuba, and appeared to be taking an improperly long time for such a simple matter. The U.S. Navy, occupied in blockading the harbor of Santiago de Cuba where a run-down Spanish squadron had taken refuge, had sent for the V Corps to flush it out, and was fretting majestically over the delay.

Washington had selected Tampa as the port of embarkation because it was close to

Cuba. However, its rail communications with the rest of the United States were poor, and the railroad management was utilizing a good deal of their existing capacity for excursion trains loaded with doting parents, anxious maidens, and ordinary gawkers eager to gaze upon the assembling soldiery. Half-organized Volunteer units, including "Teddy's Terrors" (properly the 1st Regiment, U.S. Volunteer Cavalry), with its toothy lieutenant colonel, were underfoot. Between Tampa and Port Tampa, where transports were edging into its single pier, were nine miles of single-track railroad—and unimaginable confusion. In response to goading telegrams from the War Department, Maj. Gen. Nelson A. Miles attempted to sum up the V Corps' problem:

> Several of the volunteer regiments came here without uniforms; several came without arms, and some without blankets, tents, or camp equipage.... There are over 300 [box] cars loaded with war material along the [rail]roads about Tampa ... fifteen cars loaded with uniforms were side-tracked twenty-five miles away from Tampa, and remained there for weeks while the troops were suffering for clothing. Five thousand rifles, which were discovered yesterday, were needed by several regiments. Also the different parts of the siege train and ammunition for same ... are scattered through hundreds of cars on the side-tracks of the railroads.[1]

Comfortable in Washington, the quartermaster general had not thought of having the cars labeled to show their contents or of setting up a proper railhead.

By a major feat of scrambling improvisation, the V Corps got itself aboard ship. Then it had to wait there in sweltering Tampa Bay for another week—it had just occurred to the navy that the Spanish squadron might *not* be in Santiago harbor after all, and so it cruised frantically in all directions in a belated attempt to make certain.

In 1898 the Spanish-American War found the army with an authorized strength of almost 28,000, and an effective strength of under 25,000. It was a collection of regiments, without experience or training in operating together as brigades or divisions. Many of the regiments themselves were scattered widely in small one- or two-company posts, where company commanders were apt to follow their own instincts as to proper discipline and training. Intensive work was required to reestablish uniformity when the regiment was

reassembled. On the other hand, the army as a whole was well-trained; though the major Indian wars were over, there still was enough field service to keep it tough and combat-ready. The War Department staff bureaus, rusted by thirty-odd years of nothing more demanding than the leisurely and benign neglect of a small army, now had a large-scale mobilization on their hands and a war in foreign places concerning which they knew nothing. A story—quite possible true—quoted a senior staff officer as complaining, "I just had this office working properly, and then somebody started a war!" Some of the bureaus rallied and began a frantic collection of available supplies. But meanwhile men went hungry and ragged, or died unnecessarily of common camp sicknesses.

Congress authorized increasing the Regular Army to 64,719 officers and men, permitted militia organizations to volunteer for active duty, and authorized the enlistment of U.S. Volunteers. Much of this increased strength became available too late to be of use in Cuba, but the national excitement was such that the Regular Army was able, possibly for the first time in its history, to pick and choose from the recruits available.

The Spanish-American War was followed by the Philippine Insurrection of 1899–1902 and subsequent antiguerrilla and antibandit operations in many parts of the Philippine Islands. The United States also contributed a contingent to the international force sent into China in 1900 to rescue the foreign legations besieged in Peking by the rebel Boxers. These operations, though minor, did emphasize the United States' status as a world power; more important, they brought home a disquieting realization of the army's weaknesses and primitive organization. Changes were many and rapid: the War Department was reorganized and a European-style General Staff was created to handle planning and to collect military intelligence for future national emergencies.

The outbreak of World War I in Europe led to further gradual strengthening of the army. In early 1915, it consisted of thirty-one regiments of infantry, fifteen of cavalry, six of field artillery, one hundred seventy companies of coast artillery, and three battalions of engineers, plus the Philippine Scouts, the Signal Corps, and medical units. There was a shortage of modern artillery and aircraft, and of reserve ammunition; in 1911, the decision to assemble a single "Maneuver Division" for training purposes strained the whole army.

From 1910 on, a series of revolutions and civil wars in Mexico spilled over into the United States, culminating in "General" Francisco (Pancho) Villa's raid on Columbus, New Mexico, in 1916. The United States responded by temporarily occupying Veracruz from April to November 1914, and dispatching a punitive expedition under Brig. Gen. John J. Pershing into Mexico during 1916–17 to break up Villa's forces. Much of the Regular Army and National Guard were concentrated along the Mexican border. Pershing's Punitive Expedition was, in effect, the last of the Indian wars. Hard-riding cavalry detachments probed through northern Mexico, jumped Villa's bands, and broke them. Villa's legendary skill as a guerrilla leader proved a legend and nothing more; a few months of such treatment cured him of any desire to again anger the United States.

THE REGULAR SOLDIERS

The Regular still was very much his traditional self—hardened by small wars, insurrections, and bandit suppressions, and given on occasion to the pursuit of strong drink and willing women. A fair number were expert, reliable soldiers in combat but "regular boarders at the guardhouse" when garrison duty became boring; a few were confirmed drunkards who would automatically plead "guilty" when they were brought before a court-martial because they had no idea what they had done. Gambling was a popular recreation, especially after payday.

> Sign your name on a piece of paper,
> Take it to the captain, and you get your pay.
> Take it to the squad room and put it on a blanket,
> Fellow yells "Craps" and takes it away!

Usually a half-dozen expert players would win all the money in their company and "Then that gang of highbinders would battle it out until the next pay day."[2]

A private's pay remained at the pre-Civil War level of $13 per month. Consequently, enlistments fell off and desertion increased during the first years of the twentieth century, to the extent that the army fell to barely half-strength. In 1908, Congress gave the private a dazzling $2 more a month, and raised first sergeants to $45. About this time extra pay of up to $5 a month was offered for proficiency in marksmanship, "And the shootin' in that man's army sure did get better in a hurry."[3] (This improvement was further aided by the introduction of the "Springfield '03" rifle in 1904 as a replacement for the Krag-Jorgensen. Short, beautifully made, with a substantial kick, this was probably the most accurate military rifle ever designed. During the Punitive Expedition an American captain shot a Mexican officer out of his saddle at 800 yards.)

On the whole, the army's standard of literacy had improved. Recruits included increasing numbers of sturdy farm boys looking for adventure, some of them under the official minimum age of eighteen. Their existence was Spartan, but often comfortable enough compared to the homes they had left. For many soldiers, their company ("troop" in the Cavalry, "battery" in the Artillery) became their home and family. Every outfit had its "professional privates"—competent soldiers who would refuse promotion to corporal because they wanted no responsibilities beyond a private's daily routine. When a good and faithful soldier finished thirty years of service and faced retirement, the company's first sergeant might "step down" so that he could hold that position long enough to retire on a sergeant's pay.

A good outfit *was* a tight-knit family that lived by a stark set of priorities; in the Field Artillery, "First the horses, then the guns, then the men," and when all three were properly cared for in the order so ordained, the officers could sit down. Captains made and broke their own noncommissioned officers; if they were exacting and quick to anger, their corporals and sergeants reputedly didn't bother to sew their chevrons onto their sleeves but fastened them there with hooks-and-eyes. A booster, and the knack of really managing one was high on the list of an officer's virtues.

Crack outfits would brag that *their* "Old Man" was a bastard of unbelievable parentage and ferocity, without regard for cold, heat, fatigue, thirst, hunger, and other weaknesses of the flesh, but that he never told a soldier to do anything he couldn't do himself, and he was always fair—and that *their* company mess served steak when the rest of the regiment ate beans. A captain who was weak, erratic, and harsh might find that his company always placed last on the rifle range, soldiers who had rated as "Sharpshooter" and "Expert" for years being strangely unable to get a single round into the black of the target. Forfeiture of such "proficiency pay" was a real sacrifice for the soldiers concerned, but it

was a sure way of telling the colonel that things were going sour in their company.

Beyond his formal discipline, the American enlisted man had developed a private code of etiquette, designed to make living in barracks and camps more endurable. A soldier's cot (still called a "bunk") was his castle. No other soldier sat upon it without his invitation. In the mess hall, "please" was the essential word if a soldier wanted a dish out of polite reaching distance; otherwise, it would not be passed unless he became noisily insistent, in which case he might get its contents in his lap. A man who grabbed food from a dish across the table might, quite accidentally, suddenly find a fork sticking in the back of his hand. A habitually dirty soldier would find himself in the shower room or a nearby creek with a group of his "friends" removing the dirt—and much of his skin—with stiff-bristled barracks scrub brushes and GI soap.

Some companies had an "executioner" (the term dates back at least to the early eighteenth century), who administered unofficial punishments as determined by the unofficial majority of its privates. Usually he was a steady "professional private," handy with his fists and feet but also experienced in the ways of sinful mankind. An obstreperous recruit would get kindly advice, while a hardened troublemaker would be taken to a secluded spot and slapped silly. Sergeants studiously ignored these developments—they saved paperwork and might make a good soldier out of an unruly rookie. Officers frequently were unaware of such happenings.

The Regular still was apt to be foreign-born. The 3rd Infantry Regiment had a Spanish bugler, who doubled as a company barber, and a German drill sergeant. Others were "Swedes, Irishmen, Moravians, Hungarians, and Portugee" as well as English, Polish, or Greek.[4] And there was the Polish recruit who spelled out his name "T-z-c-h-u-l-k-o-w-c-z-s-k-i" and then added "Junior."

Soldiers still were regarded with suspicion, not unmixed with contempt, by a good many of their fellow citizens. Their money was always welcome; in fact, the payroll of a little one- or two-company "hitching post" fort often was the neighboring community's major source of income. (Attempts to close such posts as a needless expense once the Indian wars were over produced violent objections by the local townspeople and their congressmen.) Even so, these communities frequently treated the soldier as a second-class citizen. Out West, ranchers and cowboys affected a lordly disdain for the army, but expected it to appear promptly whenever they got into trouble with their Indian neighbors.

Soldiers were not welcome in many "respectable" houses of prostitution—there were "soldier houses" with lower prices and less attractive women. "First she went to the dogs, then to the soldiers" was a cowboy gibe. Some towns barred soldiers from their public parks. Virtuous citizens regarded them as lost souls, apt to take up any vice, but gladly overcharged them for inferior goods. The tendency to post "No Soldiers Admitted" signs at theaters, parks, and other places of amusement finally became so blatant that Congress in 1911 decreed a fine of $500 for such conduct. In England, "Tommy Atkins" had the same experience. Tommy, however, had a champion in Rudyard Kipling, who slashed out bitter verse and stories in defense of England's "single men in barracks, most remarkable like you." America produced no Kipling, but American soldiers read him avidly.

This public attitude toward soldiers bore especially hard on the black regiments. In 1906, after much provocation and bad li-

quor, some of the 25th Infantry Regiment reportedly (accounts are far from positive) shot up Brownsville, Texas. President Theodore Roosevelt summarily broke three companies from the service, without proper investigation or attempt to distinguish between innocent and guilty. Very much to its credit, Congress took legal action three years later to force a complete investigation of this grossly unfair action and to reinstate those unjustly discharged.

All through the Philippine Insurrection a group of leading American industrialists, educators, and clergy—organized as the Anti-Imperialist League—published and circulated exaggerated reports of American brutality, and as exaggeratedly praised the Insurgents. (There was brutality: American soldiers who had found a missing comrade buried up to his chin in an anthill for the amusement of Insurgent officers tended to become somewhat careless of the laws of war and to utilize the "water cure" and other established Spanish/Filipino methods of interrogating prisoners.) Soldiers in the Philippines believed that the league furnished the enemy with money and weapons. The Philippine Insurrection was a forerunner of Vietnam, but it was only a small war and far away, and there was no radio or TV to spread the league's message.

The soldiers' attitude toward civilians was very well represented by a Regular from the 16th Infantry Regiment back from Cuba. A gushing New York lady, wearing a "Welcome home, Rough Riders" badge, accosted him with, "And are you one of our gallant heroes?" "No, ma'm," sighed the doughboy, long accustomed to peacetime public neglect. "I'm just another goddamned Regular."[5]

THE REGULAR OFFICERS

Citizens usually took a more lenient view of officers than of enlisted men. But the officer always provided a target for

frontier brawlers—they could not hit first without risk of being accused of "conduct unbecoming an officer and a gentleman."

There is a story of a second lieutenant, fresh out of West Point, traveling across Colorado by train en route to his assigned regiment. He had occasion to come to the aid of a lady who was being bothered by an overardent Texan. There were words, the Texan struck the lieutenant, and the lieutenant knocked him down. Later that day the Texan roared into the car in which the lieutenant was riding, gun in hand, and began working himself into a killing mood. No one dared interfere; but a sheepherder in the next seat, having no particular use for Texans, slipped the lieutenant a revolver. The lieutenant promptly shot the Texan dead center. No time was wasted: The train stopped at the next station, the local judge was summoned, evidence taken, and a verdict rendered of "justifiable homicide." By way of sequel, two days later the lieutenant reported to the adjutant of his regiment. It was a tough outfit that attracted tough men, enlisted and commissioned. "Mister," said the adjutant, using the contemporary title for a second lieutenant, "this is no regiment for greenhorns. Every one of our officers has been tried by court-martial at least once. Have *you* ever been tried?"

"Yes, sir. Two days ago."

"Indeed! And for what?"

"Murder, sir."

The Spanish-American War spread the available Regular officers somewhat thinly. "Political" officers reappeared in great numbers, both in the National Guard units that volunteered for active duty and in the three regiments of U.S. Volunteer Cavalry. In fact, the 1st Regiment of Volunteer Cavalry possessed two outstanding examples in its colonel, Leonard Wood, and its lieutenant colonel, Theodore Roosevelt.

Both accomplished and energetic intriguers, they did their best to run the war to their own advantage through high-level political connections and low-level leaks to sympathetic war correspondents.

One new type of officer appeared: Since 1862 some land-grant colleges had offered military training without too much help from the army. The University of Nebraska had an enthusiastic instructor in Lieutenant Pershing, and its graduates made the 1st Nebraska Infantry a first-rate outfit. New lieutenants for the larger postwar army were secured through a series of rather stringent examining boards; most of those chosen came from the Volunteers, but a fair number were former Regular Army enlisted men or graduates of military schools such as the Virginia Military Institute. (One of the latter was named George Catlett Marshall.)

The Spanish-American War saw a reconciliation of North and South. As evidence, two former Confederate generals, Fitzhugh Lee and Joseph Wheeler, received commissions as Volunteer major generals. (Both had been Regular Army lieutenants before the Civil War.) Neither proved a major asset but Wheeler did contribute the war's one classic line. At Las Guasimas, as the Spanish finally retired, he shouted to the Regulars whom he had led, against orders, into an unnecessary skirmish, "Come on, boys! We've got the damn Yankees on the run!" (Aging Jube Early's "unreconstructed" reaction was to remark that he always had hoped to go to heaven and be reunited with Robert E. Lee, but that now he'd prefer to go to hell, just to hear the devil chuckle as "he peels those blue uniforms off of Fitz Lee and Joe Wheeler.")

VOLUNTEER UNITS

The Volunteers authorized by Congress for the Spanish-American War consisted of three cavalry regiments, a brigade of engineers, and ten regiments (six white and four black) of infantry. The 1st Volunteer Cavalry Regiment obviously was created to be the personal property of its lieutenant colonel, that rising young Republican politician named Theodore Roosevelt. Totally without military experience, Roosevelt was masterful in his manipulation of the American press. Known successively as "Teddy's Terrors," "Rocky Mountain Rustlers," "Roosevelt's Rough Riders," and (in Cuba, where it served dismounted) "Wood's Weary Walkers," the unit was the war correspondents' pet darling and was credited with winning the war single-handedly. Roosevelt's canny recruiting policy, mixing genuine westerners with eastern college athletes and scions of prominent families, added to its news value. Thanks to his political pull, his unit received Krag-Jorgensen rifles, was sent to Cuba with the V Corps, and was one of the first units sent home, arriving in plenty of time for Roosevelt to run for governor of New York on his war record.

Even expert historians have difficulty tracing the progress of the other two cavalry regiments; they were organized, and one reportedly got as far as Florida before the war ended, but that was all. The Volunteer infantry was recruited in the southern states from men supposedly immune to yellow fever—hence their nickname, the "Immunes." They were employed as occupation troops in Cuba after the war. Unfortunately, some of them were not immune. An additional 35,000 Volunteers were authorized in 1899 for service in the Philippines to replace the National Guard units already serving there and overdue for discharge.

THE FORMATION OF THE NATIONAL GUARD

For a few years after the Civil War, volunteer militia units had flourished again as veterans re-formed their prewar organizations and set up new ones, which carried on the traditions and uniforms of famous wartime Volunteer regiments. But this first enthusiasm dwindled as time passed and veterans aged or moved on into the western territories. The number of effective units declined alarmingly, while growing labor unrest broke out in a series of major strikes during the 1870s. Because of the general absence of efficient city and state police forces, the militia was called out repeatedly to preserve law and order. Such employment made it unpopular with working men; the risks involved did not encourage membership in militia units.

On several occasions the militia failed badly. Its ineffective behavior during the 1877 railroad strikes forced President Hayes to employ Regulars. That same year a number of militia officers met and formed the National Guard Association to represent the collective interests of the state militias, which then assumed the title of "The National Guard." Other changes were few. In 1898 the National Guard had approximately 100,000 officers and men, but very little else—including training, equipment, and discipline. Its officers still were either political appointees or elected by their men; the state governors did not intend to yield any of the political advantages they enjoyed as wartime commanders of their state forces. Political pressures forced President William McKinley to accept the services of such National Guard regiments as might vote to volunteer their services, and to agree not to assign more than one Regular officer to each of these "volunteer" regiments.

Most of the existing National Guard regiments so volunteered but some, particularly New York's silk-stocking 7th and its more plebeian 13th, would not. The 7th, composed of men from wealthy and socially prominent families, apparently disliked the contamination of having to serve with "Tom, Dick, and Harry"; the 13th was equally unwilling to immolate itself upon the altar of patriotism.

Those regiments that saw action in Cuba behaved well, although their obsolete "trap-door" Springfields, which fired smoke-producing black powder cartridges, put them at a grave disadvantage against Spanish soldiers armed with modern smokeless-powder Mauser rifles. The 71st New York did panic at a crucial moment at San Juan Hill, but individuals from it fell in and charged with the Regulars. In the Philippines, other National Guard "volunteers" served beyond their time of enlistment because—as a result of a congressional–executive department fumbling contest—there were no troops available to relieve them, and their departure on schedule would have seriously endangered the remaining American forces. It was a little-noted act of patriotism, but some of them apparently enjoyed fighting—over 2,000 of them enlisted in the new Volunteer regiments.

But the militia's major sufferings were in the United States. Most of the regiments that volunteered for active duty were grouped in two large camps—one at Chickamauga, Georgia, the other near Washington, D.C.—for training. Practically none of these regiments were drilled or disciplined; their equipment was antiquated and worn out. (There were suspicions that some governors had kept their newer weapons and equipment in their state arsenals, and sent their National Guard units off with any available odds and ends so that the army would be forced to reoutfit them.) There was a general shortage of underwear; in the 1st Missouri Infantry a good many men were barefoot.

The army furnished adequate cooking equipment and soon had rations arriving in ample quantity, but the National Guard lacked competent mess officers and cooks. Its regimental officers and surgeons had only the vaguest concept of camp sanitation. Some regiments were ten days in camp before they bothered to dig latrines, and many soldiers didn't bother to use them after they were dug. Consequently, the camp water supply soon became contaminated, and typhoid fever and dysentery spread through the frowzy tents. Peddlers of rotgut booze and diseased prostitutes clustered along the camps' boundaries and were little hindered. A few regiments—the 8th Massachusetts was one so cited—had officers willing to do their duty. They kept their commands relatively healthy for some weeks, but eventually bad water and filthy surroundings affected them, too. Once again American militiamen died unnecessarily without ever seeing an enemy soldier.

Following the Spanish-American War, the National Guard's equipment was standardized and somewhat modernized and its training improved. In 1916 the National Defense Act placed it directly under the authority of the federal government; its officers and training were to meet army standards of efficiency. President Wilson soon thereafter ordered the whole National Guard to active duty on the Mexican border. There, the green citizen-soldiers made the acquaintance of cactus, mesquite, rattlesnakes, scorpions, dust storms, and desert heat. There never was enough water except for the rare gully-washing cloudbursts—and then there was, very briefly, entirely too much. Two regiments, the 1st New Mexico and the 2nd Massachusetts, went into Mexico to guard the Punitive Expedition's bases and convoys; for the others, there was concentrated training and toughening until early 1917. This service was hardly popular. One of the songs it inspired had the ringing chorus, "To hell, to hell with all of Texas!"—but it proved to be invaluable preparation for World War I.

During this period the small, elaborately uniformed volunteer militia units so characteristic of the nineteenth century tended to disappear. A few of the oldest, such as the Philadelphia City Cavalry, the Richmond Blues, the New York 7th Regiment, and the Georgia Hussars, retained something of their original dress and traditions; and a few new ones, like the Cleveland City Troop, the Essex Troop, and the Chicago Black Horse Troop, appeared. But in the main, a great deal of color, holiday pomp, and local pride was passing from American life.

IMPROVEMENTS IN ARMY LIFE

More Nutritious Rations

By 1898 considerably more was known about human nutrition. Canned foods having become economical and reliable, canned beef, both corned and "fresh," had been added to the army's ration. The latter was a boiling beef, intended for use in soups and stews. It was issued in large quantities to the V Corps as it embarked for Cuba, but unfortunately most of the grubby little transports lacked proper cooking facilities. During the sweltering days waiting off Port Tampa or steaming more or less toward Cuba, many soldiers had to eat this beef from the can and got heartily sick of it. Once ashore, they lived on hardtack, bacon, sugar, and coffee, and sometimes on short allowance of that because of bad roads and a shortage of transportation. (In 1895 some genius, reasoning that the Indian wars were over, had sold off most of the army's supply wagons at $15 for a $200 wagon.) This diet, hastily cooked or eaten raw, probably did as much as the Cuban fevers to debilitate the V Corps.

Serious study of the ration showed that it lacked both vitamins and sufficient nourishment; its approximately 2,300 calories were hardly adequate for hard work and cold weather. The peacetime ration introduced in 1913 was much improved, with such items as baking powder, prunes, syrup, and condensed milk added. The Philippine Scouts received a special ration in which fish and rice replaced a large proportion of the regular ration's beef and flour. An emergency ration was developed for troops in the field consisting of "evaporated powdered beef and parched cooked wheat" with a small amount of sweetened chocolate to improve its flavor. Troops traveling by train or other means that made cooking impossible received a much-appreciated "travel ration" of bread, corned beef or corned beef hash, canned baked beans, canned tomatoes, and jam. Coffee, condensed milk, and sugar were added if it were possible for the men to brew coffee during brief halts; if not, they received "liquid coffee money" for local purchases.

In addition to better food, the army had been gradually improving its preparation. Better cooking utensils and mess gear were developed, along with collapsible sheet-iron "field ranges," which replaced the flaring, smoky kitchen campfires. A school was established for army cooks and bakers; qualified company cooks were allowed the pay of an infantry sergeant. Such measures certainly improved the quality of the food, but the army cook remained a rough-hewn character. By tradition, his favorite tipples were vanilla and lemon extract. He could handle a cleaver with the dexterity of a Michelangelo, to include parting the hair of an erring KP 10 feet away. KPs (meaning "kitchen police") were privates detailed to help out around the kitchen. The hours were long and the work tedious, but a lot of it could be done sitting down and they ate well. These kitchen crews were not noncombatants; when Villa's raiders rushed the cook shacks of the 13th Cavalry outside Columbus, they were met with scalding water, butcher knives, cleavers, massive hardwood potato mashers, the hunting shotguns issued every troop, and anything else handy—and were swiftly routed.

The Design of Functional Uniforms

As the soldier's food changed, so did his uniform. The traditional blue wool was plainly unsuited for tropical service, and the Quartermaster General—once we were at war with Spain—exerted himself to procure a hot-weather uniform of drab-colored cotton "duck." It was generally available by the end of the Cuban campaign; meanwhile, a combination of blue flannel shirt and cotton trousers was frequently worn in the field. In 1902 there was a general uniform change, "olive-drab" (OD) wool replacing blue as the winter service uniform. Dress uniforms still were blue, trimmed with the distinctive branch colors, but their style was simplified, and the plumed and spiked helmets vanished. The summer uniform was a brownish cotton "khaki" which had a shiny look when new, but would fade to a creamy shade after repeated launderings. (Soldiers were apt to help the process along by a few unofficial scrubbings with strong soap and a stiff brush.)

Then, beginning in 1910, the uniform again changed: trousers were "pegged"—cut like riding britches—even for dismounted troops. The old slouch hat with its fore-and-aft crease was replaced by a stiff-brimmed OD hat, with the four quarters of its crown dimpled into a "Montana peak." Mounted troops wore a chin strap, dismounted men a "back strap" encircling the back of their head above the ears. The

old horseshoe roll of blanket, shelter half, and what-not was replaced by a carefully designed pack. The canteen was attached to the waist cartridge belt along with a pouch containing a first-aid packet.

Dandy soldiers might have specially tailored uniforms for off-duty wear. Cavalrymen sometimes fancied britches made of old overcoats, sewn up with yellow silk thread. Shirt collars and cuffs often were reinforced by an overall diamond-pattern stitching with OD-colored thread to keep them neatly stiff. A soldier received an annual clothing allowance: If he kept his uniforms in good repair, he would not have to draw all of it and so could claim the cash value of the items he had not drawn when his enlistment was up.

Progress in Medical Care

The progress of medical science during the last quarter of the nineteenth century—in particular, Louis Pasteur's work with bacteria and Joseph Lister's development of antiseptic surgery—greatly increased the soldier's life expectancy. Typhoid always had been a deadly camp disease. Unfortunately, the Medical Department was long on theory but short on administrative firmness. Although an effective antityphoid vaccine had been developed by 1896, inoculation with it remained optional. Not until the formation of the 1911 Maneuver Division was it made compulsory for all members of a large command. The results were so impressive that it thereafter became routine for the entire army. An antitoxin was found for diphtheria, a vaccine for cholera. Pasteurization of milk and water purification became common. By the early 1900s each company had a "Lister bag," in which water from doubtful local sources could be purified.

Introduction to tropical campaigning, however, brought new risks, most of them unknown to army medical officers. Yellow fever haunted the Cuban expedition, which had been launched, because of political pressure and public clamor for action, shortly before the rainy season—which was also the season for tropical fevers. Armies and fleets operating in the West Indies had been practically wiped out by yellow fever on several occasions; moreover, that disease had ravaged North American coastal areas periodically for two centuries. To further complicate the problem, the cause and method of transmission of yellow fever still were not known.

The V Corps went into Cuba thoroughly aware of the risks it was running. Once combat ended, its men—worn down by hard service, scanty and unsuitable rations, an unfriendly climate, and inappropriate clothing—fell sick in large numbers. Most suffered from sheer exhaustion, typhoid, and dysentery, but there were some cases of yellow fever, and rumor swiftly exaggerated their number.

Gen. William R. Shafter, commanding the V Corps, and his senior officers urged that it be relieved by the "Immune" regiments and returned to the United States. Immediately, influential politicians from the coastal areas objected; such action might carry the disease northward and imperil their constituents. Troop morale plummeted and the sick list increased. Eventually, the secretary of war took the courageous step of ordering the corps back to a quarantine camp at Montauk Point, Long Island—a process somewhat confused by Roosevelt's release of two rather hysterical messages to the newspapers predicting the imminent death of the whole command. Even though there was no yellow fever epidemic, the danger remained real enough.

An American medical team led by Maj. Walter Reed determined in 1900 that the disease was indeed carried by mosquitoes. The work was self-sacrificing: eighteen volunteers—sixteen soldiers (most of them hospital corpsmen), one civilian, and one acting assistant surgeon—joined Reed and three other medical officers. They were divided into three test groups. One group wore the clothing of men who had died of yellow fever and slept in the stained bedding on which they had died; the second group were inoculated with blood serum taken from yellow fever patients; the third allowed themselves to be bitten by mosquitoes that had previously bitten men sick with yellow fever. None of the first group sickened; fifteen of the other two groups did, and two of them died. With this proof that mosquitoes carried yellow fever, the army cleaned up mosquito-breeding places around Havana and other major cities. As buildings were screened and strict sanitary rules enforced, yellow fever vanished. Col. William C. Gorgas applied the same methods in Panama, which had been known as "the White Man's Grave." And so the Panama Canal was built, and yellow fever was banished from the United States and from its colonies.

In the Philippines there were even more exotic diseases. A soldier song (variously worded) went something like this:

> I've the dobie itch and the Moro stitch,
> The jim-jams and the fever!
> The burning fart and the Samar dart,
> And maybe a kris in my liver!

These problems were solved in time. In fact, the Medical Department played a potent role in the conquest of the Philippines. In addition to keeping the American soldier relatively healthy, it converted Insurgents by giving their wounded the same treatment it gave wounded Americans, by looking after the health of Filipino tribes that had never seen a doctor, and by fighting down a massive epidemic of Asiatic cholera in 1902.

The need being obvious, the Medical Department was enlarged and improved. An army Nurse Corps was activated in 1901, a Dental Corps ten years later, and a

Veterinary Corps in 1916. New medical equipment included hospital trains and motor ambulances.

At the same time another major, if self-inflicted, curse of armies came under a degree of medical control. The causes of venereal disease had been established, and a cure for syphilis discovered by 1912. Even earlier, a prophylaxis had been developed that would prevent any venereal infection if applied shortly after intercourse. The major problem was to get soldiers to take advantage of it.

During the Punitive Expedition, the situation was solved by rounding up all the "ladies of the night" who had followed the troops down from the United States and installing them in individual adobe huts inside a guarded barbed-wire stockade under the supervision of the provost marshal. A soldier could go in for a half hour, if he had the required fee; when he came out, he had to receive prophylactic treatment. There were very few cases of venereal disease among the Expedition's personnel, and the ladies concerned seem to have found their lot satisfactory—at least they prepared a fancy Thanksgiving dinner, with the provost marshal as the guest of honor.

As a further incentive to care, if not virtue, the army considered the period a soldier spent in the hospital with venereal disease as "bad time," meaning that he would have to make it up by additional service before he could receive his discharge. Periodic "short arm" inspections were held to detect unreported or unrecognized cases. It all was a trial to refined natures, but "Single men in barracks don't grow into plaster saints." They seldom do on the outside either.

Technological Modernization

The technological modernization of the army began in the Signal Corps, which was natural, since it was the army's "scientific" branch. At the start of the Spanish-American War, the Corps had eight officers, fifty-two enlisted men, an overage and leaky balloon, and $800 available for new equipment. It was quickly increased to 1,300 officers and men. In Cuba, its balloon expired of old age and Spanish bullets during the Battle of San Juan Hill, but its field telephone system—first used here by the army—proved useful.

After the war, the Signal Corps rebuilt and expanded the Cuban and Puerto Rican telegraph systems. Throughout the Philippine Islands, which had no modern communications, it installed 5,000 miles of land lines and 1,300 miles of submarine cable from 1899 to 1901. Meanwhile, in 1900 Congress had given it the responsibility for all communications, both military and commercial, to and within Alaska. By 1904 the Signal Corps had a submarine cable laid up the northwest coast to Alaska and over 3,600 miles of telephone and telegraph lines in operation. "Wireless telegraph" (the first name for radio), which the Signal Corps had been testing since 1898, was used to link this network with Nome and other isolated communities. Signal Corps personnel operated the system, but most of the actual construction, for a change, was done by civilian labor.

Another major development in Signal Corps responsibilities was its experimentation with powered aircraft. It purchased the army's first dirigible in 1907; its first airplane (built by the Wright brothers in 1908) attained the amazing average speed of $42\frac{1}{2}$ miles per hour. The Signal Corps retained its "Aeronautical Division" until 1918, since its original functions were to carry messages and take photographs—both certified Signal Corps responsibilities. Its planes were small, flimsy, unarmed, and underpowered. All eight that the Punitive Expedition first took into Mexico were wrecked or disabled within a month. The Aeronautical Division also experimented with motorcycles, equipped with sidecars and machine guns. The theory was excellent, but Mexican roads were too rough for such light vehicles.

Cargo trucks, however, were a real success in replacing the services of the unreliable Mexican railroads, and Dodge touring cars were successfully used as staff vehicles. It was a plain omen of the future that Pershing's aide-de-camp, Lt. George S. Patton, Jr.—a born cavalryman who had designed the army's last style of sword— was riding in an automobile, instead of on horseback, when he intercepted and personally gunned down one of Villa's "generals."

DUTY IN EXOTIC PLACES

The United States now had a foreign empire. Halfway around the world, American soldiers had stormed into Peking. At Nagasaki, Japan, they watched as seemingly endless lines of women carried baskets of coal to replenish their transports' bunkers. In 1912 the 15th Infantry Regiment took post at Tientsin, China, to ensure communications across warlord-ravaged China to Peking. Known as "The Forgotten Fifteenth," it remained there until 1938. It had a special reconnaissance unit mounted on shaggy, hammer-headed Manchurian ponies, Chinese "boys" to handle its fatigue details, and uniforms made by British-trained tailors.

American soldiers stood guard on Guam and the Hawaiian Islands. In the Philippines they hunted down bandits and predatory religious cults, ended the Moros' long career as pirates and slavers, and also taught school and manned public health programs. They were aided by the newly activated Philippine Scouts and Philippine Constabulary, who enlisted eagerly and served gallantly. In Alaska they again built posts in the wilderness out of green timber. Infantrymen who patrolled the Signal Corps telegraph lines there had to master the use of canoes, snowshoes, and dogsleds. In one reasonably level section they were issued bicycles, convincing the local Indians that the white man was "heap lazy; him sit down to walk."[6]

Puerto Rico was now an American possession. The American occupation of Cuba during the years 1898–1902 restored law, order, and economic stability, in addition to eradicating yellow fever. Left to themselves, the Cubans quickly fell into disorder; in 1906 their government collapsed. American military intervention restored order without bloodshed. The army supervised open elections and then went home. Eight years later army engineer and medical officers brought the Panama Canal to successful completion.

Other Americans rode unceasing patrol along the Rio Grande against Mexican bandits, who might also be unpaid Mexican soldiers or adherents of the still-mysterious "Plan of San Diego" who dreamed of the reconquest of the American Southwest. Large-scale trouble ended in 1919, but there were occasional small clashes into 1930.

These "small wars" against weak opponents killed American soldiers as thoroughly as the Civil War had done. On the whole, they had been launched on a broken shoestring and carried through catch-as-catch-can by the troops involved, amid alien cultures, unhealthy climates, and unknown, difficult terrain. The American soldier was certain that he was a bringer of civilization and the representative of a superior culture. Officers might quote Kipling's "The White Man's Burden"; privates merely noted that their coming brought order, safety, better health, and flourishing trade to places that had not known it for decades, if ever.

Meanwhile, Manila's San Miguel beer was excellent and Mexican beef from Monterrey maybe even better. It was wise to avoid Filipino *vino*, three drinks of which would make an American try to swing by his tail in the treetops with the other wild monkeys, or *tuba*, which was just as potent and produced an even worse hangover. There were pretty girls everywhere, though Hawaii had them in the greatest variety. A few soldiers married locally, others struck up temporary "jawbone marriages" by mutual consent.

Some posts had good hunting, but in the Philippines you had to avoid the domesticated water buffalo, or carabao, which hated a white man's scent. (More than one strapping American soldier was treed by a carabao, until a nine-tenths-naked Filipino tot appeared and drove the massive beast away with token slaps and shrill reproof.) There was always a Chinese restaurant where a soldier could get a tasty, cheap meal when he tired of mess hall chow. Most Chinese were honest but some needed watching; the chicken chop suey you ordered might be made with monkey meat. Also, some Chinese had a trick of hollowing out $20 gold pieces and replacing the pilfered gold with lead. You also had to be careful to take your quinine dosage, sleep under a mosquito netting, and shake out your shoes to dislodge any poisonous overnight lodger before putting them on in the morning.

And always there was the possibility of danger and excitement: another self-proclaimed "Son of Jesus" raiding across Cebu, burning villages and stealing carabao; a Moro suddenly gone *juramentado* and stoppable only by a dum-dum rifle bullet or Colt .45; big-hatted *bandidos* glimpsed sifting through the mesquite by moonlight. Even "stateside" there were forest fires, floods, and other natural disasters where the army was needed. When fire swept San Francisco in 1906 the army got the conflagration under control, put down looting, fed and sheltered refugees, and restored communications.

For married officers, foreign service could be pleasant, once American-style quarters replaced the temporary nipa huts where oversized spiders, lizards, rats, and snakes played tag in the thatched roof and periodically dropped onto the middle of the dining table. Help was plentiful, cheap, and could be expert, with Chinese cooks, Filipino house boys, an amah to care for the children, and a *lavandera* for the washing and ironing. Returning home meant a drastic increase in an army wife's workload.

Upper-class Filipinos, Cubans, and Panamanians often resented U.S. paternalism, even while they profited from it. The swagger and occasional noisy arrogance of American soldiers might spur resentment. Unable to suppress their own bandits, patriotic Mexicans nevertheless were insulted by the sudden incursions of U.S. cavalry that followed such raiders back in hot pursuit across the Rio Grande and summarily hunted them down. But this meant little to the Regular soldier; he had been sent to win an empire, and now he must keep it.

Company C, 9th Infantry Regiment, three officers and seventy-four enlisted men, is at breakfast in its mess hall off the central square of the seacoast town of Balangiga on the island of Samar. Things have been quiet for months; on the island of Luzon to the north, Emilio Aguinaldo, leader of the Insurgents, has been captured and has pledged loyalty to the United States, calling on his remaining followers to lay down their arms. In Balangiga the native police are efficient and loyal, the population friendly, the local priest cooperative. Though Company C is a veteran outfit, the soldiers no longer take their rifles with them into the mess hall, but leave them locked in racks in an adjoining supply shed. Three sentries watch the passing natives incuriously. In the little hut that serves as an aid station, a sergeant of the Hospital Corps has paused to lay out supplies for sick call.

The mess hall is filled with the satisfied rumble of men eating bacon, beans, eggs bought from local farmers, thick slabs of toast, and powerful army coffee. At the sergeants' table a skinny Filipino boy, an orphan picked up in a village wrecked by bandits, tucks food away with the best of them. Dressed in clothing improvised from worn-out shirts, he serves the company as mascot and shoeshine boy. Outside, the church bells begin ringing, but Company C has little knowledge of churches or their chimes.

The chief of police walks rapidly across the square, pushing a protesting civilian before him, two of his constables following behind. Coming up to the sentry outside the mess hall, he begins jabbering earnestly, with many gesticulations. The sentry leans down, trying to catch his meaning—and one of the constables whips a short bolo from his belt and splits the American's head. The church bells shift to a wild, swift pealing, and the place suddenly is full of screeching Insurgents, villagers jerking concealed weapons from under their shirts, wild-eyed, ragged men pouring out of the jungle beyond the houses. Screaming for the blood of the heretic invaders, the priest urges them on.

The other two sentries have been stalked and rushed from behind. The hospital sergeant is caught in the doorway of his hut. He has no weapons but he is a strong man and unafraid. Snatching up a long-handled shovel, he meets the rush. When his comrades come later to bury him, there are seven dead Insurgents around his hacked body.

The howling mob bursts through the mess hall doors. The three officers, eating together at a small table, are its first target—dead before they can get to their feet. Another assault swarms in the back way through the kitchen, chopping down the cooks. Some have rifles; a bullet catches the supply sergeant and rolls him under the table. But Company C comes up fighting— benches, table legs, and mess kit knives, thrown dishes, fists, and feet. They are bigger men and stronger than the Insurgents, and they die hard. The Filipino boy drops under the table, goes swiftly through the supply sergeant's pockets, and wiggles out of the building unnoticed.

The mess hall is full of smoke and screams and the fleshy "chunk" as bolo and club hit home. Numbers tell—four or five Insurgents throw themselves on each American, pulling down those they can isolate, forcing the rest back against the rear wall where a knot of bloody survivors make their last stand. There is window in that wall; a wounded man on the floor sees two Krag rifles, cartridge belts twined around their barrels, shoved inward across its sill. More follow as fast as two small brown hands can pitch them in—the mascot and shoeshine boy also belongs to Company C. He has taken the sergeant's keys and unlocked the rifle rack. Rifles give the Americans a new berserk fury. Steel-shod butts crunch into Insurgents' faces, gaining some men time to load. Then Krags thunder in the room, their high-velocity bullets going through three or four bodies among the packed Insurgents.

Bursting out of the mess hall, dragging what wounded they can with them, the Americans rally under their noncoms, and fight a by-the-book delaying action down to the beach to seize fishing boats and push off. There are twenty-six survivors, all but four of them wounded; they have left over two hundred dead Insurgents behind. It is a desperate voyage across the straits to an American garrison on neighboring Leyte Island, but they will make it—and come back with Brig. Gen. "Hell-Roaring Jake" Smith to sweep Samar clean.

Other posts are attacked. At some the Americans are mistrusting people who keep their rifles handy, and the attempted surprises fail. In one town the Filipino wife of an American soldier gives warning that the local priest is the ringleader. A patrol plucks him from his altar in the middle of a service and cripples the church bells.

It was all in a day's work along the frontiers of an empire. The army has a new song: "There's many a man's been murdered on Samar." Forty years later, grandsons of the Balangiga Insurgents will fight shoulder-to-shoulder with Americans against the Japanese.

143. A field hospital. In this painting of an army field hospital during the Spanish-American War, artist H. Charles McBarron shows the last use of the blue field uniform during a major war. The Medical Department major (center foreground) wears a dark blue officer's undress coat, trimmed with black mohair braid. The field artillery private holding his horse has a dark blue wool shirt, light blue wool trousers, and brown canvas leggings. He carries his blanket, wrapped in his pup tent half, slung over his shoulder; from his dark blue web cartridge belt hang the knife bayonet for his Krag rifle and his canvas haversack, stenciled with his unit's designation. Both men have drab campaign hats with the enameled red-white-and-blue badge of Headquarters, V Army Corps. Behind them are company stretcher-bearers, identified by their red armbands, and Medical Department personnel with their Red Cross brassard.

144. A first lesson in the art of war.
A veteran first sergeant eyes new recruits at Fort Slocum, New York, in early 1898. Although war with Spain brought so many volunteers that the Regular Army—for the first time—could pick the best of them, the sergeant probably is assuring these men that their mere appearance gives him indigestion and that he doubts they will ever make soldiers.

145. Krag rifle. "Underneath the starry flag, civilize 'em with a krag, and return us to our own beloved home," sang Americans in the Philippines. Designed in Denmark but manufactured in the United States, the caliber .30, bolt-action Krag-Jorgensen rifle was the first U.S. military weapon to use smokeless powder. Its magazine held five cartridges, which were loaded individually; its total length was 49 inches; its weight, approximately 8 pounds. First issued in 1892, it was modified in 1896 and 1898. Because of its long range, Crow Indians dubbed it "Shoot today, kill tomorrow."

146. Fatigue detail. The soldier's peacetime life went by daily, monthly, and yearly routines. A detail from Light Battery F, 4th Artillery Regiment, falls out in their white canvas fatigue uniforms for "stables." The noncommissioned officer in charge can be identified by his belt and saber.

147. Awaiting pay call. Battery F stands at parade rest in winter full dress, complete with white gloves. The capes of their sky-blue overcoats are thrown back to show the scarlet lining. As usual on formal occasions, a large dog has joined the formation.

148. The regimental band. Frequently cold-shouldered by adjoining communities, soldiers provided a good deal of their own entertainment. The 6th Cavalry Regimental Band, photographed at Fort Riley, Kansas, in 1906, provided music for post dances and parties as well as parades.

149. "Monkey drill" team. Mounted units organized "monkey drill" teams, such as this one of the 6th Cavalry Regiment, that performed hair-raising acrobatics and stunts.

150. *Hurdling on Three Horses.* Frederic Remington captured in this painting an example of outstanding mounted acrobatics performed by cavalrymen.

151. Home from church. Life at western army posts could still be fairly Spartan. Here an officer and his lady at Fort Huachuca, Arizona, stroll home from church.

152. Relaxing in the barracks. Soldiers at Fort Huachuca relax in a barracks squad room. It is clean and orderly, but the two stoves, the handy rifle racks, the different styles of foot lockers, the improvised spitoons, and the equipment stacked and hung above each cot give it a rough-and-ready frontier quality.

153. Return from a hunt. A hunting party comes back to Fort Huachuca with its bag. Hunting was encouraged as a means of improving the soldier's marksmanship as well as his knowledge of stalking, trailing, and looking after himself in the field. Game was always a welcome addition to the ration, particularly at Thanksgiving and Christmas.

154. Black infantrymen after a long hike. The tent (modeled on the Indian tepee) in which these infantrymen rest and their stove were both designed by Maj. Henry H. Sibley in 1855. The tent accommodated twenty infantrymen or seventeen cavalrymen, the latter having more gear to bring inside. The two diagonal bars are legs of the tripod that supports the tent pole (hidden behind the stovepipe). The men with white stripes on their trousers are noncommissioned officers. One man on the far left wears an early type of army overshoe.

155. Army mule. Confronted by what it considered an unjust burden, the army mule might simply relax. While soldiers struggle to get one wagon wheel out of a minor hole, the driver optimistically attempts to "tail up" a sulky animal.

156. "The grim three miles an hour/That is empire, that is power" **(Joyce Kilmer).** A regiment training in Florida comes into camp through the dust behind its fifes and drums.

157. Army cook. Photographed through the smoke of his fire, an army cook in Cuba whets a carving knife as he watches his pots boil. Neither the soldier's field ration nor the method of preparing it had changed much since the Civil War.

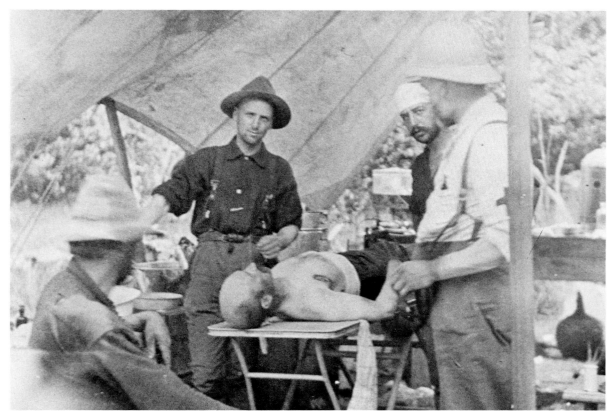

158. Spanish-American War field hospital. In a field hospital tent, surgeons treat a wounded soldier. Their hands and instruments are as sterile as is possible under such primitive conditions, but they and their patients have little protection against tropical heat, dust, and insects. The surgeon on the right wears the Red Cross brassard, now the internationally recognized symbol of medical personnel.

159. The Philippine Insurrection. Major hostilities in the Philippines ended in 1901, but it took years to establish law and order throughout the 7,083 islands of the turbulent archipelago. Much of it still was unmapped and relatively unexplored, inhabited by mutually hostile tribal groups speaking some eighty-six different languages. For the soldier it was much like the Indian wars, further complicated by tropical terrain and climate—constant patrols that suddenly might irrupt in ambush and a rush of bolo-wielding bandits. As shown in this illustration, officers discarded their regulation holsters for the western quick-draw type.

160. The 11th Cavalry in the Philippines. A detachment of the 11th Cavalry is shown landing in native boats in northwestern Luzon in 1902. Soldiers took their hardships with wry humor. Two of their favorite songs were parodies: the first, "They say I've a little brown brother," of Governor William H. Taft's pomposity; the second, "He starved on army bacon, army bacon on the rind," of the sentimental favorite "Birgen on the Rhine."

161. The San Francisco earthquake. In April 1906, San Francisco was swept by a conflagration after an earthquake that left a quarter of a million citizens homeless and completely overwhelmed the city's fire department, police, and hospitals. All available troops from the Presidio and other nearby posts were immediately ordered to assist the civil authorities. Once the fire was under control and order had been reestablished, the army took over the distribution of relief supplies. Exhausted soldiers may have envied comrades who were merely storming Moro forts in the Philippines, persuading Ute Indians back onto their reservation, or restoring peace in Cuba. The soldiers in this photo are guarding gutted buildings in San Francisco.

162. Distributing water. After the 1906 San Francisco fire, water sources were scarce or polluted. The army assisted by providing quartermaster-owned water wagons at many points around the city. In the background is a "city" of surplus army tentage, where some homeless citizens have found temporary shelter.

163. Equipment in 1910. The 1910 changes in equipment were designed to put as much of the soldier's load as possible onto his back and leave as little as possible banging against his legs. Shown here in contrast to the 1903 style of equipment, these changes promised much greater comfort and efficiency. Unfortunately, this publicity photo was carelessly posed: the soldier in the new equipment (left) was thrust into trousers, shirt, and cartridge belt that were considerably too big for him (note the rubber bands above his elbows). Also, someone forgot his hat cord.

164. Cavalry colonel. This photo of Col. Julien Gaujat, former commanding officer of the 1st Cavalry, shows the cut of the "choker-collared" blouse.

165. Philadelphia City cavalryman. The starkly functional army uniforms contrast sharply with the full dress of a captain of the First Troop, Philadelphia City Cavalry, in 1900. He wears a dark blue coat, silver lace, and red collar and saddlecloth. His sabretache (the pouch hanging beside his saber) carries the date of the troop's organization (1774) and its Revolutionary War honors for Trenton and Princeton.

166. Punitive expedition into Mexico (1916–17). The base camp at Colonia Dublan was the "windiest place in the world," noted for its barrenness, extremes of temperature, and savage dust storms. A dust storm on Christmas Day 1916 lasted twenty-four hours, making cooking impossible. Soldiers built adobe enclosures under their pup (properly "shelter") tents and furnished them with improvised bunks. A raised threshold kept out snakes, scorpions, and similar unwanted visitors. This infantryman carries the complete model 1910 equipment. His rifle is the famous Springfield caliber .30-06, which weighed slightly more than 8 pounds; its ammunition came in five-round clips, which made it easier to load than the Krag.

167. Columbus, New Mexico. A cavalry patrol moves out from Columbus, New Mexico, passing the debris of buildings burned during Pancho Villa's raid.

168. Cavalry in Yosemite Park. Cavalry units patrolling Yosemite National Park liked to be photographed against the Mariposa Grove's "Fallen Monarch," an enormous downed redwood. This is Troop F, 6th Cavalry Regiment, about 1900. Officers are on the right; in the upper right corner is an officer's wife.

173. Fighting yellow fever. The army's great victories of these years were against disease and nature. In the Philippines it conquered cholera; in the Western Hemisphere, yellow fever. It built the Panama Canal, and continued its many flood control projects within the United States. This somewhat idealized picture shows the officers and men who volunteered to be inoculated with blood serum from yellow fever patients or bitten by infected mosquitos. One officer holds a test tube containing a mosquito against the bared forearm of another. (The equally valiant men who used the dirty clothing and bedding of yellow fever victims are not included.) The civilian at the left is Dr. Carlos J. Finlay, a Cuban physician of French-Scots parentage, who was probably the first to suspect the mosquito as the carrier of yellow fever.

174. American officers in Germany. The U.S. defeat of Spain and subsequent expansion across the Pacific gave the United States a certain international military prestige. Three American officers, quietly conspicuous in their plain olive-drab uniforms and slouched campaign hats, watch the 1902 German Imperial Maneuvers.

8

Soldiers for Democracy, 1917-40

In late June 1918 a disappointed German commander wrote down some first impressions of the American soldier in action. At the full swing of a successful offensive the Germans had been stopped along the Marne River by Regulars of the U.S. 3rd Infantry Division—and then counterattacked and driven back by the Marines and Regulars of the 2nd Division. The battles at Château-Thierry, Belleau Wood, and Vaux had been smallish affairs, but they were indication enough of what might be expected in the future as more and more combat divisions joined the American Expeditionary Force in France.

The personnel must be called excellent.... The spirit of the men is high.... The 2nd American Division can be rated as a very good division and possibly be considered a special shock unit.... The various attacks of the marines were carried out smartly and ruthlessly. The moral effect of our fire did not materially check the advance of the infantry.[1]

A large part of those Regulars and Marines had been raw recruits only a few months before.

The United States came to its first European war in a state of unprepared innocence. The U.S. government has been reproached for delaying its entrance until that war was in the "eleventh hour," and for failing to prepare to do so. But such accusations ignore the fact that Germany and its allies were no threat to the United States, then or in the forseeable future. President Woodrow Wilson had hoped to preserve strict neutrality and to mediate between the belligerents, while suppressing any war fever within the United States.

When, eventually, reluctantly, America declared war on April 6, 1917—because of Germany's resumption of unrestricted submarine warfare and its attempt to reach a military alliance with Mexico—the British, French, Russian, Italian, and Rumanian armies were far superior in numbers to those of Germany and its allies, and were on the offensive on most fronts. Initially, America's new "associates" (a formal treaty of alliance was never signed) wanted mostly munitions, supplies, and money. There seemed time enough to raise, equip, and train an American Expeditionary Force for service in France, should it actually be needed.

Unfortunately, the German Army was superior in training, weapons, and leadership. During the next year it forced Russia out of the war, crushed Rumania, crippled Italy, and brought British and French offensives to bloody halts. A major mutiny in mid-1917 shook the bones of the French Army. Then in March 1918 the Germans loosed a succession of shattering offensives on the western front. With each Allied reverse, their demand for more American troops became more urgent.

THE AMERICAN EXPEDITIONARY FORCE

Like the armies of the Civil War, the American Expeditionary Force (usually called the AEF) was made up of citizen soldiers, suddenly plucked from civilian life into a strange, new existence and into equally strange foreign lands. Since 1914 they had been filled with carefully concocted Allied propaganda concerning bestial atrocities committed by the cowardly Huns—French children with their hands cut off, crucified Canadians, and other such inventions. They went, enthusiastically for the most part, as crusaders for a new and better world and with a certain swing and swagger—after all, they were Americans, and America had never lost a war. They wanted to get this war over with and go home. A German officer who interrogated wounded American prisoners noted that they seemed to be "filled with naive assurance."

When the United States declared war against Germany its active army numbered approximately 200,000, including National Guardsmen on active duty along the Mexican border. In addition, there were over 100,000 National Guardsmen on inactive status and approximately 25,000 enlisted reservists of various types. Much of the Regular Army was stationed in the Philippines, Hawaii, China, and Alaska. Both the Regulars and the National Guard were in the process of forming new units as authorized by the National Defense Act of 1916, but there was not one organized division in the country.

Manpower was the least of the many problems in creating the AEF. Congress promptly passed the 1917 Selective Service Act, and the resulting "draft," based on prewar planning by the General Staff, went into effect with surprising smoothness and efficiency. Voluntary enlistment was retained initially for the Regular Army, National Guard, Navy, and Marine Corps, but was discontinued during August and September of 1918. Both drafted men and volunteers were enrolled for the duration of the war.

The army mobilized sixty-two divisions, each with almost 28,000 men in four infantry regiments, three artillery regiments, an engineer regiment, three machine gun battalions, a signal battalion, an air service squadron, and the necessary service troops. Forty-three of these divisions served overseas. The big American division was specifically organized for sustained offensive fighting. It was the equivalent of two full-strength British or French divisions; moreover, since few of their divisions were up to full strength in 1918, the average difference probably was considerably greater. (Even respected European historians rather tend to ignore this fact.) Besides these basic divisions there were additional artillery, engineer, signal, tank, air service, and medical units attached to the various corps and field armies.

By the end of World War I the army totaled 3,710,563, of which approximately 2,000,000 were in Europe. The whole logistical system to supply them, in large part from the United States across 3,000 miles of ocean, had to be developed from scratch. Cargo ships and transports had to be built, ports along France's west coast modernized, some 1,000 miles of standard-gauge railroad built to improve the limited rail net across south-central France, and major telephone and telegraph systems installed. No nation had ever attempted anything comparable.

Originally there were three different categories of divisions: Regular Army (1st through 8th divisions), National Guard (26th through 42nd), and National Army (76th through 93rd). The first was formed around the existing infantry, artillery, and engineer regiments of the Regular Army.

These had been skeletonized to supply cadres and instructors for the rest of the army, and refilled with volunteers and draftees. Their remaining Regulars and some old regimental traditions made these divisions into the tightly disciplined spearheads of the AEF, even when half of their officers and men were green, scared replacements.

A typical infantry company in the 60th Infantry Regiment, 5th Division, was commanded by a former Regular sergeant, who had become a temporary first lieutenant. Its second lieutenant was a ninety-day-wonder ex-schoolteacher. The first sergeant was a Regular with twenty-seven years' service who would rather be a top-kick than a brigadier general and so refused a commission. The rest of the company—"they came near bein' the rookiest bunch of rookies in this man's army"—were mostly volunteers, Pennsylvania coal miners with a few New Yorkers and five western Indians for variety.[2]

The National Guard divisions varied in efficiency. Some, like the 35th Division from Missouri and Kansas, were "infested by politicians. . . . appointees with pull, untrained and incompetent."[3] The 42nd Division (known as the "Rainbow" from its insignia) had an infantry regiment from Alabama and an "Irish" regiment (formerly the "Fighting 69th") from New York. Both cherished a feud, originating from the 69th's chicken-stealing while stationed in Alabama in 1898. Sometime after the division's arrival in France, these two staged the fist-and-foot "Battle of Harp Wood"; Alabama won, capturing all of New York's supply of fresh eggs. French observers reported that the National Guard divisions' discipline was lax, and their original personnel were "men employed in banks or trade whose physique is only mediocre."[4]

In contrast, these French officers much admired the potential of the National Army divisions: "recruited by conscription from all classes. It possesses excellent qualities. It has regular officers in command of regiments, brigades, and divisions, and in the lower ranks young officers recently from camps of instruction and of the right spirit."[5] One of the best National Army divisions was the 77th, mostly from New York City. Men of other divisions claimed that the 77th's soldiers had never seen a dark night until they joined the army, that they thought the stars were distant electric lights. Without familiar street signs for guidance, its officers seldom knew where they were—naturally, the "Lost Battalion" during the Meuse-Argonne battle was from the 77th. Yet the 77th could boast that it had gained as much ground as any other division in the AEF.

Regulars might regard their regiment as their home, but the new soldier of the AEF considered his division his "outfit." Americans no longer took their colors into battle, but each man's left shoulder carried the insignia of his division. There was the "big red one" of the 1st, the star and Indian head of the 2nd, the red diamond of the 5th, the red keystone of the 28th, the Statue of Liberty of the 77th, the T-Lazy-O of the Texas/Oklahoma 90th. Nicknames evolved—"New England Division" or "Yankees" for the 26th, "Mid-West" for the 89th, "The Marne Division" for the 3rd, and "Old Hickory" for the 30th. There was a good bit of rivalry among them. Volunteers of a National Guard division greeted draftees of a National Army division with hoots of "You *had* to come!"—and were surprised to be called "Draft Dodgers!" in return. The "Rainbows" of the 42nd, made up of men from twenty-six states and the District of Columbia, thought well of themselves and enjoyed favorable publicity. (Possibly the fact that they had a smart young brigadier general named Douglas MacArthur helped.) But other divisions were less impressed; the loud jeer, "What color is the rainbow? YELLOW!" was a good way to break the monotony of a rest area.

A few months of action tended to erase the original differences among these three types of divisions, although there still were good divisions and unsteady ones. When there was a hard and dirty job, the 1st or 2nd was apt to get it. But casualties were heavy, especially officer casualties. Replacements were draftees and newly commissioned officer candidates so that the personnel of all divisions became more and more alike. They all therefore were lumped together as "divisions of the U.S. Army" in August 1918.

The orders assigning Gen. John J. Pershing to command the AEF directed that he "keep in view that the forces of the United States are a separate and distinct component . . . the identity of which must be preserved." Nonetheless, for over a year there was considerable doubt that an independent American force could be established in France. France expected an "American contingent," which could be incorporated into the French Army as they landed, and stated that "it would be very desirable to obtain from America a sufficient number of men to make up French losses." Italy was eager to secure as many Americans as possible. England was especially insistent that Americans be provided to refill her gutted divisions—as individual replacements, as American companies in British battalions, or as American battalions in English brigades.

The Allies considered their demands perfectly logical: America, they were certain, had neither military traditions nor trained officers. If left to its own untutored resources, it would not be ready to fight before 1919. Meanwhile, the great crisis of the war was coming in 1918 as Germany shifted victorious armies from Russia to the western front. Therefore, America must swallow its national pride and provide infantrymen and machine gunners to fill up veteran Allied units, which soon would whip them into useful shape. Failure to do so would practically guarantee a

German victory. This Allied pressure was adept and unceasing; Pershing had to expend far too much of his time and energy thwarting it, but his firmness preserved the AEF as a separate organization. As the Allies' defeats multiplied, they also wanted complete American divisions.

In July 1918 Gen. Ferdinand Foch, newly designated the "Generalissimo" of the Allied forces, demanded one hundred American divisions and their supporting troops (some 4 million soldiers) in France as quickly as possible to provide sufficient shock troops for a massive invasion of Germany in 1919. A rather obtuse military theorist, who preached that the moral force of an attack could overwhelm German fire power, Foch had suffered a series of costly defeats attempting to prove it. Selected as generalissimo because of his undeniable pugnacity and self-confidence, he supported the formation of an independent AEF, but attempted to divert as many American divisions from it as he could for assignment to French armies. Given enough Americans, he expected to prove his theory.

Pershing's struggle to keep the AEF from becoming a mere replacement pool for the Allied armies rested on something more than national and personal pride. American military organization and standards of discipline differed from the Allies' as much as did American rations and American social values. Language was a barrier between Americans and French (there were occasions when they had to use German as a common tongue). Even the English didn't always speak *their* language intelligibly, to Americans. Finally, there was the unvoiced fact that the average Allied commanders' professional competence was far from impressive: Their strategy was uninspired, and their tactics were incredibly wasteful; the Germans had them on the ropes. Americans hardly could do worse, and they might do much better.

Meanwhile, Americans in France caught up with their training in the art of war. The principles involved might be the same, but the great slaughters for a few square miles of blasted ground in Flanders and Champagne were far different affairs than finding and storming a Moro jungle stronghold, or a forced march through desert and mountains to pounce on a gaggle of Villa's *Dorados*. Senior officers might have studied large-scale operations in map problems at the Army Staff College or War College (by happy chance most of these problems had been based on maps of eastern France, as those were the most detailed ones available), but going from theory to its actual application was a harsh test for officers who never had commanded more than a regiment.

Americans had to master strange weapons—hand grenades, automatic rifles, trench mortars, flame throwers, tanks, and "poison" gas. Artillerymen, trained to use American-style panoramic sights, struggled with the perverse "Plateau zero, Drum 100" collimator sights of their new French guns. Infantrymen experienced the intricacies of trench warfare with its digging, sniping, and boredom. Both had to learn the modern methods of infantry-artillery cooperation. However, Pershing also emphasized rifle marksmanship and training for mobile warfare. His study of Allied operations had convinced him that trench warfare was costly and indecisive; the American soldier must be able to fight in the open.

The first American divisions received their advanced training with British and French divisions by battalions and later by regiments. While such training had its virtues, there were drawbacks. English rations could be tolerated, tea and all, since they sometimes included rum, but French food was not in the American tradition. More seriously, Allied training was largely in trench warfare. Also, there was much patronizing of American commanders and staffs as backward Johnny-come-latelys—earnest perhaps, but somewhat comic in their efforts to equal their Allied mentors. Possibly some Americans were too sensitive, but Pershing was angered enough to employ "rather forcible language" to the senior Allied commanders. Worse, many French politicians and generals tended to regard Americans as privileged to fight for France, and there were instances of American units being employed carelessly, without proper support. As a result, in June 1918 Pershing decided against any further training of American troops with the French and British.

Once they were more-or-less trained, American divisions normally were assigned to "quiet sectors" of the western front—usually to the Vosges Mountains at its southern end where there had been no real fighting since 1914. French and German divisions in such areas usually were second-class outfits of older men or badly battered units, sent there to rest and train their replacements. It was common for both sides to establish informal understandings: shelling was kept to a minimum; there was no sniping; and men from each side might take turns washing in a stream between the lines. Americans came into these sectors like the serpent into paradise. They understood there was a war going on and so shot at any German they saw. Properly irked by such unprofessional behavior, the Germans retaliated with raids and bombardments. Recuperating French units and French civilians who still lived close behind the lines were even more irritated.

The AEF never did achieve self-sufficiency or become a completely balanced organization. The shortage of transports and the Allied insistence on the priority shipment of infantry and machine gunners (to which Pershing acceded in part to obtain the use of additional British shipping) left it short of artillery, aviation, and service units. Allied promises to make up these shortages for the AEF were only partially honored.

The increasing tempo of the 1918 battles and the heavy losses they inflicted made it necessary to feed American divisions into the battle with only a few weeks of advanced training overseas. Replacements sent over from the United States might have had as little as six to eight weeks of training before they found themselves moving up into the shattered woods and battle clamor. There was little time for veterans to indoctrinate them with the fine art of winning *and* surviving. Casualties were heavy; undoubtedly the American soldier was very lucky that the Germans he fought—tough and skilled though they were—were not the German Army of 1916. A veteran Regular mused that the green replacements almost made up in courage, enthusiasm, and individual initiative whatever they lacked in technique. "They'd do things on the spur of the moment that many a trained old-timer would never even consider."[6]

The Americans went forward through the worst of weathers, wondering whatever happened to "Sunny France":

> You sleep in the mud, and drink it, that's true;
> There's mud in the bacon, the rice and the stew,
> And when you open an egg you'll find mud in it too.

They had a song with no title except its nonsense refrain, "Hinky, Dinky, Parley Vous," that ridiculed their own deeds, all French "customs quaint and rare," the method by which "The general got the Croix de Guerre," and the unseemly habits of various wenches, including the one from Saint Nazaire who "Never washed her underwear." If they sang the popular "Over There," its chorus became "Underwear! Underwear!" They claimed that AEF really stood for "Ass End First." They went up, over, through, and past the best the Germans could do to halt them. And if they did not win the war, there certainly could not have been an Allied victory without them.

Officers

The projected new army required approximately 200,000 officers. Of these, the Regular Army could provide almost 9,000, most of them well-trained in its service schools and veterans of campaigns in Cuba, the Philippines, China, and Mexico. Some 2,000 more could be drawn from the recently established Officers' Reserve Corps, composed mostly of interested civilians who had passed a qualifying examination. Also, the army finally had systematized the haphazard military training given in some colleges into a Reserve Officers' Training Corps (ROTC). The National Guard furnished most of its own officers, a good many of whom had just finished active service on the Mexican border. Lieutenants were produced by commissioning selected Regular enlisted men and through officers' training camps. In the latter, carefully selected candidates were put through highly competitive training in the duties of both enlisted men and junior officers of their particular branch of the service, to emerge as "ninety-day-wonders." The Military Academy was milked dry; its course of instruction was cut back repeatedly and finally reduced to one year in June 1918.

Promotion was rapid, if only for the duration of the war. Regular officers were advanced several grades, captains becoming temporary colonels. Regular Army top sergeants suddenly found themselves captains; regimental sergeant majors and supply sergeants, having ingrained detailed knowledge of the army's inner workings, received wartime commissions as majors and lieutenant colonels. Officer losses in combat were heavy. For example, in fighting around Soissons in July 1918 the

American divisions engaged lost 60 percent of their infantry officers; and the 26th Infantry Regiment came out of it commanded by a captain, having lost its colonel, lieutenant colonel, and all its majors. These gaps were filled by promoting the best-qualified survivors and bringing in newly trained junior officers from the United States. The majority of company commanders had only a year or less of previous service.

About one-third of the officers were commissioned directly from civilian life, with little or no military training. These were chiefly medical officers, but also included chaplains and some business or technical experts needed for supply or technical assignments. Though political influence remained helpful, especially in the National Guard, the "political officer" as such disappeared. Even Theodore Roosevelt was rebuffed when he hoped to raise from one to four divisions of volunteers and charge forth at their head to rescue democracy.

Few officers had experience in the command or staff functions of a division, let alone of a corps or field army. These had to be learned in Europe by training alongside British or French staffs, and mostly by hard experience. A whole system of officers' schools was set up in France—along with a "reassignment center" for unsatisfactory officers at Blois. (Soldier pronunciation of "Blois" was "Bloo-ey"; an officer sent there was "Blooeyed" or had "gone Blooey.") On the whole, American officers—from Pershing to the newest "shavetail"—had little or no previous experience in their assignments, but that fact did not cow them in the least. They were as well trained as their length of service could permit; they were men of energy, courage, and initiative; and they would do the best they could.

The assignment of Regular officers was considerably complicated by Allied estimates that the war would last through

1919 and could be won only by a massive invasion of Germany. Consequently, the army was careful to keep part of its Regular officers in the United States to train and command the divisions to be activated in late 1918 and early 1919—with the result that Dwight D. Eisenhower, Omar N. Bradley, and other American generals would enter World War II without ever having heard a shot fired in anger!

At all levels the AEF was tightly disciplined, possibly more so than any other American wartime army in history. A born soldier, proud of his profession and completely devoted to it, Pershing had no use for the weak and incapable. However little training his men received, they must at least know how to "shoot and salute." For all his grim pride in what his partially trained soldiers could do, he expected them to meet his Regular Army standards, both in and out of combat. Inefficiency in an officer, insubordination from an enlisted man, cowardice from anyone, he punished with a hard hand. One of his army commanders remembered: "Generally, our treatment of men who endangered others by their cowardice was lenient. We executed perhaps not more than a dozen."[7] Up in the lines, "Old Army" methods of discipline might be revived: in one Regular unit two Indians were given to drunkenness and absence without leave; rather than bother with a court-martial, their company commander cured them of such misbehavior by making them carry a heavy timber back and forth for three hours.

Black Units

Black Americans volunteered eagerly for service in World War I; over 400,000, including fifteen nurses, served in the army. Most were assigned to quartermaster, stevedore, or pioneer infantry units.

For some reason, never clearly explained, the Regular black regiments were kept in the United States or its territories, while two black divisions, the 92nd and 93rd, were activated for service in France. The 92nd was composed of draftees with mostly white officers. One of its regiments was used on the extreme left flank of the American First Army in the Meuse-Argonne to maintain liaison with the adjoining French Fourth Army, but at once panicked and had to be withdrawn. The division was put into line again during the last two days of the war and showed some improvement. The 93rd (one of several incomplete divisions that never received its artillery) was assigned to the French Army, its four infantry regiments normally serving with different French divisions. Three of these regiments were from the National Guard and had a fairly high proportion of black officers; their conduct ranged from acceptable to excellent, the 369th Regiment from New York particularly distinguishing itself on several occasions. (Also, its extra-large band was considered the best in the AEF.) These regiments wore American uniforms but had French helmets, rifles, and field equipment.

Unfortunately, since the 93rd served apart from the AEF, its good conduct got little attention, while the 92nd's unsteadiness was all too public. It was difficult to get satisfactory officers, either white or black, for black troops. Black officers often lacked sufficient education (some black colleges of this period provided only the equivalent of a sketchy high school education), and most white officers did not wish to serve with a black unit. White troops were reluctant to accept blacks as fellow combat troops and tended to ignore black officers. In their prejudice, they reflected contemporary American civilian attitudes.

Rations

In training camps, the soldier received his usual peacetime "garrison" ration—basically beef, flour, dry beans, prunes, fresh potatoes, butter, lard, coffee, syrup, evaporated milk, assorted condiments, vinegar, soap, and candles. Sweet potatoes and corn meal were added in 1918.

Overseas, the "field ration" made much use of canned meats: corned beef or corned beef hash (known as "corned willy" or "corned bill"), pink salmon (called "goldfish"), and sometimes canned beef ("monkey meat"). These were either prepared in bulk in the company "rolling kitchens"—a type of range mounted on two wheels and towed by mule teams—or issued to individual soldiers. Fresh beef and vegetables were available periodically, especially when the troops came out of the line. Now and then field bakeries provided "soft" bread, which was baked with a thick crust to protect it during hauling and distribution.

Each soldier carried two "reserve rations," for consumption in case the daily automatic supply of the field ration was interrupted. A reserve ration consisted of 1 pound of hardtack, 12 ounces of bacon or salt port (which the soldier stowed in a special "bacon can" in his pack), and coffee, sugar, and salt (all three carried in the separate compartments of a "condiment can"). When possible, soldiers would boil salt pork briefly in water to remove its excess salt before frying it. The bacon can and contents soon were replaced by canned meat. The hardtack was described as very hard indeed, needing to be fried in bacon grease or dunked in coffee or water to make it soft enough to chew. Each such reserve ration weighed 2¼ pounds and contained 3,349 calories.

The soldier also carried a lighter "emergency ration," composed of evaporated beef powder, parched cooked wheat, sweet chocolate, and salt and pepper; it was shaped somewhat like a cake of soap and marked "Not To Be Opened Except By Order of An Officer Or in Extremities." Troops overseas were supposed to receive four cigarettes a day and ½ pound of candy every ten days.

Preparation of food during combat was difficult. Smoke from campfires was likely to draw fire from German mortars and artillery, unless hidden within morning fogs. When possible, food was prepared behind the lines in the units' rolling kitchens and brought up to the troops in thick-walled, gas-proof marmite cans, either by mule cart or "carrying" details of soldiers. A good outfit would try to keep its rolling kitchens well forward so that hot meals could be served as often as possible. Here the character, or lack thereof, of the mess sergeant was all-important. A competent one possessed courage, determination, and a good nature amid frustrations. He was on his own much of the time, and a faint-heart usually could find alibis—blocked roads, heavy German fire, damaged carts—for failing to get through to his unit. But a good mess sergeant would feed his outfit at least one hot meal a day, even if bullets were "whistlin' through his whiskers," and he'd manage coffee, beef stew, or even steak with potatoes and gravy, while the less efficient companies wolfed goldfish or corned willy cold from the can. The coffee might be "black and strong enough to play Yankee Doodle," the steaks tough, but they stuck to a soldier's ribs and warmed his heart. Occasionally, to celebrate some outstanding feat, such a sergeant would achieve the small miracle of a pie.

For Thanksgiving or Christmas, soldiers overseas might barter soap, salt, and pepper from their rations for poultry and eggs. There also were informal exchanges of

American tobacco and rations for French wine. Also—having inherited his ancestors' tendency to forage liberally from the countryside—the American soldier might supplement his rations by stealthy visits to French farmyards, pastures, and cellars. Such ventures involved risks beyond those of encountering MPs or gendarmes. An American was apt to try a slug out of almost any wine bottle he found, thereby giving the medics some strange cases of poisoning to treat. Even good French food had its risks: Using a ladder, one soldier extracted a locally made cheese from the screened box where it was ripening outside a second-story bedroom window, and tossed it down to his buddy. Unfortunately, the cheese was very soft and smelled like nothing in American experience.

Troops traveling in British ships and trains complained that they were fed the same meal three times a day, every day: one hard-boiled egg, two or three strips of bacon, a big, tasteless sea biscuit, two tablespoons of orange marmalade, and a cup of tea. It probably was the first time many of them had tasted tea, and the British Army version was thick enough to chew.

When it came to alcoholic refreshment, the American soldier had reason to feel deprived. The French soldier received a liberal daily ration of wine and the English "Tommy" was solaced with high-potency rum, but the U.S. soldier was "pure." Millions of American mothers would have risen in outrage had their army tempted their sons into vice and degradation by offering them an ounce or two of potable bourbon as they wallowed through the tight-meshed German defenses of the Meuse-Argonne battleground. If the American wanted alcoholic beverages he had to procure his own. Even the more temperance-minded among them, having read how the world's elite favored champagne and cognac, were curious as to just how such drinks did taste. Naturally, the average soldier was not a discriminating con-

noisseur of European vintages; in fact, he frequently preferred a drink that made him feel as if he had swallowed a jumping jack. Shrewd French innkeepers found him a ready customer for almost anything. But even the best French beer wasn't popular with Americans: One of them invented the story of a soldier who slipped some French beer in among urinalysis specimens—and was told to get his sick horse to the vet immediately! French tobacco was regarded with the same disfavor.

Aids for Morale

Seven social welfare organizations—the Young Men's Christian Association (YMCA), American Red Cross, Knights of Columbus, Young Women's Christian Association, Salvation Army, Jewish Welfare Board, and American Library Association—operated officially with the AEF. They attempted to furnish reading rooms, help soldiers with individual problems, and assist around hospitals and rest areas. Some of them also ran canteens where soldiers could purchase candy or hot snacks; others distributed such items free. All of them did good work, though not always to the soldiers' satisfaction:

> The YMCA went over the top
> To pick up the pennies the doughboys drop!

An army medic remembered a tall, gaunt "Red Cross man" standing at the door of an aid station hour after hour, tirelessly passing out cigarettes and cookies to the wounded as they were brought in. Comparisons are invidious, but veterans remembered the "lassies" of the Salvation Army—not to mention their free coffee and doughnuts—with special fondness. Two of them set up their kitchen too far forward in the Argonne, and were buried there with full military honors.

As another aid to morale, the army instituted a hierarchy of decorations to supplement the Medal of Honor, which (once its careless use during the Civil War had been cleared away) was so difficult to win that a discouragingly large proportion of its awards were posthumous. These were the Distinguished-Service Cross, the Distinguished-Service Medal, and the Silver Star. And there was a Victory Medal for everyone in the armed forces, with a small bronze star on its ribbon for each major battle in which the wearer had served. Moreover, Congress for the first time permitted soldiers to receive and wear Allied decorations without first obtaining its specific consent. (One American service medal caused some confusion: The Indian Campaign Medal had an all-red ribbon, which Europeans took for that of the French Legion of Honor; it was subsequently given a new ribbon with alternate bands of red and black.)

Medals helped, but the average soldier's morale probably got more of a boost from the *Stars and Stripes,* the AEF's own lively weekly newspaper. Pershing knew soldiers. He gave them a newspaper run by a free-wheeling lot of soldier-newspapermen (some of whom went on to establish and work for *The New Yorker*) who took nothing—themselves very much included—too seriously. Their cartoons were howlers.

Uniforms

Clothing this mass army was another problem. The army had no reserve stocks after it had taken care of the National Guard along the Mexican border, and neither Congress nor the quartermaster general were especially quick with corrective action. There were rumors that the National Army divisions might be uniformed in hats and undershirts only. As an emergency measure, troops training in the southern states were issued summer cotton uniforms, only to have winter come

early and hard all across the United States that year (1917). Soldiers who never had seen snow before had snowball battles and caught colds. Wool uniforms and "long-handled" underwear arrived with spring.

The first Americans sent to France wore their campaign hats—which gave another exotic touch to Paris streets ("chapeaux de cow-boys," the French called them). With the issue of the steel helmets, however, these were replaced by the "overseas" cap—a rather shapeless thing, but one that could be folded and stowed in a pocket. Somewhat worse was the World War I solution to the problem of what to put on the soldier's legs between the bottom of his trousers and the top of his shoes. This was the "spiral puttee" or "wrap legging"—a band of woolen material coiled around the leg from ankle to knee. If wound too tight, it shut off circulation; if too loose, it came off. Its only virtue was that it was cheap to manufacture. The soldier's blouse with its high "choker" collar was uncomfortable in hot weather, but it did protect the throat and chest when it turned cold.

Including his wool uniform, the average soldier packed approximately 71 pounds of weapons, ammunition, field equipment, and reserve rations, along with a helmet, first-aid packet, full canteen, raincoat or poncho, overcoat, spare pair of hobnailed shoes, blanket, shelter half, toilet articles, and entrenching tool. In addition, he often was given from 8 to 20 pounds more of special equipment—wire cutters, rockets or other pyrotechnic signals, extra ammunition or grenades—to add to his personal load. His extra shirt, breeches, socks, and underwear were carried in the company wagon. When he "went over the top" he might drop the bottom part of his pack, consisting of his rolled blanket, shelter half, and raincoat. These would be left under guard, to be brought forward later— usually after he had spent a freezing night or two without them.

With some reason, American officers

considered their service uniforms drab and unglamorous. Unofficially, they began adopting the Sam Browne belt and trench coat as worn by the British. Air Service officers naturally were among the first and most enthusiastic patrons of these newer fashions. During 1925–26 the Regulars would give up the old choker-collar blouse and adopt the rolled collar with a notched lapel. This, in turn, forced the adoption of that particularly useless and unmilitary item, the necktie. There was much experimentation—white or tan shirts; black, tan, or green neckties. Officers' blouses gradually become a deep forest-green, their breeches a light rose-beige shade, irreverently termed "pinks." "Leather"—boots, belts, and various items of equipment—had to be kept polished to the proper shade, which usually was the one the regimental commander decreed, and could be anything from a light gold to an almost-black. An officer transferring from one regiment to another might have to change more than his insignia.

Medical Care

Medical attention showed constant improvement. Had it not been for the influenza epidemic that swept the world in 1918–19, casualties from disease might very well have been fewer than those from enemy action for the first time in American military history. One major threat always present was that of a typhus epidemic spread by lice. American soldiers picked up lice as they moved into old barracks, billets, and trenches. "Reading your shirt" for "cooties" or "hunting seam squirrels" was a common off-duty occupation. (The "Old Army" trick of stirring up an ant hill and then spreading your clothes on it apparently wasn't customary. Possibly French ants were not ferocious or plentiful enough.) There were outbreaks of typhus on the eastern front, but a system of delousing men and their clothing as they came out of the lines kept the west free. Troops returning to America underwent a "Farewell-to-France ritual—fumigation, shave, haircut, shower, new clothes."

There were new medical problems. One was "trench foot," a frostbite that might develop into gangrene if neglected, resulting from long periods of standing in cold, wet trenches. Dry socks were a preventative; competent officers did their best to provide frequent changes. A more serious matter was the increasing use of chemical warfare, especially the so-called "mustard gas" (actually a slowly volatilizing liquid that attacked the skin, eyes, and lungs, and might contaminate low-lying ground for days). A whole new school of military medicine would be needed to deal with such casualties.

AFTER WORLD WAR I

Demobilization after World War I ended was rapid. Draftees and National Guardsmen went home. Regular officers reverted to their permanent grades. At first eight divisions were stationed in the American bridgehead around Coblenz on the east bank of the Rhine, but this force was rapidly reduced as Germany signed the peace treaty, the last division coming home in the summer of 1919. An "American Forces in Germany" token force of some 6,800 men remained there until 1923. This service seems to have been pleasant, if boring; good wines were cheap, and Americans and Germans got along quite amicably.

Two small American forces served in Russia. One reinforced regiment was stationed in the Murmansk-Archangel area in northern Russia until August 1919, and two more were involved along the Trans-Siberian Railroad from Vladivostok westward to Lake Baikal, leaving in April 1920. Their missions were ambiguous, the government having no clear idea why it had sent them there. Duty was hard, with long winters when the ground froze 6 feet deep, and short summers when the earth dissolved into endless bog and the air was almost solid with mosquitoes. The Bolsheviks and White Russians fought a fluctuating civil war around them, full of casual brutalities and sudden betrayals. There were no comforts and few conveniences; much of the time there was nothing to do but try to keep warm. An occasional minor scuffle with Bolsheviks or Siberian bandit gangs—or a pointed disagreement with the Japanese, who hoped to seize Siberian territory—was a welcome relief from tension and boredom.

In 1920 Congress passed a new National Defense Act, establishing the Army of the United States, to consist of the Regular Army, the National Guard, and the Organized Reserves, with the Regulars responsible for the peacetime training of the latter two. A separate Air Service, a Chemical Warfare Service, and a Finance Department were added to the army. The Tank Corps was turned over to the infantry and broken up into separate companies. Maj. George S. Patton, who as a colonel had commanded the AEF's 1st Tank Brigade with distinction, found no welcome there for himself or his ideas on tank warfare and so went back to the Cavalry. A few years later his efficiency report defined him as "a disturbing element in time of peace." The Reserve Officers Training Corps (ROTC) and Citizens Military Training Corps (CMTC) were utilized to train reserve officers. The strength of the Regular Army was set at 297,717 officers and enlisted men, but a private's pay was cut back to the prewar $21 a month from the wartime $30.

The following years were full of financial troubles and pacifist agitation. Congress cut back the army's strength—to 150,000 in 1921; to 137,000 in 1922; and to 118,750 in 1927. At least 1,000 Regular officers were forced out as "surplus"; promotion for the rest was slowed drastically. There was no money for new equipment, weapons, or research. The army lived on supplies left over from World War I. The National Guard, with an authorized strength of 435,000, had half that number or less because of the shortage of drill pay and proper equipment. Young reserve officers felt themselves lucky if they could secure two weeks of active duty training every other summer; most of their advanced education came from correspondence courses or evening classes held in the larger cities by Regular officer instructors. All told, the Regular Army of the 1930s stood approximately seventeenth in size among the armies of the world. Its divisions were skeletons, its weapons and equipment largely obsolescent.

Nonetheless, the army managed certain changes. The Artillery School at Fort Sill was evolving a new "fire direction" technique that would permit the rapid massing of fire from widely separated battalions on the same target. There was more experimentation with radio, motor vehicles, and new weapons. An embryo armored force began developing at Fort Knox.

The Air Service, which had been demanding coequal status with the army and navy to better develop its capabilities for "strategic" bombing of enemy industry and civilian populations, became the Air Corps in 1926. In 1933 it received a degree of autonomy, which it exploited in developing a heavy bomber while neglecting fighter aircraft and air-ground cooperation. As an additional duty, President Franklin D. Roosevelt, in a typical political flourish, ordered it to fly the U.S. air mail—a mission for which its planes were unsuited and which resulted in the death or injury of a shocking number of pilots.

West Point in 1919 was in disarray. It had on hand one Plebe (freshman) class that had expected to finish its year of instruction and be commissioned the coming June, and a new "emergency" Plebe class admitted in November 1918. To these were added members of the last class previously graduated, already commissioned but now brought back for six months of additional instruction and not happy about it. All three groups wore different uniforms and had different disciplinary status. Brig. Gen. Douglas MacArthur, twice wounded, with twelve decorations, was appointed superintendent. Devoted to the Academy, he attempted to broaden the curriculum, increase cadet responsibility, and produce graduates trained to lead citizen soldiers as well as Regulars. This alone would have been a major pill for the permanent professors to swallow—five of them had been professors in 1899 when MacArthur was a Plebe—but MacArthur's aloof, authoritative personality made him even less welcome. He avoided the Academy staff socially, ignored uniform regulations, and returned salutes (if at all) by a careless flip of his riding crop. He was able to expand the athletic programs, give definite form to the traditional Academy honor code, improve instructor training, and modernize the course of instruction, but his attempt to introduce realism into the cadets' summer camps (expressed as "How long are we going on preparing for the War of 1812?") was abolished by his successor.

As for the Regulars, wherever American bugles sounded, from Tientsin eastward to Puerto Rico, they remained "single men in barracks." The Great Depression brought in a higher class of recruits, but the soldier's image, as perceived by the public, was not much improved. Payday nights still were a time of public rejoicing, if not some uproar. A few had a weakness other than wine and women—marijuana. Such "goof burners" then were usually Mexican-Americans or poor whites from the Southwest; there weren't many of them and their pet vice was considered a low one.

Little had changed around the typical army post, although the army had acquired motor vehicles and needed drivers and mechanics. Except for sergeants, not many soldiers were married—a private or corporal couldn't afford either a wife or an automobile. Sometimes the row of "enlisted married quarters" was known as "Hungry Hill." Down in the barracks, a soldier short of cash might borrow from one of the company "Shylocks" at "one for one" interest—which meant repaying $2 for $1 borrowed. If money were really tight, the rate might be five for three.

Athletics were becoming more organized. The old-time company ball team, sometimes including both officers and enlisted men, which played for the fun of it was being replaced by scheduled events that took on all the solemnity of a general inspection. In those units or posts where the commanding officer was a sports addict, military training might be neglected under the theory that a good athlete just naturally was a good soldier. In such outfits ball players and boxers were pampered—excused from duty, fed at special training tables, given cushy jobs. To the average soldier they were "jockstrappers" or "jocks" whose work had to be done by the company's nonathletes. However, a well-organized athletic program that allowed the maximum possible number of soldiers a chance to play, and gave no special privileges, could be a boost to unit morale and a good physical conditioner.

In 1933 the army was brought in to supply and administer the camps of the Civilian Conservation Corps (CCC), sometimes known as "Roosevelt's Tree Army," after it became apparent that there was no other national organization capable of handling the job. Since President Roosevelt had applied a 15 percent pay cut to federal employees, soldiers regarded the $30-a-month CCC enrollee as a pampered pet, even though he supposedly sent $25 of his pay home to his family. Once the Regulars, officers and enlisted men, got the camps running, most of the responsibility was taken over by selected Reserve officers. Though often presented as an extra bur-den on the army, the CCC actually gave it the experience of a small-scale mobiliza-tion, and taught thousands of officers the arts of leadership and company adminis-tration. That experience would be invalu-able in just a few years.

Chill dusk on a back road in northeastern France, the last of September 1918. Rain drives down relentlessly, as if preparing a second Deluge. The road is narrow, an inch deep in slippery mud that cakes the soldiers' hob-nailed shoes and sprays from under the tires of passing trucks. Ditches be-side the road are swirls of dirty water and foul debris, the woods beyond smashed into splintered stubs. Through the rain comes the sickening-sweet stink of corrupting flesh, sometimes touched with the garlic scent of mus-tard gas. The few houses, the rare small village the column passes are tum-bled heaps of broken brick and stone.

These are Regulars and veterans. They have won a battle at St. Mihiel, and they are moving north to add their weight to the just-begun American drive in the Meuse-Argonne. The planning for this complex movement—among the best non-German staff work of the war—has been done by Col. George C. Marshall, but to the doughboys moving up through the wind and wet under 80-pound packs it's only another long night march. By now they are so numbed that they hardly notice the rain and the cold or the unceas-ing jar and rumble of artillery fire ahead of them. They are still too far away to hear the rattle of German machine guns, like a world of maniac wood-peckers, but they know it is there. The ambulances that come swaying and skidding along the other side of the road get no attention. The broken men in them are out of the war.

A soldier, glassy-eyed and swaying, slips and goes down with a rattle and thud, taking two men with him, shoving another halfway into the ditch. Someone spits mud and curses with tired conviction. Even before a sergeant gets there, the men are up, hunching their packs into place, and moving again. "Sorry," the soldier mumbles, "guess I just dozed off." The dark comes down; muzzle flashes of the massed guns up ahead whip across the black horizon like endless sheet lightning. The column plods on.

Up ahead a hooded light sparks briefly; hoarse shouts echo through the rain. The column lurches to a halt. Men bring their rifles down behind them to prop up the bottom of their packs and take the weight momentarily off their shoulders, too thankful for the pause to wonder why. Then officers be-gin checking their companies—"Get those rifle butts out of the mud!" (A soaked rifle butt may warp, throwing the sights out of line.) More hoarse shouts, and the march picks up again. Why they halted, no one knows.

Hours later, still in the rain, the column turns off onto a rutted side road. Mounted officers direct each company off into a section of what once was an orchard. Most of the trees are broken but enough remains of them to give some concealment—and also to drip on men passing among them. Soldiers collapse wearily into shell holes, pulling their ponchos around them and their rifles. Puddles may form under them, but they have learned that if they lie quietly the water inside their clothes will get warm enough to let them sleep.

Walking as if his boots were full of broken glass, a captain checks his company area. His first sergeant and dog robber (orderly) have found a piece of sheet iron and rigged it over a shell hole to make a crude shelter. The captain slips off his pack and peers inside. "Thanks, sergeant. It reminds me of home—it's so damn different!"

175. The World War I soldier. World War I added the "tin hat" (steel helmet) and the gas mask to the soldier's equipment. The first sergeant wears his gas mask pouch in the "alert" position on his chest; the lieutenant colonel's is slung over his right shoulder. In the background is a field telephone crew and a 75mm field gun, in full recoil after firing.

176. "Uncle Sam wants you." Poster art became extremely important in boosting popular support for the war effort. James M. Flagg's "I Want *You*" remains a masterpiece.

177. Postcard from camp. The soldier who sent home this postcard from Camp Upton wrote, "I am almost a soldier. Expect to get uniforms in a day or two and then I will feel like one anyway. I think I am going to like the life very much."

178. Doing the laundry. Once soldiers got uniforms and equipment they had to keep them clean, as a corporal and his buddy are doing.

179. Training recruits. New soldiers were taught close-order drill and the manual of arms—often by new officers who were about one lesson ahead of them. With a shortage of uniforms and equipment, many units had a rather irregular appearance.

180. Training equipment. Much training equipment was obsolete. The soldiers in Illustration 179 are drilling with Krag-Jorgensen rifles. Those in this illustration are training with a wooden copy of a Vickers machine gun. Their tripod is real, but all others issued their company were substitutes, improvised out of pieces of water pipe. Each gun crew took turns using the real tripod.

181. On the obstacle course. The World War I version of the obstacle course may have been crude, but it was rough, inspiring one verse of a soldiers' song: "He bruised his belly on a tack,/ He tore it on a nail!/He have made a damn good lizard/If he'd only had a tail!"

182. "They took him to the rifle range/ 'Way out beyond the hill,/To teach to him the trigger squeeze/And how the foe to kill./His rifle kicked him in the jaw—/ He missed the bull a mile!/For the messhall is the only place/He shows off any style!" Wearing "fatigues" over their uniforms, new soldiers take turns getting acquainted with the Springfield rifle.

183. The model 1910 infantry equipment. Designed to give the soldier a convenient place for everything he was supposed to carry at that time, the 1910 equipment unfortunately left no extra room for anything else, such as another blanket or a pair of shoes and an overcoat. The soldier could only somehow attach the first two to the outside of his pack—which made it necessary to hang his entrenching tool from his belt again. As for his overcoat, he could wear it or carry it over his arm. Naturally, a good deal of equipment was soon "lost."

184. Gas mask drill. The introduction of chemical warfare during World War I made "gas mask drill" an essential part of every soldier's training. Army nurses in their long white skirts scramble down into a "gas chamber"—a dugout filled with tear gas. If their masks are properly fitted and adjusted, they will have no trouble; if not, they'll come out weeping.

185. After the drill. A soldier expresses his joy over having completed his gas mask drill.

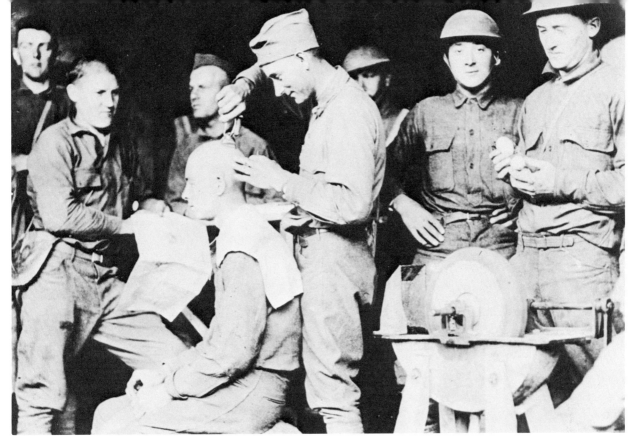

186. Haircuts. A soldier of the 128th Infantry Regiment, 32nd Division, gets a close haircut in an improvised barbershop just behind the lines. The ever-present French cooties made short hair popular.

187. "Reading" underwear. Taking advantage of a sunny day and a lull in the fighting, a soldier "reads" his undershirt to get the lice out of their hiding places along its seams.

188. Foreign hosts. Following traditional European practice, when out of the line soldiers might be "billeted" in the homes of local civilians. While the equally traditional occasional result inspired numerous verses of "Parley Vous," soldiers who had left families at home were quick to share their rations, tobacco, and candy with their hosts.

189. A typical canteen. This canteen in France (managing organization unknown) offered hot chocolate, cigars, cigarettes, pipe and chewing tobacco, matches, playing cards, cookies, candy, and chewing gum.

190. Canteen at home. The canteen at Camp McArthur in Waco, Texas, offered the usual items plus French lessons.

191. A "rolling kitchen." Sometimes called a "slum gun," the rolling kitchen was a busy place at mealtimes. One KP ladles out coffee while a cook serves the meal—stew, from the looks of it, and a slab of bread from the stack on top of the range. Balancing a loaded mess kit in one hand and a canteen cup, with its tricky folding handle, in the other was a definite skill. Every company had its ever-hungry "chow hounds" who were always first in the mess line.

192. Inspection. A guard detail from the famous 2nd Division falls in for inspection in late August 1918. On the back of this photo (reproduced below it), the photographer noted the fates of the eight enlisted men—in the remaining two and a half months of war, three were gassed, two wounded, one killed.

193. Sleep. While a sentry watches, exhausted infantrymen sleep sprawled in a shallow trench they have scooped out at the end of their advance. Sleep was as important as food—sometimes more so.

194. The 396th Infantry Regiment (formerly the 15th New York). This corporal has a French pack, gas mask carrier, canteen, and cartridge belt. His rifle is the comparatively awkward French Mannlicher-Berthier. Most photographs of this regiment show its men in French helmets.

195. Studying the German lines. From his "observation post," a precarious perch at the corner of a ruined house, an artillery officer uses his "battery commander's telescope" to study the German lines in search of targets. His telephone operator crouches below him, ready to relay his fire commands to the guns, which are in a concealed position farther to the rear. A mile or so to the east, German artillerymen undoubtedly are trying to locate this position, so it is wise to be inconspicuous. American gunners sometimes adapted a largely unprintable little poem about the engineers that began, "Cannoneers have hairy ears. They live in drains and ditches. . . ."

196. Going to the front. An American tank unit, equipped with French Renault light tanks, advances into the Argonne Forest in September 1918. The Renault, considered an excellent tank, could travel at 5 miles an hour along good roads and go 22 miles without refueling. It weighed a little over 7 tons and had almost an inch of armor over its vital parts. Some, like the leading tank, were armed with a single machine gun; others, with a short 1-pounder cannon. The crew consisted of a driver and a gunner, who also acted as tank commander. The soldiers on top of the tanks are officers, who usually advanced on foot to maintain better control of their units.

197. Outpost in Russia. Soldiers of the 339th Infantry Regiment man a fortified outpost on the Archangel front in northern Russia during the winter of 1918–19. The sentry at the left wears canvas arctic boots over several layers of wool socks—warm, but not suitable for fast movement. His rifle is a 7.62mm Moisin, manufactured in the United States for the Russian Army, and used here because large stocks of ammunition were available. The man kneeling behind him has a Lewis gun, a British light machine gun that functioned effectively in cold weather.

Opposite, above:
198. Russian entertainment. On the Vladivostok front, clear across Russia, American soldiers listen to an afternoon concert by a White Russian military band. The armored car at the right is an Austin, built in England for the Russians.

Opposite, below:
199. Field Artillery School. An instructor at the Field Artillery School gives a group of officer-students a critique of a just-completed firing problem, sometime in the early 1920s. All of these officers wear Sam Browne belts, but only a few have the light-colored "pink" breeches. Several have reversed their caps for greater convenience in using the battery commander's telescopes. The officer seated at the left, who will "fire" the next problem, meanwhile checks his data.

200. Loading a howitzer. Artillerymen load an 8-inch howitzer, a massive weapon that was English-designed, but manufactured in America. Some saw service in World War I, but they were little used after 1920. Loading required precise, quick teamwork from every member of the gun crew.

201. Coast Artillery Corps. Established as a separate arm in 1907, the corps continued to improve its defensive works around the United States, the Panama Canal Zone, and Hawaii. (Those on Guam and in the Philippines were not modernized as a concession to Japan at the 1921–22 Washington Naval Conference.) This photo shows a 12-inch "disappearing" gun as it is fired by members of the Reserve Officers' Training Corps at Fort Monroe, Virginia, in 1925. The force of such guns' recoil was utilized to bring them back down into their loading position, below the level of the battery's ramparts.

202. Fire control center. A team of coast artillerymen compute the range and direction of a target from reports phoned in from widely separated observation posts. The rest of the army tended to deride coast artillerymen as "the branch of the women and the wine"—semi-soldiers who could neither hike nor ride.

203. New uniforms. Modernization was laggard during the 1920s and 1930s. The 30th Infantry Regiment parades at the Presidio of San Francisco, showing its new uniforms with civilian-style collars and neckties, but still enduring the abomination of wrap leggings, in July 1926.

204. "Portee" artillery. The Artillery School demonstrates "portee" artillery with field guns carried in trucks rather than pulled by horses. The artillerymen have the new uniform and a new style of gas mask, but the truck is an automotive antique with solid tires, and the gun is a "French seventy-five," little modified from its 1897 original model. It was still an effective weapon, but European armies were adopting 105mm field guns, longer ranged and more powerful.

205. Some things never change. While equipment and uniforms were changing, soldiers in 1930 still had to shave and brush their teeth, as shown by men of the 27th Infantry Regiment (nicknamed the "Wolfhounds").

206. Army Air Corps. As always, the army had a number of odd jobs. These included such missions as Army Air Corps assistance to the National Geographic Society in the exploration of the earth's stratosphere.

207a and 207b. Civilian Conservation Corps. The army also organized and handled the administration of the Civilian Conservation Corps. In the photo at left, a detail builds latrines for public camp grounds. In the photo at right, another detail of CCC "enrollees" engaged in an insect control project in northern Utah falls in for a hot lunch. Their vehicles, mess gear, and most of their clothing are from army stocks.

9

Soldiers of the Long Wars

Maj. Gen. John P. Lucas, who is usually remembered as the unfortunate commander sent with insufficient forces to make a landing at Anzio behind the German front in Italy during early 1944, was also a soldier of perception and feeling. He had watched the grim Allied advance northward across Italy's sheer mountains and swift-running rivers, through winter rains and snow, against a tenacious and skillful enemy. "I don't see how our men stand what they do," he wrote. "They are the finest soldiers in the world and none but a humble man should command them."

The army's existence since 1940 has been something like that of an accordion—violent expansions and contractions accompanied by both stirring music and discordant noise. When World War II began in 1939, the Regular Army had been increased to almost 190,000 officers and men—still an inconsequential force by international standards, without a single combat-ready unit. Its weapons and equipment were largely those of World War I. In 1940 the National Guard and Organized Reserves were summoned for a year's active duty, and the Selective Service and Training Act authorized the first peacetime draft in American history. Even so, mobilization did not really get under way until the Japanese attack on Pearl Harbor in December 1941. Thereafter the army was rapidly increased. However, because of the need for manpower for an immensely expanded navy and for a war industry capable of supporting both our armed forces and those of our allies, its peak strength (reached in May 1945) was not quite 8,300,000.

In previous wars, most American soldiers had been combat troops who actively engaged the enemy. Now, out of that 8,300,000, some 2,400,000 men were required for the Army Air Forces; of these, only a small percentage actually participated in combat missions. Another 1,800,000 were assigned to noncombatant duties with the Army Service Forces, which was responsible for the procurement and distribution of supplies. Out of the remaining 4,100,000, barely 2,000,000 were actually ground combat troops—the balance included men undergoing training, replacements en route to the front, men in hospitals, or noncombatant ground forces such as medical or ordnance units.

The fighting man now was the sharp tip of a military iceberg: Infantrymen made up only 11 percent of the total army, including the Air Forces, yet they sustained 60 percent of its total battle casualties (approximately ten times as many as the Air Forces suffered). The army could field only eighty-nine divisions, consisting of five airborne, sixteen armored, one cavalry (serving dismounted), sixty-six infantry, and one mountain, and their supporting troops—a force that proved barely adequate. These divisions were roughly half the size of the World War I division but, even so, the army had great difficulty in keeping them filled up to strength.

Combat soldiers came in more varieties than ever. There were airmen of many types; tank troops and their associated "ar-

mored" infantry and artillery; airborne troops, both parachute and glider units; specially trained mountain troops; and tank destroyer formations. Rangers reappeared as separate battalions for such traditional ranger missions as long-distance raiding.

The training of a modern army was handicapped by equipment that was generally obsolescent, often obsolete, and always in short supply. The new weapons, vehicles, and airplanes that American industry was beginning to churn out went in large part as "Lend-Lease" to England, Russia, and China. Meanwhile, American soldiers trained with lengths of stovepipe to simulate trench mortars, with wooden-barreled cannon, and similar let's-pretend weapons.

Demobilization was swift—in some respects almost frantic—at the war's end. By December 1945 the army was down to 4,230,000; a year later, its strength was 1,320,000. In 1947 the Army Air Forces became a separate armed service, coequal with the army and navy. By mid-1948 the army numbered only 575,000.

Unlike the years following previous wars, however, the Regular Army did not go back to its normal stark and isolated existence. It remained much in the public eye, involved in the occupation and military governments of Germany, Austria, and Japan—a mission it handled with remarkable overall success, though with many minor blunders. Its senior generals were men of vast popularity and influence in American and international affairs. But the army also became the target of heavy criticism from people who had found it unkind during the war. There were demands that the army be rebuilt on democratic principles, that its "regimentation" and "caste system" be abolished, along with saluting and all other possible differences between officers and enlisted men.

Seeing no danger of another war in the near future, faced with the need of attracting more volunteer enlistments than ever before once the draft expired in 1947, and wanting to remain popular, the army high command gave in. Their "New Army" stressed athletics, education, and "learning a trade." Training standards were relaxed; any officer who insisted on realistic exercises that might occasionally get a man hurt was inviting trouble. Following the recommendations of various study groups, particularly the Doolittle Board of 1945–46, the authority of company officers and their NCOs was considerably reduced. In 1950, Congress replaced the stern old Articles of War with a more liberal Uniform Code of Military Justice, which put the army's courts-martial system firmly under civilian review, and threw out the traditional punishment—unconditional dismissal from the service—for officers convicted of "conduct unbecoming an officer and a gentleman." Somewhere along the way, too, the principle that soldiers must make up the "bad time" they spent hospitalized with venereal disease was dropped.

At the same time, these were years of professional uncertainty. The introduction of the atomic bomb in 1945 had convinced some people that the very nature of warfare had been changed and that there might well be no need for the ground soldier in the future. The army regularly came out a poor third in the division of an ever-tighter defense budget. For lack of funds, most infantry regiments lost one of their three battalions, and artillery battalions one of their three firing batteries. The army sought to work out new organizations, weapons, and tactics for nuclear warfare, but there was little money for new equipment. It accordingly lived off the dwindling leftovers from World War II, and could not match Russian progress in guns, armor, and missiles.

It was therefore a limp army that responded to the Communist invasion of South Korea in 1950. The regiments that went into Korea from occupation duty in

Japan were Regulars, with battle honors from many wars, but the recruits who filled their ranks were "New Army"—poorly trained, soft in body and mind from easy living. Also, they had neither effective antitank weapons nor reliable radios. Wilting in the blazing heat of a Korean summer, they abandoned their weapons and wounded in action; some of them behaved disgracefully in Communist prisoner-of-war camps. Other Americans of the same breed—but properly disciplined and led—fought the Communists into the ground for a victory of sorts in 1953.

The army increased to almost 1,700,000 men. After the war, because of the generally unstable world situation, it was kept at about 870,000. Congress enacted a Universal Military Training and Service Act in 1951, placing an obligation of eight years' military service—two years active, six (later five) in reserve status—on all men between 18½ and 26 years of age. This was subsequently extended until 1973; that year the army returned to voluntary enlistments.

During these years the army changed. The Coast Artillery ("In my cottage, by the sea, I shall sit and drink my tea, while the didies hang out on the line!") was abolished, along with its comfortable and sedentary life. Armor was made a permanent branch as a continuation of the cavalry; the Military Police and Transportation Corps likewise became permanent. New missiles, helicopters, and armored vehicles gave the army greater mobility and flexibility. The army developed its own Army Aviation for reconnaissance, evacuation of wounded, adjustment of artillery fire, courier flights, and similar short-range work; in 1965 the 1st Cavalry Division was made into an "airmobile" organization moving by helicopter. Consequently, the army needed more soldier mechanics, technicians, and pilots.

A series of big and small international crises—Lebanon in 1958, the Berlin blockade in 1961, the Cuban missile crisis in 1962, and the Dominican Republic in 1965—led to some increases in army strength and readiness. The growing utilization of guerrilla-type warfare in Communist-backed "wars of liberation" led President John F. Kennedy to beef up the Special Forces, which the army had begun organizing in the 1950s for irregular operations in any future war. Known by their special headgear as the "Green Berets," they were qualified paratroopers, linguists, and experts at guerrilla warfare and living off the countryside; they also were trained for underwater work and in medical techniques. When the decision was made in 1965 to commit Americans in strength to South Vietnam, the army was better prepared than in any previous wars.

Vietnam remains a frustration to American soldiers. Contrary to their usual fortune, they won their first battle. They also won every other major fight and almost all the small ones. But, even more so than in Korea, most of them never had much idea of why they were fighting. Prominent Americans loudly opposed their war; some openly praised their enemies. They came home unwelcomed. Veterans expressed it bitterly: "When I came back from World War II, everyone bought me a beer. When I got back from Korea, I had to buy my own. When I got back from Vietnam, everyone expected me to buy *them* a beer!"

THE GIs OF THE 1940s

The American "GI" of the 1940s came to Europe and Asia as a liberator and a conqueror. In World War I the AEF had been but one of several large Allied armies; now the U.S. Army provided the major ground and air forces on most of the war's fronts, and all our allies depended to a considerable extent on American supplies. The American soldier was fully conscious of his contribution. Once he had measured himself against the Wehrmacht's best, he went with a self-confidence that might have a tinge of arrogance; "free men who fear nothing on this earth" is how a Czech doctor described the 2nd Infantry Division in the war's last days.

The GI was better educated than the doughboy of World War I and knew something more of the world, superficial though much of his knowledge was. Foreign places and peoples seldom impressed him; he was apt to drive recklessly, without much concern for local pedestrians and to regard most "furriners" with reservation. (One of the odder little episodes of World War II was Gertrude Stein—longtime American expatriate and author—scolding a group of GIs for their standoffishness toward the French.) From most accounts, the major exception was the Dutch, with whom American soldiers got along famously.

The GI was open and unabashed in his off-duty pursuit of pleasure, causing Englishmen to remark that the trouble with Americans was that they were "overpaid, oversexed, and over here." This attitude could and did spill over into a quick grab for "a fast buck" by officers and enlisted men alike, adding a dirty fringe of looting, black marketing, and related malfeasances to the army's history through western Europe and Japan, and later in Korea and Vietnam. Infantrymen in the "death factory" of Hürtgen Forest in the bitter December of 1944 got few cigarettes because a rear-area railway battalion, possibly with the connivance of some of its officers, had diverted them by the carload to the Paris black market. Cold-weather clothing, urgently needed at the front, was purloined to keep noncombatants comfortable—and probably to help their egos by making them think that they looked like combat soldiers.

On the whole the World War II GI probably was less disciplined than the AEF's doughboy. There were exceptions—especially Patton's Third Army—where the old Pershing emphasis on military bearing and conduct still ruled. But he fought magnificently and endured greatly. Gen. John Lucas' tribute to him (see chapter opening) was well earned. He also had a certain common sense not always present in the highest levels of the army or the United States government.

With the war won, soldiers in Germany found themselves confronted by an official policy of nonfraternization, dreamed up in Washington and very popular in influential American media and intellectual circles. There were to be no personal relations whatever between American soldiers and the German population; in those areas of military government where a certain degree of association between Americans and Germans was necessary there must be separate facilities, including toilets. For the first time in known history, victorious soldiers in a conquered nation were to be held in monastic seclusion, forbidden to enjoy the company of pretty girls or to make friends with frightened small children. This asinine directive ignored the basic facts of life. When soldiers began ignoring it, the army soon gave up attempting to enforce it.

Soldier Morale

The soldier could count on the Red Cross for many small amenities; in particular, for help with personal matters and communications with his family. It was the only nonmilitary agency allowed to operated overseas with the army during World War II—selected because of its international character and experience in working with the military. In addition, there was the United Service Organizations (better known by its initials, USO), which secured the services of a wide variety of actors and actresses, from top stars to young hopefuls, to entertain the troops in the United States and overseas. Some formed small mobile groups that gave pick-up shows at rest areas. Female singers were popular, but a good magician or comedian could really hold an audience. One of the original USO entertainers, Bob Hope, kept up the practice through Korea and Vietnam. There were USO "canteens" in towns adjacent to military bases and ports of embarkation where a soldier could get a snack, write a letter, dance, or pick up information, and small ones in many railroad stations. Some of this care and comfort still continue.

Some people (including Allied soldiers) thought the World War II GI was coddled with his candy and cigarette ration and his access (infrequent if he was in the average combat unit) to post exchange (PX) supplies. Possibly the American cigarette was the most envied item; once GIs learned that it could be bartered for practically anything it became a sort of international currency. The *Stars and Stripes* was revived as the soldiers' own newspaper; operating under very light control, it gave a number of senior officers heartburn, not always undeserved, and had an excellent cartoonist, Bill Mauldin with his "Willy and Joe." At the war's end, some of its issues went from the bratty to the semihysterical in urging the immediate demobilization of the army. There also was *Yank,* a weekly magazine, for which George Baker drew his "Sad Sack" strip. Opinions on its usefulness varied, but most soldiers liked its pin-ups.

The Korean War, which dragged on under miserable conditions and without the stimulus of hope for a clear-cut victory, required something more to help soldier morale. Every company had its little post exchange, selling everything from soft drinks and candy bars to cameras and radios. Something much better was "R & R"—the soldier's typical abbreviation of "Rest and Recreation"—which meant a five-day period in Japan to rest, get cleaned up, and see the sights. On the whole, it seems to have been reasonably decorous until the last of the war when only the front-line units were under heavy strain. Then the men going to Japan often had other things in mind, and R & R became "I & I"—"intercourse and intoxication."

In Vietnam there was the equivalent of R & R in adjacent countries. The army had its own television and radio stations; there was air conditioning in many of its bases along with refrigerators and hobby shops. It made the soldier's lot more comfortable, but maintaining that style of living diverted even more manpower away from the combat troops and into supply and service units.

The soldier's pay increased steadily. In 1940 a private received $21 a month for the first four months of his service, after which he drew $30. This rose to $50 in 1942, and to $75 in 1946. By 1972, as the army put more emphasis on voluntary enlistments, it was up to $286 a month, and more increases followed. Moreover, the soldier could draw additional "jump pay" if he served as a paratrooper, or "flying pay" if he became a member of an army aviation aircraft crew. Special qualification with his weapons brought him extra pay, as did promotion and length of service. There were generous bonuses for enlisting in the combat arms, bonuses for reenlisting, and increased rental allowances for married soldiers who had to live off-post because of the lack of sufficient quarters.

Similarly, the number of decorations and service medals multiplied. New decorations included the Legion of Merit, the Distinguished Flying Cross, the Soldiers Medal (given for acts of heroism not involving combat or "aerial flight"), the Bronze Star Medal, the Air Medal, the Commendation Ribbon, and the Purple Heart (given for a wound that "necessitates treatment by a medical officer"). A bronze "oakleaf cluster" on the ribbon of a decoration indicates that the wearer has won it on two occasions. A silver cluster is the equivalent of five bronze. The service medals included the major campaigns of World War II, with later ones for Korea and Vietnam, and miscellaneous issues such as the Women's Army Corps Service Medal, the World War II Victory Medal, and the Army of Occupation Medal. Battles and amphibious landings in which the wearer had participated were indicated by small bronze stars or arrowheads on the medal ribbons. Congress having again authorized the acceptance of foreign decorations, the chests of many American soldiers began to glow with ribbons of many colors. The soldiers had their own name for these displays—"fruit salad."

TODAY'S SOLDIERS

The life of today's soldier is very different. In his barracks the long rooms with their lines of cots and footlockers are being broken up into smaller ones with better furnishings and a degree of individuality in their decoration. Some single soldiers, wanting more privacy, obtain permission to rent apartments at their own expense in nearby towns rather than live in barracks. Various methods of allowing the soldier to express his individuality and to communicate freely with his superiors have been established. One, first tested at Fort Carson, Colorado, in 1970, is the "Enlisted Men's Council," a group of enlisted men selected by their peers who meet regularly with their commanding officer to discuss complaints and carry back information. There also are "Racial Harmony" councils for soothing friction among the army's different ethnic groups. The latest method is "Dial-a-Boss": If a soldier has a problem and has not been able to resolve it through normal channels (his company commander, the inspector general, the chaplain, or various aid programs), he can phone the senior commander of his post and leave a tape-recorded message. The commander will review it and initiate any necessary action. The only certain result is that the commander will have less spare time than ever.

MINORITY SOLDIERS

The black soldier's service in World War II began under the handicap of his comparatively poor showing in World War I. The Air Corps in particular was more than reluctant to accept blacks, especially for flying personnel. Training involved unexpected problems. Black units, especially those from northern states, were unwelcome in many southern areas, and there were occasions when black soldiers and their officers were victims of unprovoked assault by state or local police, even while on duty. (Also, some black units were exceptionally rowdy and undisciplined.) As in 1918, there was a shortage of suitable black officers and noncommissioned officers. ROTC graduates from Howard and Wilberforce universities were useful but far too few in number. A large proportion of black draftees was assigned to quartermaster, transportation corps, and engineer units, but others formed separate tank battalions, light bomber and fighter squadrons, and field artillery, tank destroyer, chemical corps, and military police units. The 9th and 10th Cavalry regiments, however, were inactivated and their personnel transferred to other units. The 92nd and 93rd Infantry divisions reappeared, the first serving in Italy, the second serving in the Pacific.

Initially, black troops made a favorable impression in England. In combat, their record was spotty. The 92nd Division which, on General Marshall's insistence "had been nursed and trained and strengthened more than any division we have," repeatedly came apart in action, its infantry literally dissolving each night, whether under fire or not, abandoning equipment and even clothing. The 93rd Division was largely employed as security and labor troops, but some of its units were involved in combat and performed satisfactorily. During the last months of the war the army experimented with attaching platoons of black volunteers to white infantry companies—a move that had considerable success.

Growing discontent among blacks after World War II affected the army's black units. In spite of the increasing number and higher rank of black officers, all-black units came to be regarded as another form of segregation and discrimination. Black units increasingly showed a sullen inferiority complex, and in Korea they were undependable. Consequently, with some reluctance, the army began the full application of President Harry S. Truman's 1948 executive order, decreeing equality of treatment for all members of the armed forces, by integrating black soldiers into white units. This adjustment is not yet perfect and will not be for years to come. Racial prejudices and resentments still exist; units with a large proportion of black recruits may be troubled by the formation of racial cliques and even racial clashes. In Vietnam it was notable that white and black soldiers might serve and fight efficiently together, but took their recreation separately.

Soldiers from another minority group, the Nisei (Americans of Japanese descent), served in another segregated unit—the 442nd Infantry Regiment. This was regarded as one of the outstanding American combat units of World War II.

In Korea, especially during the desperate days of 1950, skeletonized American units were hurriedly filled up with South Koreans, termed KATUSAs (Korean Augmentation United States Army). These were civilians, many of them refugees from areas overrun by the Communist invasion; they knew no English, had no training, and often were in poor physical condition. Most had to be used as stretcher bearers or ammunition carriers; few developed into useful combat soldiers.

The Philippine Scouts had passed from the army's strength in 1947, shortly after the Philippines became a fully independent nation. Their veterans who had been in the Scouts before World War II were allowed to claim American citizenship if they so desired. The army placed most of those who did in divisions stationed in the southern United States, but it was a "blue norther" winter in Texas and amazed ex-Scouts found themselves shoveling a strange, cold substance called "snow."

The army had had permanent women officers since the introduction of the Nurse Corps in 1901. World War II saw women enlist in large numbers to help meet the manpower shortage. This began with the formation of the Women's Army Auxiliary Corps (WAAC) in May 1942; in July 1943 this became a permanent part of the army and was renamed the Women's Army Corps (WAC). The WAC had the same pay and allowances as the rest of the army. It was organized into military units under its own officers for administrative and disciplinary purposes, and had its own separate barracks areas. Its individual members (known, naturally, as WACs) were detailed to noncombatant duties in various headquarters and installations. While most had some type of clerical, medical, or communications assignment, some were interpreters, meteorologists, cartographers, intelligence analysts, or air controllers.

OFFICERS

The "Old Army," in which officers and men often spent most of their service in a single regiment, is long gone. Officers especially are shifted every few years—to schools, to duty with the Organized Reserve or National Guard, to various boards and staffs. Enlisted men are almost as mobile. "This isn't a battalion," one officer groused. "It's a damn hotel." Under such conditions it is harder to build and main-

tain a sense of unit teamwork, pride, tradition, and morale.

With World War II, the Organized Reserve became the army's first source of extra officers. These "reservists," mostly graduates of the ROTC program, had kept up their training through correspondence courses, short tours of active duty when funds were available, or duty with the Civilian Conservation Corps. As a group,

resembling a moss-grown scouring pad. The quartermaster corps attempted to develop types of chocolate and butter that would not melt and run, even in the Southwest Pacific's heat. Unfortunately, these products also were issued to troops in Europe during the hard winter of 1944–45; nobody considered them recognizable substitutes for the real thing. Soldiers did speak kindly of the "Ten-in-One" ration—45 pounds of Field Ration B items, enough to give ten men 4,100 calories apiece for one day, along with a supply of cigarettes, water purification tablets, salt, matches, toilet paper, paper towels, and a can opener. Its items were all nonperishable and could be eaten either hot or cold.

The combat soldier, however, usually dined on C or K rations when he was in the line. The C ration consisted of six cans—three of meat and three of "biscuits," soluble coffee, and candy. Supposedly, the meat came in several tasty varieties, but most of the army fought most of the war on meat-and-vegetable hash and meat-and-vegetable stew, with pork and beans as a rare treat. It was edible but monotonous, not quite filling, and short of vitamins. The lighter K ration, packaged in a weatherproof box, was designed for paratroopers but issued to combat troops in general. It came in three general types—breakfast, dinner, and supper—and included cigarettes, chewing gum, water purification tablets, and toilet paper. The contents were fairly tasty, but not for prolonged consumption; the powdered lemonade and bouillon in, respectively, the dinner and supper packets were violent concoctions, designed for stainless-steel stomachs; the "meat" item for supper was processed cheese, which might have qualified as an appetizer but not as a main course.

For emergencies, when no other rations were available, each soldier was issued a D Bar Ration, an enriched chocolate-and-oat-flour bar, fortified with vitamin B_1—nourishing but practically impervious to the human tooth. These standard rations were supplemented periodically by extra distributions of candy and cigarettes, and sometimes beer. (To provide the last, the army took over several French breweries.)

The outstanding weakness of the C and K rations was that front-line troops normally had to eat them cold, even in bitter winter weather. Tank crews and truck drivers usually worked out some method of warming them on their vehicles' engines, but few infantrymen had any such opportunity. Englishmen and Germans, who did their best to feed their men at least one hot meal a day, usually accompanied by a comforting slug of hard liquor, considered such neglect of good fighting men a barbarous procedure. American soldiers remembered that German prisoners of war protested when they were fed C rations, refusing to believe that American soldiers ate such stuff regularly.

There was a liquor ration for American officers—usually two bottles a month of assorted alcoholic beverages procured from local sources or low-voltage wartime Scotch whiskey purchased in England—but none for enlisted men. This was grossly unfair; the fact that many officers shared their allowance with their men hardly provided a drop of moisture for the army's collective thirst. On occasion, there were fortunate captures of German depots of drinking liquor—achievements usually reported to higher headquarters only well after the fact. In static situations, American mechanical know-how could convert various bits of scrap into functioning stills; in Italy, such were used to convert wine or vermouth into a crude brandy that soldiers called "Kickapoo Joy Juice." Otherwise, soldiers bought what they could from local civilians, and some of it was dreadful stuff indeed. (Cynics made the peddler swallow a good swig of his stock before they closed the deal.)

The old peacetime company messes

gradually were replaced by centralized mess halls that feed whole battalions, using monthly master menus provided by far-away army nutritionists. There is no more KP duty for soldiers, hired civilians having taken over that drudgery. The average quantity, quality, and variety of their food is good though the overall system might prove musclebound. For example, the problem of providing an alternate meal for a Muslim visitor, when the official menu proclaimed pork, could completely confuse a 1950 consolidated mess officer's mental processes. A 1940 company mess sergeant would have grinned and produced a spare can of goldfish, suitably camouflaged, on five minutes' notice.

Combat rations during the Korean and Vietnam wars were an improved version of the old C ration. Profiting from World War II experience, however, there was an intensified effort to serve hot food, including the traditional Thanksgiving and Christmas turkey dinners with all the trimmings in the field. But in 1950, with Americans fighting desperately to keep from being driven completely off the Korean peninsula, certain virtuous American civilians suddenly became aware that the army's field rations now included beer. Outraged over this degradation of clean-living American boys, they demanded its abolition. There was speechifying in Congress, much of it undoubtedly tongue-in-cheek, but no one in the army high command had gumption enough to speak up against this minicrusade. So "virtue" triumphed and battered soldiers on steamy-hot Korean hillsides were told to be content with chlorinated water. One group of well-intentioned ladies did seek to supply them with fruit juice, but soon were shocked to learn that the ungrateful recipients of their bounty were converting it into home brew.

In Vietnam by 1967, approximately 93 percent of the meals served to soldiers in the field were hot and consisted primarily of fresh foodstuffs. Sometimes they included ice cream. Recently the army adopted a new type of ration—dehydrated foods in plastic packets—for troops in actual combat or on patrols where cooking is simply not possible.

Feeding the American soldier is no easy problem. More than ever, today's army is a mixture of different ethnic groups, each with its own dietary preferences. Moreover, the average American is accustomed to far more variety in his meals than was the case forty years ago, and also has developed a great fondness for "takeout" and "junk" foods. The army mess hall must deal with these preferences (periodic surveys attempt to determine which foods are the most popular), and in the process, it must feed the soldier a nutritious, balanced diet. Today, the American soldier is probably the best fed in all the world's armies. Nevertheless, in keeping with American military tradition, he continues to find fault with his rations.

Medical Care

Medical attention continued to improve during World War II. Vaccination and a formidable series of "shots" protected the soldier against all common diseases and some uncommon ones. Water supply points furnished chlorinated water. Outbreaks of disease in surrounding civilian populations were checked—as in Naples in 1943 when a typhus epidemic was stopped by delousing all civilians with DDT. The shortage of quinine (caused by the Japanese seizure of the Dutch East Indies, its chief source) was met by the development of a synthetic drug, Atabrine, which was just as effective, though it could give the skin a yellow tint. Other new drugs were equally important; penicillin was highly effective against venereal diseases as were the sulfa drugs in the treatment of wounds and injuries.

In combat, the emphasis was on quick

emergency treatment and the prompt evacuation of the seriously wounded to a hospital. The latter proved extremely difficult in the twisted Korean hills, but this problem was solved by using helicopters to lift the wounded, a technique further improved and employed in Vietnam. This ability to rush the seriously wounded to the rear, often in a matter of minutes, combined with progress in surgical techniques and the use of blood plasma to counteract shock, saved thousands of lives.

Veterans of World War I felt that American soldiers of the 1940s were more likely to succumb to that state of scrambled nerves known as shell shock or combat fatigue than soldiers of 1917–18. In part, this may have been the result of the increased understanding of psychiatric afflictions since World War I, and the consequent greater readiness of medical officers to detect and accept such disabilities. Unfortunately, malingerers and deadbeats found it relatively easy to fake the appropriate symptoms. Some dedicated officers, like Patton, considered most cases of combat fatigue tantamount to plain cowardice; probably a majority of American soldiers were in general agreement. Still, even Patton agreed that the best soldiers might be worn down by continuous combat. Most units worked out a system of pulling such soldiers back out of line for two or three days of sleep, hot food, and cleaning up.

Peacetime medical care is generally thorough for soldiers, but, because of a continuing shortage of army doctors, in some areas it is less than satisfactory for their families or for retired military personnel, creating definite morale problems.

Uniforms

The army's uniforms changed, too. New types of clothing were required for armored, airborne, and aviation personnel and for a wide variety of climatic conditions. Breeches were replaced by trousers, and officers discarded their Sam Browne belts and riding boots. The campaign hat was discontinued as inconvenient to wear in motor vehicles. Low "combat boots" (naturally, the paratroopers had a special model) were issued in place of the canvas leggings. During World War II the short "Ike" jacket was worn in both olive drab and officers' "green" in place of the blouse. (Its prompt abolition after the war was attributed to the fact that it was not becoming to plump "chairborne" officers.)

During the late 1950s the olive drab uniform was replaced by one of "army green," which now comes in summer and winter weights. This green uniform is identical for officers and enlisted men; the former are distinguished by black braid stripes on their trousers and cuffs, and a different cap ornament. With this changeover in the shade of its uniform, the army also changed the color of its leather from brown to black. Service in Korea led to the development of special cold-weather "shoe-pacs" (also called "Mickey Mouse Boots"); Vietnam required mildew-resistant, hot-weather "jungle boots."

A lightweight olive green uniform is worn for warm-weather fatigue and field duty; "camouflage" pattern clothing is also issued for the latter. Certain minor distinctions exist: Military Police are distinguished by their white cap covers or white-painted helmets; the Special Forces have their green berets; and drill sergeants in army training centers have resumed the campaign hat. Honor guard units and army bands have special blue dress uniforms. Some units adopted special headgear or scarves while serving in Vietnam. Officers of armored cavalry units wear spurs with their full-dress blue uniform. Recently, the secretary of the army ordered some of these unit distinctions discontinued. Such things, however, tend to continue, with or without official approval.

Morning over Fort Missoula in the clear gold and pine green Montana mountains in early summer. Opened in 1877 to watch Hell Gate Canyon while Chief Joseph's band of Nez Percé were on the war trail, kept in existence ever since to pacify Montana politicians, the fort has been a quiet, shabby-genteel battalion post. A trout stream runs behind the bachelor officers' quarters, and deer come down to graze in safety on the parade ground when snow falls deep in the peaks behind it. (Some socially ambitious army families do regard an assignment to Missoula as exile to "Siberia.") Now its neat, old-fashioned quadrangle of barracks, married quarters, warehouses, and workshops is unwontedly cluttered with boxed organizational property and crated household goods. Trucks come and go, the buildings are emptying. Half the world away eastward, Hitler's *Blitzkrieg* has ground across France; in America the army has begun to concentrate its scattered regiments. Fort Missoula's resident infantry battalion is moving out, leaving the place to a few caretakers and the officer candidates of the annual Citizens' Military Training Camp. Preparations move easily; another "permanent change of station" is nothing new to Regulars or their families. Moreover, there aren't many families. Most of the enlisted men and a good many of the junior officers are bachelors. There aren't many household goods. A life of frequent moves has taught army people to travel light. The battalion will go in the old style: enlisted men in tourist sleepers, field ranges set up in sandboxes in box cars quickly modified for use as traveling kitchens, a few Pullman cars for families. The only moderately flurried individual is the post quartermaster—his responsibilities include a dozen-odd dogs, many of them mutually incompatible, and one aging and contrary Shetland pony.

They go without excitement or wasted motion, trim in fitted uniforms, faces impassive under their bone-deep tan, individual equipment in perfect order. The adjacent city of Missoula ignores their going. At the station a small draggle of tawdry, overperfumed women watch almost silently; one or two are crying. An anguished local Shylock scurries along the platform from coach to coach, clutching a cigar box filled with loose money and a bundle of IOUs.

The locomotive's whistle suddenly blasts echoes from the mountains; the train creaks, groans, gathers itself into smooth movement. A few loud good-byes, waving hands and handkerchiefs, and the train dwindles down the tracks. The Regulars are gone, and will not be returning.

208. The American soldier, 1945. Somewhere in Germany in early 1945, a major from an infantry regiment of the 5th Infantry Division, followed by his radio man, passes halted M4 Sherman tanks of the 37th Tank Battalion, 4th Armored Division. The dismounted tanker with a Thompson submachine gun at the left is about to scramble up the ridge behind him to act as a sentinel.

209a and 209b. A military career. If he were capable and hard working, the American citizen turned soldier could achieve a successful military career. As one example among thousands, in 1927 the young Ohio National Guard artilleryman on the right in the photo above was a sergeant. In 1945, as a battle-proved lieutenant colonel commanding a 240mm howitzer battalion (in the photo at right), he congratulates one of his lieutenants who has just received the Air Medal. (The peculiarly textured background is a camouflage net covering one of the big howitzers.)

210. The end of the army horse. Suddenly, the American army became motorized and mechanized. Its proud cavalry regiments were converted to armored units or infantry, or broken up. (There are still veterans who feel that something vital went out of soldiering with them.) In July 1941, troopers of the 1st Cavalry Division watered their horses at a Texas railroad siding with water pumped from tank cars; other units at the right rear waited their turn. Later, the army would find cavalry reconnaissance units useful in the Italian mountains, and thousands of pack animals were necessary in both Italy and Burma. Soldiers who could ride, handle mules, or serve as horseshoers, saddlers, and packers were needed once again.

211. The M5 light tank. The speed and ruggedness of the M5 is shown at the Indio (California) Desert Training Center. It was an excellent vehicle but its 37mm gun was ineffective against German panzers.

212. Horse artillery. The artillery had prided itself on its horse mastery since at least 1838. A 3rd Field Artillery Regiment reel cart lays telephone wire across country during 2nd Cavalry Division maneuvers in March 1942.

213. Armored field artillery. A unit conducts a demonstration at Fort Sill with its M7 "motor carriages" mounting 105mm howitzers.

214. The K-9 Corps. World War II's new breeds of soldier included dog handlers of the K-9 Corps. The corps trained 10,526 dogs, most of which went overseas; 2,290 were killed in action.

215. Machine Records Unit. The technicians of this unit maintained up-to-date personnel returns, giving commanders current information on their divisions' combat effectiveness.

216. Paratroopers. Tough paratroopers risked their necks in their daily training, then spearheaded major offensives. This illustration shows men of the 82nd Airborne Division taking part in a mass jump during a training demonstration for Department of Defense officials at Fort Bragg, North Carolina.

217. Mail call. For the average soldier, mail call was a big event. Successful Lotharios were showered with letters from anxious girls, but many lonesome boys never received a letter. There were wives who wrote only to heap their troubles and discontent on their soldier-husbands, while a single soldier could be stunned by a "Dear John" missive from a girlfriend, announcing that she had found someone new. In this mail call in an artillery unit, note that the censor has blocked out the division shoulder patches.

218. Chow call. Every outfit had its "chow hound," who was first in the mess line. Here a jeep's hood makes a handy dining table. The fatigue hat worn by the soldier gave him the look of a wilted mushroom; it was very unpopular.

219. "Beer and Ballads." Soldiers' off-duty relaxations were generally those of young men away from home. Good liquor seldom was plentiful, even in the United States, as World War II lengthened; and the army had surprisingly few songs of its own. Hollywood and Broadway cranked out many tunes; some were excellent but all were somehow untouched by military realities. Soldiers adopted the English "Bless 'Em All" and "I've Got Sixpence," and the German "Lili Marlene." Their own training camps inspired "Sound Off"; "Dog-Face Soldier" and "Roger Young" came later, out of foreign service and combat.

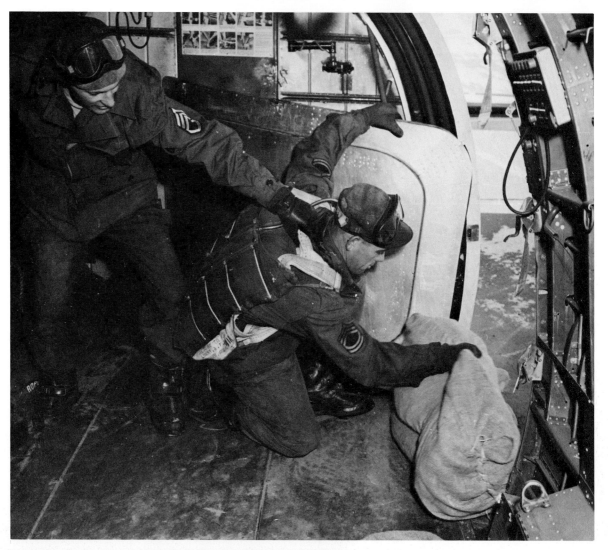

224. After the war. A time of change for the American soldier followed World War II. The Army Air Force became the coequal U.S. Air Force, though it continued some of its former missions, such as dropping feed cakes to cattle isolated by a Dakota blizzard.

225. Nuclear war. Nuclear weapons required extensive tests and new doctrine. Soldiers of the 31st Infantry Division watch a nuclear explosion at the Nevada Proving Grounds.

226. Carrying cargo. Methods of moving heavy equipment by air were improved after the war. Here 82nd Airborne Division soldiers maneuver a small bulldozer aboard an Air Force C-82 cargo plane.

227. The Korean War. The savage, frequently short-range hill fighting in Korea meant heavy casualties in the front-line units, jamming the forward aid stations with wounded soldiers. Here, the soldier in the foreground is receiving blood plasma. A chaplain kneels in prayer behind him, as medics labor over other patients.

228. At the forward lines. Exhausted survivors of a unit that took and held its objective catch their breath. "Oh they've got no time for glory in the infantry, Oh they've got no use for praises loudly sung. . . ."

229. The American soldier in Korea. Once the Korean front was stabilized in mid-1951, reserve units could live in some comfort. Two 25th Infantry Division soldiers, carrying Korean "A-frames" loaded with straw matting and sections of stovepipe to make their bunkers more comfortable, trudge past abandoned rice paddies. Their rifles are the Garand caliber .30 semiautomatic, which the army had adopted in 1940—a sturdy, reliable weapon, not as accurate as the Springfield '03, but able to fire its eight-round clip in 20 seconds.

230. Adopting a friend. With the soldier's traditional fondness for pets, this 2nd Infantry Division soldier has adopted an orphan fawn. More important, American soldiers and marines established and supported orphanages and schools for South Korean children.

232. West Point summer camp. A sergeant from the 101st Airborne Division, on temporary summer camp duty at the Military Academy, trains cadets on the new M108 105mm howitzer.

231. U.S. Military Academy Band. The efficiency of the U.S. Military Academy depends in good part on the enlisted soldiers assigned there to guard the post, operate its utilities, and assist in the cadets' practical military instruction. Above, the drum major of the U.S. Military Academy Band—formed in 1813 and the oldest one in the army—checks his ranks just before evening parade. His broad baldric with its miniature drum sticks is a drum major's traditional insignia.

233. The jungles of Vietnam. Vietnam was an uncomfortable place for a war—jungle, swamp, muddy rivers, and mountains, insects, humid heat, and an average of 6 feet of monsoon rains. Keeping soldiers healthy and effective under such conditions was a major feat. Two men from the 9th Infantry Division struggle out of a bog hole.

234. Getting some sleep. Flooded out of his sandbagged emplacement, a soldier proves that a veteran can sleep anywhere, anytime he gets the chance.

235. Riding shotgun. Men of the 1st Cavalry Division ride shotgun on a small river gunboat during a patrol in Vietnam.

239. The USO show. The big USO shows did not come around very often or go very deep into the combat zones. But small groups like the Philippine Troupe shown entertaining soldiers of the 9th Infantry Division were always welcome.

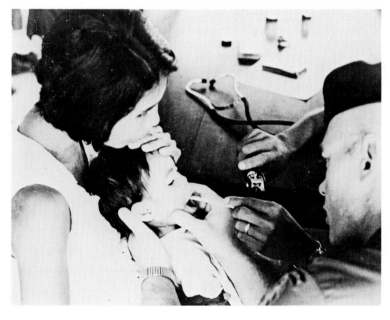

240. Medical help for civilians. Out in the wild frontier hill country of Vietnam, Green Berets of the U.S. Special Forces made themselves welcome among the small Montagnard tribes by offering modern medical and veterinary services. The medic checking the child's throat is from the 8th Special Forces Group.

241. Soldiers at sea. Special Forces' soldiers master many forms of warfare. A detachment prepares to transfer from a landing craft to a submarine that will land them after dark on a debatable beach.

242. Training irregulars. In Vietnam, one specialty of the Special Forces was the organization of irregular forces to block the enemy's supply routes. Here a sergeant trains Montagnard recruits—small, but effective fighters—to use M16 rifles.

243. Protest. Antiwar protests in the United States culminated in October 1967 in the "siege" of the Pentagon. Soldiers of the 503rd Military Police Battalion—one of the units that met obscenities, brandished Vietcong flags, spitting demonstrators, and thrown rocks and garbage with restraint and firmness—march across the Pentagon grounds after the last demonstrators were removed.

10

Soldiers of Tomorrow

New men, new weapons bear the brunt.
New slogans gild the ancient game.
The Infantry is still in front.
The mud and dust are much the same.

The army prefers its recruits at least eighteen years old, with a high school diploma. It may, under certain circumstances, accept seventeen-year-olds, and the diploma is not essential. All recruits must pass an English-language "selection test." Enlistments are for three years' service. Qualifications may be eased or raised, depending on the number of recruits needed and available. Usually the army has difficulty securing enough qualified personnel. As Thomas Jefferson said early in the nineteenth century, Regulars "are not to be had among a people so easy and happy at home as ours." Young Americans are restless, impatient of restraint and regimentation. Consequently, Congress and the armed forces periodically consider the revival of selective service in some form, to bring the Regulars up to their full strength of approximately 774,000 and especially to rebuild the Organized Reserve.

Today's American soldier is an expensive article. A private's pay on enlisting is $501.30 a month, plus his food, housing, uniforms, and medical and dental care. If he meets the required standards of training, his pay goes up to $558.60. When he has completed basic training (which is the same for all recruits), he goes into advanced training or special schooling for the specific combat arm or service of his choice. This satisfactorily finished, if he enlisted in the infantry, armor, or artillery he then is entitled to an enlistment bonus, ranging from $1,000 to $3,000. He is assigned to a unit, either in the continental United States, Alaska, Hawaii, Europe, or Korea. When possible, the army tries to assign him to the unit and place he desires.

In his unit he has the opportunity to be trained in one of several hundred types of professional skills. If he has the ambition to earn college credits in his spare time, the army will pay up to three-fourths of the tuition for approved courses. If he wants to put money aside regularly for further education, he can utilize the Veterans' Educational Assistance Program (VEAP); under its provisions the army will add double his contribution up to a total of $8,100.

A married soldier receives a monthly housing allowance (from ($179.70 to $322.50, depending on his grade); those serving abroad in high-cost countries also get a special monthly cost-of-living allowance that may amount to over $200 and is periodically adjusted. (It must be noted that the figures given above are those of mid-1981: They are liable to change, but any change will be an increase.)

Finally, the soldier has thirty days' leave with full pay every year. Practically all military posts have excellent sports facilities, clubs, theaters, libraries, commissaries, and post exchanges—the last including gas stations, snack bars, and various useful concessions. In Europe, there are a number of army-run resort areas for soldiers and their families. The USO still helps.

There are few better prospects for an eighteen-year-old with limited education and no special skills or talents.

THE MODERN SOLDIER—MALE AND FEMALE

Whether Regular, National Guard, or Reserve, today the American soldier is increasingly likely to be a woman. In 1981 the Regular Army had approximately 69,000 enlisted women and women officers, more than 8 percent of its total strength. There were plans to increase this to 11 percent by 1983, but those are now under review. The Women's Army Corps has been abolished, and women now serve as members of all the army's different branches, "except in battalion-size and smaller units of infantry, armor, cannon field artillery, combat engineer, low-altitude air defense artillery, and other direct combat-related specialties." These, however, constitute only 34 of the army's 636 different jobs.

One reason for this growing proportion of women was the army's shortage of suitable male recruits. Originally, women had to be high school graduates to enlist, but their entrance requirements have been steadily reduced because too few women volunteers could meet them.

Women soldiers live, train, and work with the unit to which they are assigned. Except for a degree of privacy in their quarters, there is no official difference between their lot and that of the men in the same outfit. In practical application, however, their comparative lack of physical strength restricts the types of training and work that most of them can handle.

Also, there is the sticky problem of male/female social relationships off duty. If an officer dates an "enlisted person" of the opposite sex, any promotion the latter receives will be viewed with vast suspicion by the unpromoted. And how does a male captain deal with an unsatisfactory female lieutenant who is the romantic interest of his battalion commander?

Marriages between military men and women add other problems when the wife remains on active duty. The army tries to keep such couples together, but that is not always possible. If they have children, one of them may not be available in emergencies. The "single parent," either male or female, who is responsible for a child's care is a similar difficulty, as is the "pregnant soldier," married or unmarried.

Above all is the uneasy question of whether women actually will be used in combat. No current law specifically forbids their employment there, but the whole idea runs head-on against the traditional Western/Christian ethos, with notions ranging from a man's lighting a lady's cigarette and opening doors for her to the code of "women and children" first on a sinking ship. There is no historical example of the successful employment of mixed-sex military units in sustained combat, just as there is no reason to believe that healthy young male and female soldiers can work in close contact and share the same foxholes without experiencing emotions other than the stern call of duty. There will be no easy solution.

American military families overseas—especially those living in rented private housing—have faced increasingly hard times as the value of the U.S. dollar has dropped during recent years. In 1980 a dollar wouldn't buy a cup of coffee in the average German restaurant. Looking after its own, the army has opened its mess halls to soldiers' wives and children, arranged shuttle bus runs to get them there, and scraped up money for extra allowances.

The modern army is reflected in changes at the U.S. Military Academy. It now is coeducational. Although attendance at Sunday religious services is no longer compulsory, a course on philosophy, which stresses ethics, is. The instructional system has been revamped to make it less competitive. There will be no more "goats"—the cadet with the lowest standing in each graduating class who, by tradition, received a dollar apiece from his classmates. A recent superintendent even decreed a reduction in military instruction. Fortunately, public and service disapproval forced its restoration.

The night wind comes down out of Siberia, over Manchuria and the Yalu River, across the wilderness of the Demilitarized Zone. It blows through the young pine woods, the thickets of wild plum, the tall grasses that cover collapsed bunkers and gullied roadways along lonely ridges that once had famous names—Heartbreak, Bloody, The Hook, Pork Chop, Arrowhead, and White Horse Mountain.

The sentry leans on the outpost's sandbagged parapet and peers into the wind and the night. There is live ammunition in his rifle's magazine, for the Korean War has never ended. There is only a cease-fire—a fragile truce that the Communists began violating before the ink of their signatures to it was dry. Through the years since then, Americans have died suddenly in Korea, truce or no.

Nothing moves in the starlit dark but the flowing wind. The Demilitarized Zone—"DMZ" to soldiers who watch its southern border—is 4 kilometers wide, all across the Korean peninsula. Wildlife flourishes in its empty reaches—even the great Siberian tiger, some say. But deadlier things than tigers may run those empty ridges in the night. And tonight something nags the sentry's senses—something just beyond perception.

"This," he thinks, "is the way they'll come when they do come—straight south down the old Uijongbu gap toward Seoul. We'll be ass-deep in North Joes [North Koreans] before anyone back home remembers we're still here. They're mean little bastards too—I knew one of the men they chopped to death there at Panmunjom when we wanted a tree trimmed. How they get away with that stuff all the time I'll never . . ."

The explosion had been very faint, maybe a couple of kilometers away—but there is a vibration through the soles of his boots and the sandbags against his chest. Wind ruffles the grass out beyond the barbed wire while he strains to listen. Another muffled-down thud comes, and the tremor through the earth, on the same general bearing. The sentry reaches for the telphone. "Sounds like the North Joes are building themselves another cute little tunnel under the DMZ." The north wind carries the smell of wild plum and forsythia blooms as it flows around the outpost and on across the hills to the Yellow Sea.

244. Charcoal-broiled. A soldier of the 1st Armored Division has charcoal-broiled hamburgers for lunch during maneuvers. Instead of the traditional mess kit and canteen cup, he eats from a compartmented tray and paper cup carried in his company's field kitchen.

245. Recruiting. To attract recruits today, posters stress military qualities such as leadership, as well as the chance to learn a trade or complete education.

246. The C-5 Galaxy. New air force cargo planes, such as this C-5 Galaxy, can "airlift" army forces vast distances. With fifty soldiers plus equipment weighing 256,000 pounds aboard, the C-5 can fly more than 2,900 miles nonstop.

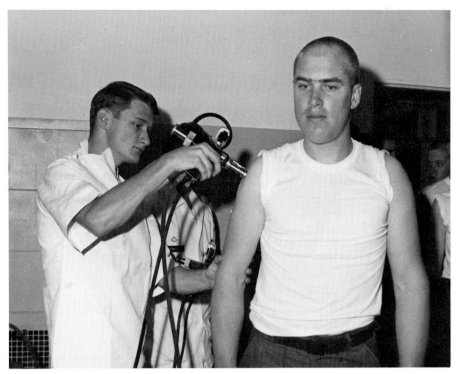

247. A shot in the arm. The soldier still gets his "shots" (inoculations) for typhoid and other communicable diseases, but the old-style hypodermic needle has been replaced by a fast, relatively painless pneumatic "gun." Waiting in line for your shots, however, is no more pleasant than it ever was.

248. Women's barracks. For greater privacy in this older-style barracks, used by women basic trainees at Fort McClellan, Alabama, wall lockers have been placed to form two-bunk compartments. Note the precise uniformity and spotlessness.

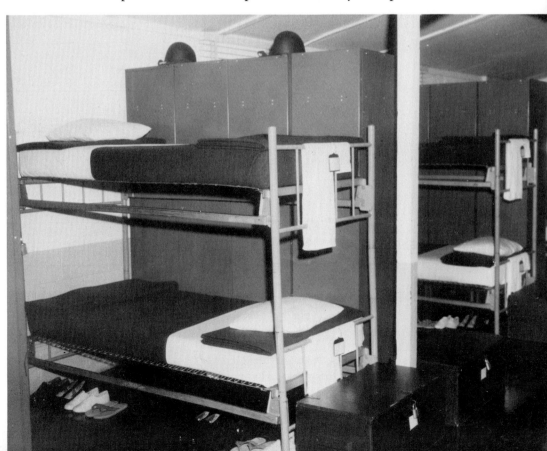

249. New weapons. Artillerymen have new weapons to master as improved guided missiles replace earlier models. Here, soldiers prepare a "Lance" surface-to-surface tactical missile for a field test.

250. Time for coffee. Soldiers of the 197th Infantry Brigade relax with a cup of coffee after a meal at Fort Benning, Georgia. Light plastic-ware cups have replaced the former massive white china mugs because, according to some Old Army sergeants, the modern VOLAR (Volunteer Army) soldier isn't man enough to lift one of them!

251. The "slide for life." Knee-deep in water, a West Point cadet stands at attention after completing the "slide for life." He has dropped from a trolley (as the cadet behind him is about to do) into the lake and then swum ashore. Cadet summer camps emphasize weapons and survival training and small-unit tactics.

252. Policing the area. Women soldiers do their share of all duties for which they have the necessary physical strength, such as the time-honored army detail of policing up the area.

253. Reception Day at West Point. A newly arrived Plebe reports to a cadet officer on Reception Day at West Point.

254. Today's army mule. The last of the World War II army mules, Wind River, died at Camp Carson, Colorado, in 1978, aged forty-six. The remaining representatives of his kind are the official mascots of the U.S. Military Academy. One of these, Buckshot, appears here in full ceremonial regalia, ready for a half-time show at a football game.

255. Stressing the practical. A sergeant instructor at the Armored School at Fort Knox, Kentucky, shows two officer students how to charge a tank's damaged bogie wheel when no jacks, lifts, or other heavy maintenance equipment are available. In this "field expedient," the tank is hung up between the banks of a dry creek, allowing its suspension system to hang loosely.

258. Continental Color Guard. Because of its mission as the army's official ceremonial unit, the 3rd Infantry has several special features. Its Continental Color Guard dresses in replicas of the 1784 infantry uniform—blue coats with red facings and white waistcoats and overalls. The central flag, between the National Color and the regiment's Color, is the U.S. Army flag—a top-heavy load for a strong soldier with its one hundred sixty-five battle streamers, representing every major action in which the army has participated. (The 3rd took part in fifty of these.)

259. Fife and Drum Corps. The 3rd Infantry's Fife and Drum Corps wears the uniform of the Color Guard, but in the reversed colors—red coats with blue facings—typical of early army musicians.

260. Burial at Arlington. Military funerals of deceased soldiers at Arlington National Cemetery require burial parties from the 3rd Infantry—a detail to handle the casket, a firing party, and a bugler to sound *Taps*. Meticulously trained, they serve with quiet dignity and sympathy. The 3rd Infantry is also a combat unit, responsible for the security of the capital during national emergencies and civil disturbances. Its army name—"The Old Guard"—was bestowed by General Scott for its valor and efficiency in Mexico.

261. The Caisson Platoon. The army's only remaining mounted unit, the Caisson Platoon participates in all Arlington funerals, whatever the deceased's branch of service. It has two sections, one with black horses, one with light grays, normally used on alternate weeks. The duty section normally averages two funerals a day.

262. Training with the British. Pennsylvania National Guard infantrymen train in England with a Territorial unit, their British equivalent. Emphasis was on familiarization with British weapons and combat problems.

263. Disasters. In natural disasters America depends on its armed forces, particularly its National Guard—supplemented, if necessary, by Reserve and Regular Army units. Here Tennessee Guardsmen battle a Memphis grain elevator blaze during a firemen's strike.

264. Civil disturbance. Pennsylvania Guardsmen maintain order after Pittsburgh riots in 1968, making some young friends in the process.

265. Brushfire. A Guardsman works on a fire break during a California brushfire. Other members of his unit, the 149th Armored Regiment, hauled supplies and equipment to firefighters.

266. Blizzard. A Delaware Army National Guard crewman guides travelers to his helicopter for evacuation after a blizzard in early 1978. Tanks were used to tow stalled trucks through drifts that blocked the highways.

267. The Berlin Wall. Today, as throughout American history, the soldier serves the United States on lonely and hazardous frontiers. Two East German border guards, in their Russian-style uniforms, peer over the Berlin Wall into the American zone, where an isolated garrison maintains a tiny island of freedom. The cross in the foreground is a memorial to a young East Berliner killed while trying to escape.

268. Still in Korea. The tunnel on the left was dug under the Demilitarized Zone by the North Koreans, in complete violation of the 1953 Korean armistice. On the right is a countertunnel constructed to intercept the North Korean tunnel.

269. The Unknown Soldier. Day and night, in all weather, a soldier of the Old Guard's picked Tomb Sentinels paces his round before the simple memorial to the Unknown Soldier of World War I and the graves of the Unknown Soldiers of World War II and Korea that flank it—a comrade's tribute to their courage and self-sacrifice.

HERE RESTS IN
HONORED GLORY
AN AMERICAN
SOLDIER
KNOWN BUT TO GOD

Picture Credits

The following abbreviations are used for sources cited most frequently.

AAH	*Album of American History*, published by Charles Scribner's Sons
ABM	Anne S. R. Brown Military Collection, Brown University Library
AIO	U.S. Army Information Office, West Point, N.Y.
ANF	Army News Features
CSS	Charles Scribner's Sons
JRE	John R. Elting Collection
MHR	U.S. Army Military History Research Collection
NA	National Archives
OGM	Old Guard Museum, Fort Myer, Va.
USA	U.S. Army photograph
WPM	West Point Museum Collections

1. Painting by Gary Zaboly, 1978.
2. AAH, I, 352.
3. Hexham, *Principles of the Art Military*, 1637. Property of the New York Public Library Collection.
4. Hexham, *Principles of the Art Military*, 1637. Yale University Library.
5. Drawings by Jacques Le Moyne in De Bry, *Grands Voyages*, 1592.
6. Engraving by F. O. C. Darley.
7. Carnet de la Sabretache, 1897. JRE.
8. From the Collections of Old Sturbridge Village, Sturbridge, Mass. JRE.
9. Frick Art Reference Library. JRE.
10. William H. Guthman. JRE.
11a and 11b. Paintings by H. Charles McBarron, *The American Soldier* series, Army Historical Program.

12. Courtesy of the New-York Historical Society.
13. JRE.
14. By Baron von Clausen, 2nd Regt. R. I. (?) ABM.
15. Believed to be from various engravings made by Daniel N. Chodowiecki for the *Allgeimeines historisches Taschen buch . . . fur 1784.* ABM.
16. ABM.
17. Ibid.
18. Ibid.
19. Ibid.
20. Reprinted from *The Book of the Continental Soldier*, by Harold L. Peterson, Stackpole Books, 1968, Harrisburg, Pa. From the collection of the late Harold L. Peterson.
21. JRE.
22. *Merry Christmas*, painting by H. Charles McBarron. WPM.
23. *In the Trenches Before Yorktown—Washington Inspecting the French Batteries*, drawn by Rufus F. Zogbaum. ABM.
24. Painting by G. A. Roth. WPM.
25. ABM.
26. WPM.
27. New York Public Library.
28. *Washington Crossing the Delaware* by Emmanuel Leutze. Courtesy of the Metropolitan Museum of Art.
29. WPM.
30. ABM.
31. Painting by H. Charles McBarron, *The American Soldier* series, Army Historical Program. JRE.
32. Carse, *The River Men.* *KSD American Pioneer, I, frontis. Chillicothe, 1842. Rare Book Division, New York Public Library, Astor, Lenox, and Tilden Foundations.
33. Painting by H. Charles McBarron. JRE.
34. From an original painting in possession of Chicago Historical Society; a soldier in Wayne's army was credited. Chicago Historical Society. Property of the New York Public Library Picture Collection.
35. JRE.
36. Montana Historical Society, Helena. JRE.
37. Painting by H. Charles McBarron. JRE.
38. Fort Adams State Park.
39. ABM.
40. Public Archives Canada, Ottawa, C-25697. JRE.

41. From *History of the U.S. Navy.* CSS.
42. WPM.
43. Painting by H. Charles McBarron. JRE.
44. Stokes Collection, New York Public Library. Property of the New York Public Library Picture Collection.
45. From Edwin James, *Account of an Expedition from Pittsburgh to the Rocky Mountains Performed in the Years 1819, 1820* (1823).
46. Painting by Samuel Seymour. From Edwin James, *Account of an Expedition from Pittsburgh to the Rocky Mountains Performed in the Years 1819, 1820* (1823).
47. WPM.
48. Ibid.
49. ABM.
50. Artist unknown. WPM.
51. WPM.
52. Ibid.
53. Painting by H. Charles McBarron, *The American Soldier* series, Army Historical Program. JRE.
54. *The Army on the March in the Valley of Mexico* by James Walker. WPM.
55. Painting by H. Charles McBarron. JRE.
56. Portrait by Robert Weir. WPM.
57. ABM.
58. From *Recollections of a Rogue* by Samuel E. Chamberlain. WPM.
59. Ibid.
60. Ibid.
61. Ibid.
62. ABM.
63. Ibid.
64. From a sketch by J. G. Bruff. The Henry E. Huntington Library and Art Gallery, San Marino, Calif.
65. Howard Stansbury, *Exploration and Survey of the Valley of the Great Salt Lake of Utah in 1849–50.*
66. *Message for the President of the United States*, 1846. Abert's Journal in U.S. Engineer Bureau.
67. *The Camel Express—1857.* Courtesy of Bureau of Public Roads, Department of Commerce.
68a and 68b. *Second Half Hour* and *Last Half Hour!* by James McNeill Whistler. WPM.
69. From a picture in possession of 7th Regt., N.Y. N.G. CSS.
70. ABM.

71. Ibid.
72. WPM.
73. Ibid.
74. Eno Collection, the New York Public Library.
75. Painting by H. Charles McBarron, *The American Soldier* series, Army Historical Program. JRE.
76. WPM.
77. ABM.
78. From Billings, *Hard-Tack and Coffee.* CSS.
79. From the etching by Adalbert John Volck, "Confederate War Etchings," No. 7, in the Library of Congress. CSS.
80. WPM.
81. Ibid.
82. Reprinted with permission of Michael G. McAfee. JRE.
83. Frank M. Betz, photographer, 137 Santa Clara Ave., Dayton, Ohio. WPM.
84a, 84b, and 84c. "Detail from Co. C. Reported for Duty," "Teaching a Baltimore Secesh Manners," and "Our Guard Duty at Hamtion was very severe, some of us being on post all the time." WPM.
85. CSS.
86. From Freeman, *Lee's Lieutenants,* Arlington edition. Virginia Historical Society. Print from Dementi Studio.
87. WPM.
88. From Edwin Forbes, *Life Studies of the Great Army,* 1876. New York Public Library.
89. ABM.
90. Collection of Michael G. McAfee. JRE.
91. WPM.
92. ABM.
93. Ibid.
94. WPM.
95. Lithograph after Winslow Homer. WPM.
96. Photo embossed Signal Corps U.S. Army. CSS.
97. National Park Service Museum Lab copy negative of a Brady photograph. Property of the National Park Service.
98. WPM.
99. From the photograph taken by Brady in the Library of Congress.
100. "Capture of the forts at Hatteras inlet.—Fleet opening fire and boats landing through the surf, August 28, 1861. Boats of the fleet: Pawnee, Minnesota, Cumberland, Susquehanna, Harriet Lane, Wabash." From *Naval History of the Civil War* by David D. Porter.
101. Sketched by A. R. Ward. ABM.
102. WPM.
103. "Army of the James—Signaling by torches across James River from General Butler's Head-quarters.—Sketched by William Waud." ABM.
104. CSS.
105. Ibid.
106. The Collections of the Library of Congress.
107. *R. E. Lee,* IV. The Collections of the Library of Congress.
108. From *Harper's Weekly,* July 12, 1862, wood engraving. Prints Division, the New York Public Library, Astor, Lenox, and Tilden Foundations.
109. The Collections of the Library of Congress.
110. Ibid.
111. WPM.
112. "Pickets Fraternizing over Coffee and Exchanging Papers." Scenes In and About the Army of the Potomac—Sketched by A. R. Waud. ABM.
113. WPM.
114. Collection of Michael J. McAfee. WPM.
115. WPM.
116. Ibid.
117. Painting by H. Charles McBarron, *The American Soldier* series, Army Historical Program. JRE.
118. Original sketch by Col. Harry C. Larter, Jr. (?) Company of Military Historians.
119. NA.
120. William Walton, *Army and Navy of the United States.* USMA Library, West Point, N.Y.
121. Picture by Henry Alexander Ogden. WPM.
122. Woodcut cartoon by Thomas Nast, from *Harper's Weekly,* March 16, 1878. WPM.
123. Photo by A. F. Randall. NA.
124. NA.
125. Library of Congress.
126. Ibid.
127. ABM.
128. Photo by S. J. Morrow. NA.
129. Ibid.
130. ABM.
131. Leon Kelly Co., Columbia, MO.

132. Photo by Frank F. Currier. NA.
133. NA.
134. Photo by J. C. H. Grabill.
135. From *Settler's West.*
136. Photo by S. J. Morrow. NA.
137. Nebraska State Historical Society.
138. Photo by C. S. Fly. The Bureau of American Ethnology, Smithsonian Institution.
139. Kansas State Historical Society.
140. JRE.
141. Drawn by Otto Walter Beck. ABM.
142. By R. G. Zogbaum, *ca.* 1887. WPM.
143. Painting by H. Charles McBarron, *The American Soldier* series, Army Historical Program. JRE.
144. "First Lesson in the Art of War.—Recruits for the Two Additional Artillery Regiments at Fort Slocum, Davids Island, Long Island Sound." Drawn by Frederic Remington. ABM.
145. WPM.
146. JRE.
147. Ibid.
148. Tom McGuir. JRE.
149. Fort Huachuca Historical Museum.
150. ABM.
151. Ford Huachuca Historical Museum.
152. Ibid.
153. Ibid.
154. Ibid.
155. MHR.
156. Ibid.
157. Ibid.
158. Ibid.
159. By Frederic Remington. ABM.
160. CSS.
161. California Historical Society Library.
162. Ibid.
163. Carter Rila Collection. NA.
164. USA.
165. WPM.
166. Carter Rila Collection. NA.
167. National Archives Record Group III, Records of the Office of the Chief Signal Officer.
168. National Park Service photograph.
169. Ibid.
170. Ibid.
171. JRE. USA.
172. JRE.
173. Tom McGuir. JRE.
174. CSS.

175. Painting by H. Charles McBarron, *The American Soldier* series, Army Historical Program.
176. The Collections of the Library of Congress.
177. Postcard addressed to Mrs. W. H. Smith, Binghamton, N.Y., postmarked March 1, 1918, Brooklyn, N.Y., and signed "Louis."
178. JRE.
179. Photographed by F. W. Dresser, International Film, 80 Summer Street, Boston, Mass. CSS.
180. JRE.
181. Postcard produced by W. R. Thompson & Company, Publishers, Richmond, Va.
182. CSS.
183. Carter Rila Collection, U.S. Army Signal Corps. NA.
184. Photo by U.S. Army Signal Corps.
185. MHR.
186. USA.
187. MHR.
188. Ibid.
189. USA.
190. National War Work Council, YMCA of the United States.
191. Personal collection, Barry E. Thompson.
192. Ibid.
193. MHR.
194. WPM.
195. MHR.
196. Musée de l'armee, Paris, France, Service photographique. U.S. Signal Corps. JRE.
197. MHR.
198. JRE. Tom McGuir.
199. ANF.
200. JRE. Tom McGuir. USA.
201. JRE. USA.
202. USA.
203. Tom McGuir. USA. JRE.
204. Tom McGuir. U.S. Army Field Artillery and Fort Sill Museum, Fort Sill, Okla. JRE.
205. Tom McGuir. JRE.
206. Photograph by Richard H. Stewart. Copyright National Geographic Society.
207a and 207b. JRE.
208. Painting by H. Charles McBarron, *The American Soldier* series, Army Historical Program. JRE.
209a and 209b. JRE.
210. USA.

211. JRE. USA.
212. USA.
213. JRE. USA.
214. MHR.
215. Ibid.
216. USA.
217. MHR.
218. War Department, Public Relations Dept., Lowry Field, Denver, Colo.
219. WPM.
220. Ibid.
221. USA.
222. Defense Dept. photo (Marine Corps) SRW.
223. USA. OGM.
224. USA. Washington, D.C.
225. USA.
226. Fairchild Aircraft, Hagerstown, Md. Photo by Dan Frankfurter.
227. USA.
228. MHR.
229. Ibid.
230. Ibid.
231. Photo by PFC Levicoff. JRE. USA.
232. JRE. USA.
233. MHR.
234. United Press International photograph.
235. MHR.
236. Ibid.
237. Ibid.
238. Ibid.
239. Ibid.
240. 8th Special Forces Gp (Abn), Public Information Section, Fort Gulick, Canal Zone.
241. Army photo by SAFAsia.
242. Information Office, 5th SFGA.
243. Photo by SFC Martin Kendreck. USA.
244. Photo by David Marrquin. ANF.
245. WPM.
246. Newsbureau, Lockheed-Georgia Company, Marietta, Ga.
247. Photo by SSG James R. Powell. ANF.
248. Photo by Kavie Cole. ANF.
249. USA.
250. ANF.
251. USA. U.S. Military Academy.
252. USA. AIO.
253. Ibid.
254. Ibid.
255. USA. Patton Museum, Fort Knox, Ky.
256. Photo by Sp5 Craig Wellman. ANF.
257. USA. OGM.
258. Ibid.
259. Photo by Sp4 Steve Geary. Ibid.
260. USA. OGM.
261. Ibid.
262. National Guard Association of the United States.
263. Photo by David R. Crowell.
264. Photo by WO Arthur Kramer, PARNG.
265. National Guard Association of the United States.
266. Delaware Army National Guard.
267. ANF.
268. United Nations Command photograph.
269. USA. OGM.

Notes

CHAPTER 1.
The Colonial Soldier

1. J. S. McLennan, *Louisbourg* (Sidney, N. S.: Fortress Press, 1969), p. 241.
2. Ibid., p. 152.
3. S. McC. Pargellis, *Lord Loudoun in North America* (New York: Archon Books, 1968), p. 130.
4. From an ancient British soldiers' song: "And never a lassie wherever we came,/ but packs up her placket and follows the drum."
5. J. Shy, *Toward Lexington* (Princeton, N.J.: Princeton University Press), p. 173.
6. John R. Cuneo, *Robert Rogers of the Rang-ers* (New York: Oxford University Press, 1959), p. 42.
7. McLennan, *Louisbourg*, p. 241.
8. Douglas E. Leach, *Arms for Empire* (New York: Macmillan, 1973), p. 439.
9. Pargellis, *Loudoun*, p. 103.
10. Francis Parkman, *The Conspiracy of Pontiac* (New York: Collier Books, 1962), p. 110.
11. Pargellis, *Loudoun*, p. 97.
12. Douglas S. Freeman, *George Washington* (New York: Charles Scribner's Sons, 1948), vol. II, p. 332.
13. *Orderly Book of General Phineas Lyman*, 4 August 1757.
14. Pargellis, *Lord Loudoun*, p. 95.
15. Cecil C. P. Lawson, *A History of the Uni-*

forms of the British Army (London: Norman Military Publications, 1961), vol. III, p. 205.

16. Alfred P. James and Charles M. Stotz, *Drums in the Forest* (Pittsburgh: Historical Society of Western Pennsylvania, 1958), p. 103.

17. Shy, *Toward Lexington*, p. 100.

18. Ibid., p. 173.

19. James and Stotz, *Drums in the Forest*, p. 166.

CHAPTER 2.
Soldiers for Independence

1. T. Harry Williams, *The History of American Wars* (New York: Alfred A. Knopf, 1981), p. 71.

2. John C. Miller, *Triumph of Freedom, 1775–1783* (Boston: Little, Brown, and Co., 1948), p. 562.

3. Charles K. Bolton, *The Private Soldier Under Washington* (Port Washington, N.Y.: Kennikat Press, 1964), p. 133.

4. Peter Force, *American Archives, Series 4*, vol. II, 1029, 1472–1473.

5. John R. Elting, *The Battle of Saratoga* (Monmouth Beach, N.J.: Philip Freneau Press, 1977), p. 26.

6. William Duane, trans., *The Journal of Claude Blanchard* (Albany, N.Y.: J. Munsell, 1876), p. 115.

7. Elting, *Saratoga*, p. 12.

8. Miller, *Triumph of Freedom*, pp. 236–237, 548.

9. Elting, *Saratoga*, p. 25.

10. John R. Elting, *The Battle of Bunker's Hill* (Monmouth Beach, N.J.: Philip Freneau Press, 1975), p. 26.

11. Richard M. Dorson, *American Rebels* (New York: Pantheon Books, 1953), p. 216.

12. Joseph R. Riling, *Baron von Steuben and His Regulations* (Philadelphia: Ray Riling Arms Book Co., 1966), p. xi.

13. Christopher Ward, *The War of the Revolution* (New York: Macmillan, 1952), vol. II, p. 613.

14. Freeman, *George Washington*, vol. V, p. 177.

15. Ward, *War of the Revolution*, vol. II, pp. 715, 718.

16. Ibid., pp. 825, 844; Miller, p. 678.

17. Albigence Waldo, *Dr. A. Waldo's Diary* (*Historical Magazine*, May 1861), p. 131.

18. *Elijah Fisher's Journal While in the War for Independence* (Augusta, Me.), p. 7.

19. Freeman, *George Washington*, vol. IV, p. 578.

20. Bolton, *Private Soldier*, p. 99.

21. Miller, *Triumph of Freedom*, p. 221.

22. Ibid., p. 545 n.

23. Freeman, *George Washington*, vol. V, pp. 174–175.

24. Alfred H. Hall, *Valley Forge* (New York: Harper and Brothers, 1952), p. 243.

CHAPTER 3.
The Frontier Soldier, 1784–1845

1. Francis P. Prucha, *Broadaxe and Bayonet* (Madison, Wis.: State Historical Society of Wisconsin, 1953), p. 105.

2. James R. Jacobs, *The Beginnings of the U.S. Army, 1783–1812* (Princeton, N.J.: Princeton University Press, 1947), p. 69.

3. Ibid., p. 382.

4. Prucha, *Broadaxe and Bayonet*, p. 210.

5. Ibid., p. 49.

6. Russell F. Weigley, *History of the United States Army* (New York: Macmillan, 1967), p. 107.

7. William H. Guthman, *March to Massacre* (New York: McGraw-Hill, 1970), pp. 37, 63–69.

8. Ibid., p. 218.

9. Ibid., p. 29.

10. Jacobs, *Beginnings of the U.S. Army*, pp. 261–262.

11. Charles James, *An Universal Military Dictionary in English and French* (London: T. Egerlon, 1816), pp. 223–224.

12. James W. Elliott, *Winfield Scott: The Soldier and the Man* (New York: Macmillan, 1937), pp. 147, 270.

13. Guthman, *March to Massacre*, p. 240.

CHAPTER 4.
Soldiers of Manifest Destiny

1. George W. Smith and Charles Judah, *Chronicles of the Gringos* (Albuquerque: University of New Mexico Press, 1968), p. 30.

2. Samuel Chamberlain, *Recollections of a*

Rogue (London: Museum Press, 1957), p. 68.

3. Smith and Judah, *Gringos,* pp. 127, 133–134.
4. Ibid., p. 47.
5. Ibid., p. 44.
6. Bernard De Voto, *The Year of Decision, 1846* (Boston: Little, Brown, and Co., 1943), p. 236.
7. Weigley, *History of the U.S. Army,* p. 185.
8. Chamberlain, *Recollections,* p. 68.
9. Smith and Judah, *Gringos,* p. 29.
10. Ibid.
11. Ibid., p. 54.
12. Chamberlain, *Recollections,* p. 68.
13. Smith and Judah, *Gringos,* p. 301.
14. Elliott, *Winfield Scott,* p. 583 n.
15. Smith and Judah, *Gringos,* p. 128.
16. K. Jack Bauer, *The Mexican War, 1846–1848* (New York: Macmillan, 1974), p. 278.
17. Smith and Judah, *Gringos,* p. 377.
18. Chamberlain, *Recollections,* pp. 83–84.
19. Ibid., p. 78.
20. Smith and Judah, *Gringos,* p. 331.
21. Chamberlain, *Recollections,* p. 72.
22. Smith and Judah, *Gringos,* p. 283.
23. Chamberlain, *Recollections,* p. 69.
24. Alfred H. Bill, *Rehearsal for Conflict* (New York: Alfred A. Knopf, 1947), p. 83.

CHAPTER 5.
Soldiers of the Civil War

1. Henry S. Commager, *The Blue and the Gray* (New York: Bobbs-Merrill, 1950), vol. I, p. 272.
2. Robert M. Utley, *Frontiersmen in Blue* (New York: Macmillan, 1967), pp. 211–212.
3. Bell I. Wiley, *The Life of Billy Yank* (New York: Bobbs-Merrill, 1951), pp. 343–344.
4. Allan Nevins, ed., *A Diary of Battle* (New York: Harcourt, Brace, and World, 1962), pp. 33–34.
5. Elbridge Colby, *Army Talk* (Princeton, N.J.: Princeton University Press, 1942), pp. 52–53.
6. John W. De Forest, *A Volunteer's Adventures* (New Haven, Conn.: Yale University Press, 1946), p. 221.
7. Lloyd Lewis, *Sherman: Fighting Prophet* (New York: Harcourt-Brace, 1932), p. 495.
8. Bruce Catton, *Mr. Lincoln's Army* (Garden City, N.Y.: Doubleday, 1951), p. 180.
9. *Personal Memoirs of John H. Brinton,* pp. 120–121.
10. Ibid.
11. Ibid.
12. Nevins, *A Diary of Battle,* p. vii.
13. De Forest, *A Volunteer's Adventures,* p. 44.
14. David S. Sparks, ed., *Inside Lincoln's Army* (New York: Thomas Yoseloff, 1964), p. 157.
15. *Photographic History of the Civil War* (New York: Review of Reviews, 1912), vol. IV, p. 334.
16. Charles W. Cowtan, *Services of the 10th New York Volunteers ...* (New York: Charles Ludwig, 1882), pp. 50–51.
17. De Forest, *A Volunteer's Adventures,* p. 46.
18. Ibid., pp. 166, 167, 169.
19. Catton, *Mr. Lincoln's Army,* p. 20.

CHAPTER 6.
The Indian-fighting Soldier, 1866–97

1. Oliver Knight, *Life and Manners in the Frontier Army* (Norman: University of Oklahoma Press, 1978), p. 196.
2. John G. Bourke, *Mackenzie's Last Fight with the Cheyennes* (New York: Argonaut Press, 1966), pp. 8–9.
3. Ibid., pp. 10–11.
4. Richard Upton, ed., *Fort Custer on the Big Horn, 1887–1898* (Glendale, Calif.: Arthur H. Clark, 1973), p. 60.
5. Ibid., pp. 79–80.
6. Bourke, *Mackenzie's Last Fight,* pp. 2–3.
7. From the old song, "The Regular Army, Oh."
8. Odie B. Faulk, *The Geronimo Campaign* (New York: Oxford University Press, 1969), p. 182.

CHAPTER 7.
Soldiers of Empire, 1898–1916

1. Walter Millis, *The Martial Spirit* (Cambridge, Mass.: Literary Guild of America, 1931), p. 245.
2. Lowell Thomas, ed., *Woodfill of the Regulars* (London: William Heinemann, Ltd., 1930), p. 58.
3. Ibid., p. 25.

4. Ibid., p. 79.
5. A. C. M. Azoy, *Paul Revere's Horse* (Garden City, N.Y.: Doubleday, 1949) p. 252.
6. Thomas, *Woodfill of the Regulars,* p. 102.

CHAPTER 8.
Soldiers for Democracy, 1917–40

1. T. Dodson Stamps and Vincent J. Esposito, *A Short Military History of World War I* (West Point, N.Y.: U.S. Military Academy, 1954), p. 292.

2. Thomas, *Woodfill of the Regulars,* p. 222.
3. Robert L. Ballard and Earl Reeves, *American Soldiers Also Fought* (New York: Maurice H. Louis, 1939), p. 99.
4. Thomas C. Lonergan, *It Might Have Been Lost* (New York: G. P. Putnam's Sons, 1929), p. 261.
5. Ibid., pp. 99–100.
6. Thomas, *Woodfill of the Regulars,* p. 260.
7. Ballard and Reeves, *American Soldiers Also Fought,* p. 69.

Bibliography

CHAPTER 1.
The Colonial Soldier

Cuneo, John R. *Robert Rogers of the Rangers.* New York: Oxford University Press, 1959.

Doughty, Arthur G., ed. *The Journal of Captain John Knox.* Toronto: The Champlain Society, 1916.

Freeman, Douglas S. *George Washington.* Vols. I and II. New York: Charles Scribner's Sons, 1948–49.

Hamilton, Edward P., ed. *Adventure in the Wilderness: The American Journals of Louis Antoine de Bougainville, 1756–1760.* Norman: University of Oklahoma Press, 1964.

James, Alfred P., and Charles M. Stotz. *Drums in the Forest.* Pittsburgh: The Historical Society of Western Pennsylvania, 1958.

Leach, Douglas E. *Arms for Empire.* New York: Macmillan, 1973.

McLennan, J. C. *Louisbourg.* Sydney, Nova Scotia: Fortress Press, 1969.

O'Connor, Norreys J. *A Servant of the Crown.* New York: D. Appleton-Century Co., 1938.

Pargellis, Stanley, ed. *Military Affairs in North America, 1748–1765.* New York: D. Appleton-Century Co., 1936.

———. *Lord Loudoun in North America.* New York: Archon Books, 1968.

Parkman, Francis. *The Conspiracy of Pontiac.* Boston: Little, Brown, and Co., 1903.

Shy, John. *Toward Lexington.* Princeton: Princeton University Press, 1965.

Stacey, C. P. *Quebec, 1759.* Toronto: Macmillan, 1959.

Stanley, George F. G. *New France: The Last Phase.* Toronto: McClelland and Stewart, Ltd., 1968.

CHAPTER 2.
Soldiers for Independence

Andrist, Ralph K., ed. *George Washington: A Biography in His Own Words.* New York: Harper & Row, 1972.

Bellamy, Francis. R. *The Private Life of George Washington.* New York: Thomas Y. Crowell, 1951.

Berg, Fred A. *Encyclopedia of the Continental Army.* Harrisburg, Pa.: Stackpole Books, 1972.

Bill, Alfred H. *Valley Forge.* New York: Harper and Brothers, 1952.

Bolton, Charles K. *The Private Soldier Under Washington.* Port Washington, N.Y.: Kennikat Press, 1964.

Dorson, Richard M. *American Rebels.* New York: Pantheon Books, 1953.

Elting, John R. *The Battle of Bunker's Hill.* Monmouth Beach, N.J.: Philip Freneau Press, 1975.

———. *The Battle of Saratoga.* Monmouth Beach, N.J.: Philip Freneau Press, 1977.

———, ed. *Military Uniforms in America: Volume I, The Era of the American Revolution, 1755–1795.* San Raphael, Calif.: Presidio Press, 1974.

Higginbotham, Don. *The War of American Independence.* New York: Macmillan, 1971.

Miller, John C. *Triumph of Freedom, 1775–1783.* Boston: Little, Brown, and Co., 1948.

Peterson, Harold L. *The Book of the Continental Soldier.* Harrisburg, Pa.: Stackpole Books, 1968.

———. *Arms and Armor of Colonial America.* New York: Bramhall House, 1956.

Riling, Joseph R. *Baron von Steuben and His Regulations.* Philadelphia: Ray Riling Arms Book Co., 1966.

Smith, Samuel S. *A Molly Pitcher Chronology.* Monmouth Beach, N.J.: Philip Freneau Press, 1972.

Wade, Herbert T., and Robert A. Lively, eds. *This Glorious Cause.* Princeton: Princeton University Press, 1958.

Ward, Christopher. *The War of the Revolution.* 2 vols. New York: Macmillan, 1952.

CHAPTER 3.
The Frontier Soldier, 1784–1845

Adams, Henry. *The War of 1812.* Washington, D.C.: The Infantry Journal, n.d.

Buley, R. Carlyle. *The Old Northwest.* 2 vols. Bloomington, Ind.: Indiana University Press, 1951.

Elliott, Charles W. *Winfield Scott: The Soldier and the Man.* New York: Macmillan, 1937.

Elting, John R., ed. *Military Uniforms in America: Volume II, Years of Growth, 1796–1851.* San Raphael, Calif.: Presidio Press, 1977.

Guthman, William H. *March to Massacre: A History of the First Seven Years of the United States Army.* New York: McGraw-Hill, 1970.

Hay, Thomas R., and M. R. Werner. *The Admirable Trumpeter: A Biography of General James Wilkenson.* Garden City, N.Y.: Doubleday and Co., 1941.

Jacobs, James R. *The Beginnings of the U.S. Army, 1783–1812.* Port Washington, N.Y.: Kennikat Press, 1971 (originally published, 1947).

James, Marquis. *The Life of Andrew Jackson.* Garden City, N.Y.: Doubleday and Co., 1940.

Kohn, Richard H. *Eagle and Sword.* New York: The Free Press, 1975.

Mahon, John K. *The American Militia: Decade of Decision, 1789–1800.* Gainesville, Fla.: University of Florida Press, 1960.

Prucha, Francis P. *Broadaxe and Bayonet.* Lincoln, Neb.: University of Nebraska Press, 1967 (originally published, 1953).

Swanson, Neil H. *The Perilous Fight.* New York: Farrar and Rinehart, 1945.

Van Every, Dale. *Ark of Empire: The American Frontier, 1784–1803.* New York: William Morrow and Co., 1963.

CHAPTER 4.
Soldiers of Manifest Destiny

Ambrose, Stephen E. *Duty, Honor, Country: A History of West Point.* Baltimore: Johns Hopkins Press, 1966.

Bauer, K. Jack. *The Mexican War, 1846–1848.* New York: Macmillan, 1974.

Bill, Alfred H. *Rehearsal for Conflict.* New York: Alfred A. Knopf, 1947.

Chamberlain, Samuel. *Recollections of a Rogue.* London: Museum Press, 1957.

De Voto, Bernard. *The Year of Decision, 1846.* Boston: Little, Brown, and Co., 1943.

Elliott, Charles W. *Winfield Scott: The Soldier and the Man.* New York: Macmillan, 1937.

Elting, John R., ed., *Military Uniforms in America: Volume II, Years of Growth, 1796–1851.* San Raphael, Calif.: Presidio Press, 1977.

Lewis, Lloyd, *Captain Sam Grant.* Boston: Little, Brown, and Co., 1950.

Pourade, Richard F., ed. *The Sign of the Eagle.* San Diego, Calif.: Copley Press, 1970.

Smith, George W., and Charles Judah. *Chronicles of the Gringos.* Albuquerque, N.M.: University of New Mexico Press, 1968.

Utley, Robert M. *Frontiersmen in Blue: The United States Army and the Indian, 1848–1865.* New York: Macmillan, 1967.

Walker, Henry P. *The Wagon Masters.* Norman, Okla.: University of Oklahoma Press, 1966.

CHAPTER 5.
Soldiers of the Civil War

Billings, John D. *Hard Tack and Coffee, or the Unwritten Story of Army Life.* Boston, George M. Smith & Co., 1888.

Forest, John W. De. *A Volunteer's Adventures.* New Haven, Conn.: Yale University Press, 1946.

Lanier, Robert S., ed. *The Photographic History of the Civil War.* 10 volumes. New York: Review of Reviews, 1912.

Leech, Margaret. *Reveille In Washington.* New York: Harper and Brothers, 1941.

Nevins, Allan, ed. *A Diary of Battle.* New York: Harcourt, Brace, and World, 1962.

Schuff, Morris. *The Battle of the Wilderness.* Boston: Houghton Mifflin, 1910.

Sparks, David S., ed. *Inside Lincoln's Army.* New York: Thomas Yoseloff, 1964.

Stilwell, Leander. *The Story of a Common Soldier of Army Life in the Civil War, 1861–1865.* Erie, Kans., 1920.

Wiley, Bell I. *The Life of Johnny Reb.* New York: Bobbs-Merrill Co., 1943.

———. *The Life of Billy Yank.* New York: Bobbs-Merrill Co., 1951.

CHAPTER 6.
The Indian-fighting Soldier, 1866–97

Bourke, John G. *Mackenzie's Last Fight with the Cheyennes.* New York: Argonaut Press, 1966.

De Barthe, Joe. *Life and Adventures of Frank Grouard.* Norman, Okla.: University of Oklahoma Press, 1958.

Chappell, Gordon, *The Search for the Well-Dressed Soldier, 1865–1890.* Tucson, Ariz.: Arizona Historical Society, 1972.

Faulk, Odie B. *The Geronimo Campaign.* New York: Oxford University Press, 1969.

Knight, Oliver. *Life and Manners in the Frontier Army.* Norman, Okla.: University of Oklahoma Press, 1978.

Rickey, Don, Jr., *Forty Miles a Day on Beans and Hay.* Norman, Okla.: University of Oklahoma Press, 1963.

Steffen, Randy. *The Horse Soldier, 1776–1943.* Norman, Okla.: University of Oklahoma Press, 1978.

Upton, Richard, ed. *Fort Custer on the Big Horn.* Glendale, Calif.: Arthur H. Clarke Co., 1973.

Utley, Robert M. *Frontier Regulars: The United States Army and the Indian, 1866–1890.* New York: Macmillan, 1973.

———, ed. *Life in Custer's Cavalry.* New Haven, Conn.: Yale University Press, 1977.

CHAPTER 7.
Soldiers of Empire, 1898–1916

Clendenen, Clarence C. *Blood on the Border.* London: Collier-Macmillan Ltd., 1969.

King, Dale M., ed. *The Army Almanac.* Washington, D.C.: U.S. Government Printing Office, 1950.

Millis, Walter. *The Martial Spirit.* Cambridge, Mass.: Literary Guild of America, 1931.

Sargent, Herbert H. *The Campaign of Santiago de Cuba.* Chicago: A. C. McClung and Co., 1907.

Sexton, William T. *Soldiers in the Sun.* Harrisburg, Pa.: Military Service Publishing Co., 1939.

Thomas, Lowell, ed. *Woodfill of the Regulars.* London: William Heinemann, Ltd., 1930.

CHAPTER 8.
Soldiers for Democracy, 1917–40

Ballard, Robert L., and Earl Reeves. *American Soldiers Also Fought.* New York: Maurice H. Louis, 1939.

Chapman, Guy. *A Passionate Prodigality.* New York: Holt, Rinehart and Winston, 1966.

Eaton, Ralph P. *Recollections of World War I By a First Aid Man.* Privately printed.

Historical Section, Army War College. *The Genesis of the American First Army.* Washington, D.C.: Government Printing Office, 1938.

Lonergan, Thomas C. *It Might Have Been Lost.* New York: G. P. Putnam's Sons, 1929.

Thomas, Lowell, ed. *Woodfill of the Regulars.* London: William Heinemann, Ltd., 1930.

CHAPTER 9.
Soldiers of the Long Wars

Ambrose, Stephen E. *Duty, Honor, Country.* Baltimore: Johns Hopkins University Press, 1966.

Fehrenbach, T. H. *This Kind of War.* New York: Macmillan, 1963.

Murphy, Robert. *Diplomat Among Warriors.* New York: Doubleday and Co., 1964.

Palmer, Dave R. *Summons of the Trumpet.* San Raphael, Calif.: Presidio Press, 1978.

Pogue, Forrest C. *George C. Marshall: Organizer of Victory, 1943–1945.* New York: Viking Press, 1973.

Weigley, Russell F. *History of the United States Army.* New York: Macmillan, 1967.

Index

The numbered references in this index refer either to textual material, which is designated by page numbers in lightface, or to caption material, which is designated by illustration numbers in boldface.